WHEEL
of
INITIATION

PRACTICES FOR RELEASING YOUR INNER LIGHT

JULIE TALLARD JOHNSON

Bear & Company
Rochester, Vermont • Toronto, Canada

Bear & Company
One Park Street
Rochester, Vermont 05767
www.BearandCompanyBooks.com

Bear & Company is a division of Inner Traditions International

Library of Congress Cataloging-in-Publication Data

Johnson, Julie Tallard.
  Wheel of initiation : practices for releasing your inner light / Julie Tallard Johnson.
    p. cm.
  Includes bibliographical references and index.
  Summary: "A guide to personal spiritual initiation through the transformation of habitual patterns, apathy, and resistence"—Provided by publisher.
  ISBN 978-1-59143-111-4
  1. Spiritual life. 2. Symbolism (Psychology) I. Title.
  BL624.J6388 2010
  204'.4—dc22

                                                                    2010012576

Printed and bound in the United States by Lake Book Manufacturing
This book is printed on 100% certified SFI paper. The Sustainable Forestry Initiative is a program that promotes sound forestry practices.

10   9   8   7   6   5   4   3   2   1

Text design and layout by Virginia Scott Bowman
This book was typeset in Garamond Premier Pro, Legacy Sans, Agenda, and Gill Sans with Civet, Frutiger, and Legacy Sans as display typefaces
The cover art and chapter art is by Kathy Kershaw
Thunderbird petroglyph image by Lydia Ishmael

"Grace" and "To Know the Dark" by Wendell Berry, © 1999 by Wendell Berry from *The Selected Poems of Wendell Berry*. Reprinted by permission of Counterpoint.
"A Purification" by Wendell Berry, © 1987 by Wendell Berry from *The Collected Poems of Wendell Berry, 1957–1982*. Reprinted by permission of Counterpoint.
"Quo Vadis," "The Way It Is," "You Reading This, Be Ready," "A Message from the Wanderer," "A Ritual to Read to Each Other," and "Ask Me" by William Stafford, © 1998 by The Estate of William Stafford. Reprinted from *The Way It Is: New & Selected Poems* with the permission of Graywolf Press, Saint Paul, Minnesota.

To send correspondence to the author of this book, mail a first-class letter to the author c/o Inner Traditions • Bear & Company, One Park Street, Rochester, VT 05767, and we will forward the communication.

CONTENTS

★

Initiation represents one of the most significant spiritual phenomena in the history of humanity. It is an act that involves not only the religious life of the individual, in the modern meaning of the word "religion"; it involves his entire life. It is through initiation that, in primitive and archaic societies, man becomes what he is and what he should be—a being open to the life of the spirit, hence one who participates in the culture into which he was born.

MIRCEA ELIADE, *RITES AND SYMBOLS OF INITIATION*

The initiation circle, the Wheel, the experiences and lessons themselves have become more than threads woven into the fabric of my life. They are an inner current, a seventh sense even . . . in my actual physical being and on out into my subtle body as well. I feel them humming through me at all times like a new life-nourishing fluid. They surround me at all times as a new layer of skin. The great beauty of this is that they will always be with me despite a changing of the guard of my individual cells and reconfigurations of my energies. They will always be part of me.

LISA HARTMAN, 2007 INITIATION CIRCLE

A USEFUL TENSION

Religious Beliefs and Spiritual Practices

Spirituality I take to be concerned with those qualities of the human spirit—such as love and compassion, patience, tolerance, forgiveness, contentment, a sense of responsibility, a sense of harmony—which brings happiness to both self and others. While ritual and prayer, along with the questions of nirvana and salvation, are directly connected to religious faith, these inner qualities need not be, however. There is no reason why the individual should not develop them, even to a highest degree, without recourse to any religious or metaphysical belief system. This is why I sometimes say that religion is something we can perhaps do without. What we cannot do without are these basic spiritual qualities.

THE FOURTEENTH DALAI LAMA,
ETHICS FOR THE NEW MILLENNIUM

I agree with what the Dalai Lama has stated: there should be a distinction, a useful tension, between religious beliefs and spiritual practices. I do not consider myself a religious person. Consciously choosing various spiritual practices does not mean I am in agreement with their various religious assumptions.

Since beginning my spiritual search at the age of eight, I found myself in the presence of awakened ministers, fundamentalist preachers, wounded healers, narcissistic medicine men, authentic gurus, spiritual masters, and everyday goddesses. I relied on the written word of ancient masters and the I Ching to guide me when there were no teachers available. I chose to be baptized at thirteen by a Lutheran minister who later left the clergy. I also participated in rituals with African shamans and sweats with a Lakota medicine man, and later attended teachings and empower-ments by His Holiness the Fourteenth Dalai Lama. From him I took the Bodhisattva vow in 1995, a vow to live a conscious life in order to benefit others. I began my meditation practice at the age of sixteen, nearly forty years ago, and have studied many psychological as well as spiritual teach-ings in search of truth and peace.

My core practice is the Mahayana path within Tibetan Buddhism. In the spiritual practice of purification I borrow from both Tibetan and yogic practices as well as psychological and Native American methods. I do not jeopardize my faith or practice when I do yogic breathing to purify my mind and body, nor do I piss off the gods when I do a Buddhist chant in the sweat lodge.

I do not consider myself a master of any kind. I *can* call myself an initiated adult—I do know and practice my principles and live an inten-tioned life. I am a Bodhisattva* *in training,* and that's good enough for me. I have traveled many unusual and usual places in search of the truth and learned that the Holy One is in us all, all along, all the time. Others can point the way for us and show us the means to get to the root of our difficulties, but in the end it is up to each of us to release the inner light within ourselves and commit to living a full and honest life.

Too often I find that religious beliefs divide and separate us.

Ritual, for example, can be experienced as a religious belief or as a

---

*Bodhisattvas are "Heros of Enlightenment"—individuals who generate an altruistic mind of compassion in order to help free all beings from suffering.

spiritual practice. Various traditions bring out inherent qualities such as compassion, insight, mindfulness, wisdom, love, understanding, and patience in a spiritual practice. If a ritual or any other act is based on an attempt to fulfill a codified religious goal such as reaching nirvana or obtaining salvation, then it is an expression of a religious belief. A spiritual practice such as meditation can be used to calm and train the mind. As a religious expression, guided meditation can be used as a directive to keep people in line.

"Sin" in a religious context may be looked upon as an act against god wherein the sinner is fundamentally flawed and needs an outside source to forgive and release him from his sins. As a spiritual practice, sin can be more personally understood and used symbolically as a means to become more conscious and compassionate to self and others. In a spiritual context, sins are seen as acts against one's true nature wherein the individual is the only one who can forgive and act more enlightened.

No one can take our spiritual journey for us. *We don't become initiated based on the wisdom path of others. We become initiated based on our own choices, practices, and actions.* Thus is the Wheel of Initiation a spiritual path, where your initiation results in a more conscious, ethical life, a life that benefits both yourself and others.

In general, religious beliefs rely on dogma, rules, and traditional methods, while true spiritual practices are more intuitive and flexible, blending both the richness of tradition and the freshness of contemporary and scientific wisdom.

In every tradition there are those who feel called upon to protect the history and guard the pure form of the tradition. Equally so, there are those who intuitively grasp the essence within the tradition. Understanding the spirituality within the cultural mythology and ancient rituals, they extract the inner meaning and spiritual science from the tradition. True masters understand that there is dialectic between these two—tradition and pulling out the present essence. The ones who guard can err on the side of dogma and the ones that are more intuitive can miss the richness and power that the tradition

*holds. This tension is useful. There is value in holding within our
awareness these two polarities.*

A'CHA'RYA JINA'NESHVAR (JAMES POWELL)

You can even approach your religious tradition with the heart of a spiritual
practitioner. Honor various traditional practices for what they bring forth
and symbolize for you. Hold in your heart how any given practice may
bring forth those inherent qualities mentioned in the quotation from His
Holiness, the Fourteenth Dalai Lama at the beginning of this preface.

Practice walking around a stupa or entering a sweat lodge in the traditional clockwise fashion because it keeps your mind focused and opens
you up to the experience, not because someone somewhere said that this
is how it should be done. Learn about your chosen traditions and intuit
which ones work for you, which ones bring forth your true nature.

Follow your heart.

EAGLE MAN (ED MCGAA)

ENTERING THE WHEEL

Truth is within ourselves, it takes no rise
from outward things; whate'er you may believe
there is an inmost center in us all
where truth abides in fullness; and around,
wall upon wall, the gross flesh hems it in,
this perfect, clear perception which is Truth.
A baffling and perverting carnal mesh
Binds it and makes all error; and to know
rather consists in opening out a way
whence the imprisoned splendor may escape
than in effecting entry for a light
supposed to be without.

ROBERT BROWNING, FROM "PARACELSUS"

Imagine yourself being pulled away from your life and, in the middle of the night, taken deep into the woods where darkness and the unknown prevail. The intention of those who take you from your comfortable home is to offer you a personal spiritual initiation. Their purpose is to free you from whatever binds you, knowing that whatever binds you binds us all. They intend to do whatever it takes to help you awaken to all your potential. They know your destiny, but at this point you do not.

1

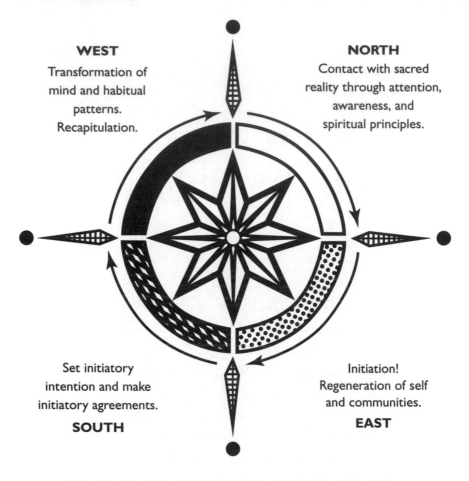

WEST
Transformation of
mind and habitual
patterns.
Recapitulation.

NORTH
Contact with sacred
reality through attention,
awareness, and
spiritual principles.

Set initiatory
intention and make
initiatory agreements.
SOUTH

Initiation!
Regeneration of self
and communities.
EAST

*Fig. I.1. The Wheel of Initiation and what you will address
in each of its four quadrants as you travel through
it on your spiritual journey.*

To survive the time in the woods, your old ways must die. To return home transformed, you will have to tap the inner resources that may be buried deep under habitual states. What worked in your day-to-day life won't work in the inner recesses of the deep, dark woods. Those who stole you from your comfortable life know you cannot hold onto the old paradigm, the comfort of which might be killing you, if what you want is personal initiation. Once they get you into the deep of the bush, you will be left on your own, for days, weeks, maybe even years.

The Wheel of Initiation, as revealed in the pages of this book, will take you on an initiatory journey, a personal spiritual pilgrimage of initiation, with me as your guide. Since the late 1980s I have taken individuals and groups through personal initiations. I went on my first initiatory journey at the age of thirteen. And at the age of sixteen, I had my first initiation into the Buddhist tradition.

Later, in 1991 I took another initiatory journey and spiritual pilgrimage to Bear Butte Mountain in South Dakota with Eagle Man (Ed McGaa), where I attended my first sweat lodge and participated in an overnight vision quest on Bear Butte. I have experienced several other personal initiations since, many of them through my Buddhist practice and others through this Wheel. Each one has taken me deeper into the woods and out again.

The Wheel of Initiation opens "out a way whence the imprisoned splendor may escape." It is an inner pilgrimage where you free yourself from that which ties you to habitual and even harmful ways of being. It opens you into a more natural state of expression wherein you see through the mirage of the life you have created for yourself.

You *come as you are,* and you will not be expected to embrace any particular spiritual practice.

THE CIRCLE OF LIFE

In the sky there is no East or West. We make these distinctions in the mind, then believe them to be true.

RUDOLPH WURTLIGZER, *HARD TRAVEL TO SACRED PLACES*

The circle or spiral is our most universal symbol; it is found in every spiritual tradition, as well as in the natural world. It is the shared symbol of unity and synthesis. The universal Wheel expresses our underlying dependence on each other and the universe. In a circle, everything is connected to everything else; there is no separation. So when we enter such a Wheel, we enter into an ideal.

Mandalas are like maps used in spiritual practices for healing, transformation, meditation, and insight. They give us a means to travel in both the mundane and sacred worlds. The universal mandala represents the whole and true self as well as the entire universe. The world and so much in it is understood as cyclical, round, a spiral going in and out. It represents both the spiritual ideal (i.e., initiation) and the more ordinary realities of cyclical existence (stages of life). The sacred Wheel is then both internal (within us) and external (in the world). The internal journey of initiation represented by the Wheel is also taken out into the physical world through the practices used to move us toward initiation.

There are typically four aspects within the symbolism of the Wheel—the four directions, the four seasons, and the four stages of life. In the Wheel of Initiation the four directions are used to carry us through the process of initiation, beginning in the South, moving East through the West, then the North, and into the East. The image of the Initiation Wheel gives us a visual template; the practices give us the tools of initiation.

The directions of the Wheel are not associated with any particular tradition or belief system. The Wheel is just a finger pointing, a visual template, and a means for you to experience personal initiation. The totems, symbolic images, animals, and deities of each direction are chosen for their *symbolic* meaning within the Wheel. There is no push for you to choose them for your practice; you may come up with your own if you so desire.

When you enter the Wheel of Initiation in the South, you will set your intentions, thereby agreeing to the precepts of your journey. Then, when you move into the West, you will learn how to free yourself from habitual patterns, beliefs, and negative mind-sets that are limiting you; this is essential for spiritual transformation. In the North you will apply the skills of meditation and contemplation that further enhance your journey, and in the East you will experience regeneration.

Because there are no elders to personally conduct you into the heart of the woods, your soul has stepped in and awakened you to the call of an initiation. If, however, we refuse to heed the call to enter the Wheel consciously and on our own, the circumstances of our lives may see to it that we are summoned. Each of us has experienced wake-up calls of illness, loss, close calls, or radical change. Sometimes we heed the wake-up call, and sometimes we run from it. These wake-up calls are asking for your attention; they want you to take the journey of your life. To go by choice means to listen to your soul's calling and to wisely and consciously step into the Wheel.

Listen to the call to go deep into your being and bring forth the imprisoned light. For at least several months, if not for a year, take yourself into the woods on the inner pilgrimage of personal spiritual initiation.

HEEDING THE CALL

The Wheel of Initiation, once entered, can offer you skillful and personal means of freedom from painful habitual states. But be warned, you will be leaving the shores of your comfort zone behind you. As André Gide so rightly stated, "One doesn't discover new lands without consenting to lose sight of the shore for a very long time." You will need a willingness to let go of old beliefs and assumptions about yourself and the world in order to "see" anew.

However, you will not be offered someone else's beliefs to replace the ones that you are dispensing with. This spiritual initiation is simple but not easy, and it opens inner doors so that you can access and discern truth *for yourself*. It is accessible to all because the splendor is indeed hidden within each one of us. The Wheel, as an organic template, presents you proficient means to open the inner doors for yourself, choose for yourself, and initiate yourself.

Many of us are now living various degrees of an uninitiated life. We are living in a false dream, a life that is more like sitting on the soft-cushioned deck chair on a cruise ship (that may or may not be heading for an iceberg). We tend to choose comfort to get us through the rough seas and the difficulties of life, but these insular comforts too often keep us a spectator of life rather than a participant. We all want happiness, yet we tend to do that which causes more pain. If outward comfort freed us from our suffering, we wouldn't need bigger toys or more potent drugs. Those who experience personal initiation have left the comfort of the deck chair and the sight of their own familiar shoreline.

Michele Chooses Initiation:
You Can't Serve Two Masters

MICHELE WAS IN HER *second year of retirement when she had a wake-up call. She had recently had a mammogram. Late on Christmas Eve day, she received a letter in her mailbox. That day she had been busy getting ready for an evening of baking with her daughter. In fact, when she opened the letter, her loved ones were in the kitchen ready to decorate cookies. She had opened many such letters in the past, all of which had given her a clean bill of health. So she opened it expecting the best. Instead, she read that her mammogram results revealed something of concern and she needed to go in for more tests.*

It was Christmas Eve. She couldn't contact her doctor and had to wait out the weekend. She shared the letter's contents, but not with her daughter. Immediately she began to worry and stress out, as most of us would. She had several friends and colleagues who had become ill soon after retirement, and she knew of one individual who had died within a year or two of leaving his job of thirty-five years.

Even though she was worried, she tried to share and enjoy the holiday with her family. She called me on Sunday morning and, as a friend, asked for some intuitive insight. What I got immediately was for her to view this as a wake-up call, to know it was a call for her to put her spiritual/creative life first. I suggested she put her hands on her body, confirm her commitment to her spiritual life, and let her body know she was listening to it. This seemed right to her, and she agreed to do this. I also understood that her response to the wake-up call could influence the results of her follow-up test.

Later that I day when I shared all this with my husband, he said, "The technician probably made a mistake," and we both felt strongly that she was all right. Certainly, Spirit was trying to get her full attention. She told me that the entire weekend, for her, had been like "walking between two worlds" (she had scheduled an X-ray for Monday). This sense of a dual reality is often something we experience when being called to leave the shore of an old way of life.

Trust, for her, became essential. She needed to trust in the process, trust her body, trust Spirit. The call had been made, and now she also needed to trust that she would heed the call. She made a commitment to herself to honor this experience as initiatory, no matter what the outcome. *Even before the follow-up testing, by doing all these things, she had entered the Wheel. On Monday she went in for the X-ray, which didn't take long. Throughout the entire process, it seemed to Michele that the nurse was emanating light and love. Of course, Michele was worried and yet, at the same time, she was doing her best to trust the process. The nurse looked at her at one point and said, "You know, you can't serve two masters. You can't serve god and worry. You need to choose."*

At that moment Michele realized how, for much of her adult life, she had tried to serve two masters—worry and spirit, control and trust. She knew that she was being shown what she needed for her spiritual, mental, and physical well-being. She needed to serve one master and not two.

The nurse then went out and returned with the X-ray results. The technician at the clinic had indeed made a mistake. They had put a piece of tape on her breast where a natural mark existed. But the tape had been folded over, causing it to appear as an abnormality. "When I heard this, I knew I could have gotten angry, but I felt no anger. I only felt humbled and grateful, and I vowed to not forget this, because I want to be able to honor it for the rest of my life. The anger would have kept me back, focused on what was going wrong on the outside. I am taking this gift and moving forward. I entered a new room, and I am not sure what is on this path, but I vow to keep on walking. I know I can no longer serve worry and spirit; I cannot serve both trust and control."

At the entrance to the Wheel, we can't be in control of our true initiatory process—we must trust in ourselves, our choice to hear the call, and we must enter the Wheel being open to the journey.

Rule of thumb: The more important a call or action is to our soul's evolution, the more Resistance we will feel toward pursuing it.

STEVEN PRESSFIELD, *THE WAR OF ART*

Refusing to Heed the Call

If you begin your spiritual journey and don't go all the way with where it wants to take you, then you may end up worse than when you began. Students and spiritual seekers often encounter adversity and resistance along the way, and somewhere in the middle of their effort it can become quite a challenge to stay with the journey. They are enthused or motivated in the beginning, and then something happens. It gets difficult. Resistance arises (as it always will): They get angry at the technician and miss their opportunity. They blame circumstances outside themselves. They give up. They blame their past. They blame the conditions of their life. They never leave their soft-cushioned deck chair long enough. They give in to old familiar patterns rather than pushing onward through the tight, uncomfortable spots.

In many myths, "Refusing to Heed the Call" is a refusal to heed the call of the spiritual path—the person declines the adventure of personal or heroic transformation. Depending on the myth, sometimes the one who refuses suffers as a result, and perhaps it is the case that later he or she will choose to listen and follow the call. To decline the call completely means to live a life directed by the false self, wherein a great part of you remains unilluminated. But *once you say yes to the call and experience personal initiation, you find yourself responding differently, and therefore experiencing everything from a more awakened mind.*

Because the patterns that keep us asleep, that keep us among the uninitiated, are deeply rooted, there will be deal-breakers along the way. Be ready to break deals with old, deeply rooted patterns and the pain stories that you carry. Be ready to break the deal with "cult time" (time spent following other's paths, or two masters) rather than your own.

Parker Palmer, writer and activist, encourages us not to give in to the existing illusions of the social environment and remain asleep to our potentialities. He writes of "the illusion that violence solves problems, that both rich and poor deserve their fate, that the young sent to die in wars fought to defend the rich are heroes rather than victims, that the murderous drugs are the way beyond despair—just to name a few. These illusions serve a societal function: They keep us in place." They keep us on the deck chair.

Initiation has always been a risk. People have gone off into the bush and not survived (while others get stolen back by their mothers or lured back by other societal obligations). Some have relied on bread crumbs or bent twigs to get them back to their old ways of being. Leave the bread crumbs at home, jump off the deck of the ship, enter the woods, and don't leave a forwarding address!

TOOLS FOR YOUR JOURNEY

This process of initiation does not rely on being taken into the bush and dropped off. You may only be making a pilgrimage within your own heart and mind. You also will not be able to meet with me every week in an initiation circle. Thus, we will use spiritual journaling as a means to move through the Wheel.

Spiritual Journaling: Creating an Outer Temple

> Writing, above all, is seeing clearly.
>
> PETER MATHIESSEN,
> *LETTERS FROM THE WILD*

Consider your journal as one of your outer temples, a place where you can engage the practices of the Wheel. Also use it to document your pilgrimage. The exercises and inquiries within each chapter deepen your experience within the Wheel and are sequential. At the very least, you will want to *contemplate* each query or exercise. Better still, give yourself the time to actually journal and practice the given exercises. I would give yourself at least six months to go through the Wheel and to experience your personal spiritual initiation. (Those individuals in my Initiation Course allow a year for the journey.)

Throughout the Wheel, writing exercises can be practiced to increase insight and your ability to stay focused. Spiritual journaling is a universal means to access your Inner Teacher and a means to give yourself a personal spiritual initiation without the direct guidance of a group or teacher. Within each direction of the Wheel will be valuable writing exercises and contemplative questions. These will help direct your experience toward your intention and initiation. Take the inquiries and write about them, as well as carry them in your consciousness as questions. Maintain a curiosity with these questions rather than search for answers. In other words, *live the questions*. Do all this from a compassionate position. We are not looking to blame here; we are looking for personal truth.

When journaling, date and title each entry. That way you can find the piece in your journal that relates to what is in the book. Take some time to write about what you hope to get out of this experience. What do you hope will be different for you after you have completed the Wheel? What do you want to no longer be true for you when you have completed this journey of spiritual initiation? What is your idea of what your spiritual initiation will bring you? Write a wish list and include every financial, spiritual, relational, physical, and global desire. This list could go on for several pages.

Journal about where you feel you didn't belong and don't belong now. Did you belong to a certain group of friends while in elementary school? Do you feel like the Ugly Duckling, a swan among ducks, lost to your true tribe? Where do you lack a sense of belonging now?

The Initiatory Journey through Dreamtime

All the things one has forgotten scream for help in dreams.

ELLIAS CANETTI, *DIE PROVINZ DER MENSCHEN*

While you move through the Wheel of Initiation, listen to and journal your dreams as well. Particularly notice dreams that come up during specific practices within the Wheel. For example, the evening you set your initiatory intention, notice the dream that may be speaking to you about this commitment. Throughout the Wheel you will use your dreams to gain further insight into your personal initiation. During Amy's entrance into the Wheel, she had the following dream: "I am with my initiation circle, we are on a retreat. . . . Julie's there. We walk down a path to a lake, around the bend of the path lies the shore, the dock, and a boat just arriving. I start to sob . . . almost uncontrollably. I see my grandma's father, my great-grandfather whom I have never met. Julie and the group hold space for me. I get introduced to my great-grandfather. He's pleased I am doing this work. He's been waiting and floating out in that boat. Now it's safe for him to come to shore."

Because you will not be stolen from your home and taken into the bush—go find the deep wood for yourself. Spend some time meditating and journaling in nature. Ideally, take yourself away from the sounds and sights of the city and into some bush or wood somewhere when possible. Sit in one spot for a while and feel your connection to all the sights, sounds, and scents around you. Feel the earth holding you. Watch the night sky. Make a greater connection between you and the natural world.

Initiation

Into the Wheel
I pried my lacquered self:
A solid work of years.
Linear and on a path
But wondering . . .
Wondering . . .

We circled sacred air
With breath.
Wind moved between my parts

Gave voice to Spirit:
Harmony;
The echoes split my heart

We grew into the earth below
Rooting
I stretched beyond my skin

We opened to the All above,
Rising.
My passion blazed within

And now the wind has caught these pieces of my soul
And scattered them
Around.

With breath and song

And roots and sky
And wondrous spirit sisters and brothers,
I will pick them up
One by precious one,

And form a new being

A round being

In this
Moving
Loving
Wheel

PRUDENCE TIPPINS,
POET AND TEACHER, 2008 INITIATION CIRCLE

1
ENTERING THE SOUTH
The Power of Agreements

Everybody walks in the street, more or less straight down the middle, and if a car comes while somebody's having a good conversation or telling a good story, the car has to wait till the story finishes before people will move out of the way. Stories are important here, and cars aren't.

ANN CAMERON,
THE MOST BEAUTIFUL PLACE IN THE WORLD

Is not the South the source of life, and does not the flowering stick truly come from there? And does not man advance from there toward the setting sun of his life? Then does he not approach the colder North where the white hairs are? And does he not then arrive, if he lives, at the source of light and understanding, which is the East?

BLACK ELK, *BLACK ELK SPEAKS*,
AS TOLD TO FLAMING RAINBOW
(JOHN G. NEIHARDT)

STEPPING IN TO INITIATION

The medicine wheel, circle, or spiral represents the never-ending cycle of life even as it represents the healing journey. It is based on an understanding of the cyclic nature of life and the importance of universal principles of behavior: sharing, caring, kindness, honesty, respect, trust and humility. Its circular nature ensures that the whole is addressed. It informs us that all its elements are related to each other.

LEWIS MEHL-MADRONA, *COYOTE HEALING*

One enters the Wheel of Initiation in the South, the direction of agreements, intentions, and aspirations. As with everything in your life, what you will experience in the Wheel comes down to your agreements and intentions. Your life and its conditions show you what you believe, what you are in agreement with, and what intentions you hold. Basically, what you experience in the outer world is what you are in agreement with internally. In Ann Cameron's tale of the most beautiful place, the power of story was given a priority. Entering the South means you choose consciously to identify your agreements and develop conscious intentions. You choose what is truly a priority. As a result, you become the cause rather than the effect of your life.

If you step in to the Wheel, you are expressing an agreement that you want to experience a personal initiation. The Initiatory Wheel, in response, will initiate aspects of yourself that lie dormant or in states of resistance.

Agreements are energetic contracts that are in alignment with unconscious and consciously held intentions and beliefs. Wherever there is a decision or action, there is an agreement; wherever there is an agreement, there is a belief sustaining it. I *believe* we can all become awakened in a single lifetime, I *agree* that I am responsible for my life, I *choose* to have everything in my life become an opportunity for awakening. Agreements are an invisible force, contracts that bind our lives together. They are why we do what we do. Each and every decision we make is acting out or supporting an agreement (mind-set) that we have made.

The momentums of your old agreements are what get shaken up first in the initiatory journey. This is because for initiation to take place, you have to let go of some old agreements and embrace some new ones. In every relationship I enter into, including facilitating various classes and circles (and now my relationship with you as a reader), I begin with agreements and bring them to a conscious level.

For me, stating agreements means that people are now being called to know what is driving their life. I know your experience of initiation will be determined by what you carry in your heart-mind (what you're in agreement with and what your intentions are). So as you enter the Wheel, let's introduce several new agreements—*agreements that your initiation depends upon.*

The First Agreement

The first agreement is for you to take 100 percent responsibility for your experiences. On the deepest of levels, you are responsible for your life (you can't blame circumstances, others, god, time, etc.). You don't get mad at the technician for his mistake; you choose one master to serve. Imagine yourself alone in the woods, and a large crashing sound is coming toward you. How will it help you to blame those who left you there? What is likely to happen if you say to yourself, "Why me? Why is this happening to me?" Much like getting shot with a poison dart, you had best put your energy into removing the dart and finding an antidote. Wasting time on blame and shame could ultimately kill you.

Thus, when entering the Wheel, you agree to take 100 percent responsibility for your *experience* in the Wheel and for your life. You agree to serve one master at a time. As long as you assign credit or blame to someone or something outside yourself, personal initiation will not be possible. Fools Crow, a Teton Sioux holy man, nephew of Black Elk in his profound healing work with others, understood this agreement. He attributed a successful healing to the intentions of the patient. The initiate takes the primary load of responsibility, Spirit then shows up to help, and the healer, teacher, or group takes on the task of holding space.

The Second Agreement

Along with the agreement to take 100 percent responsibility for your own life comes the agreement to *be willing to do whatever it takes.* This agreement will be in alignment with your personal intention of initiation (which you will set here in the South). *Be willing to do whatever it takes to bring your spiritual intention to fruition, to experience your personal initiation*, to bring forth your inner light.

"Whatever it takes" will arise as you move through the Wheel. It will likely touch every area of your life and bring forth the tight spots where habitual states are strong. It will bring forth those places where you have not, up until now, been willing to do whatever it takes to live a fully engaged life. When we are not willing to do whatever it takes, we either do not want to leave the comfort of our deck chair, or we don't trust ourselves or the world in which we live. We don't value our ability to decide for ourselves what we need in order to experience initiation.

If you have heard the call, follow that call all the way. Agree to do whatever it takes to fulfill your spiritual intentions, and you will experience a personal spiritual initiation. When you align your life with this agreement, you find the energy and ability to live a more creative, awakened life. Don't hesitate too long here; *say yes!*

The Third Agreement

> When gazing at sentient beings,
> one should do so candidly and lovingly,
> "In reliance upon them, I shall attain Buddhahood."
>
> SHANTIDEVA*

This next agreement is that we are in this together, that we belong to one another. Consider the earth a lifeboat; how you occupy your place in the boat impacts me and everyone else in your boat. You may think that this agreement is something everyone knows and understands. Isn't it obvious that we are all in this together? In reality, however, many people are *not* in agreement with this and see and experience themselves as separate from others. In fact, the closer we are to each other in the boat, the more

---

*All Shantideva quotes throughout this book are from Shantideva, *A Guide to the Bodhisattva Way of Life (Bodhicaryāvatāra),* translated from the Sanskrit and Tibetan by Vesna A. Wallace and B. Alan Wallace. New York: Snow Lion, 1997.

we are impacted by this truth. I belong to you, the reader. I belong to all those who have taken the Initiation Course. I belong to the president of the United States. I belong to my brothers. I belong to my husband and daughter. I belong to my daughter's piano teacher.

When we consciously agree (form a deliberate agreement) with this truth, it impacts us more directly (and usually more quickly). When you enter the Wheel, you are in deliberate agreement with *belonging to one another*. Whoever you are in intimate contact with is in close quarters to you on the boat. (Your spouse or partner, close friends, and dependent children are those to whom you have deliberately chosen to belong.) I do belong to my daughter's piano teacher and the president, but the agreement is not consciously made between us. So it is still true, but the truth is a bit softer, you might say. *When I uplift my life, I will improve the lives of all those I belong to.* I cannot actually make someone else happy, but I can create positive conditions for myself and then be one who is dispensing happiness.

In reality, we witness many of those around us suffering. I appreciate the metaphor of "holding one's seat" on the boat while someone may be suffering. Holding our seat means we offer love inwardly and outwardly. We hold our seat while we pay attention to our own stuff (taking 100 percent responsibility for it). We attend to what is arising in ourselves with compassion. And we don't interfere or separate ourselves from another's suffering. We stay present.

Belonging to someone doesn't mean taking care of or being dependent upon that person being a certain way or curing them of their problems. There will be times that the person sitting next to us in the boat is simply suffering; they are angry and depressed, and we didn't do anything to create this. But because they are in our boat (and nearby), and there is an agreement that we belong to one another (deliberate or not), we need to respond by staying present, not interfering or trying to control but not separating ourselves either. This is the dance of belonging—being present without interfering. If you are going through the Wheel on your own, take the time to commit to this agreement and the previous two agreements before continuing.

With this particular agreement, get a mirror and, looking into it, say, "I belong to you." Now, this may sound like a strange thing to do. But how true has this been up until now? How well have you belonged to this body, this spirit, this person that is you? Didn't Michele (in the Introduction) learn, in her wake-up call, who she first belongs to?

Next, close your eyes and bring to mind all the people sitting close to you in your lifeboat and imagine saying to them, "I belong to you." You can include whomever you want and then imagine this truth going out to everyone on the planet.

If you are in an initiation circle, take the time to make this agreement known to one another. In the yearlong course, we go around and say to one another, "I belong to you." This is intense but necessary, because otherwise we hesitate. If we cannot do this, we remain in an agreement that we *don't* belong to one another. As you enter the Wheel and deliberately choose to walk this journey of initiation, know too that *I belong to you.*

> Finding what we already possess may seem like a strange goal for a spiritual path. Yet the process of finding may provide us more joy than if the universe delivered all its secrets to us without any effort on our part.
>
> Neil Douglas-Klotz, *The Sufi Book of Life*

KNOW WHAT YOU ARE SIGNING UP FOR

The universe conspires to make us whole and to offer us the means to spiritual initiation. But it is up to us to get on the horse and ride.

One afternoon when my daughter was eight, she came home from school, upset with a bully she repeatedly encountered in her classroom. The bully teased her, telling her, "You're stupid," and was generally unpleasant. This confused and upset my daughter.

"What makes her do this?" she asked me.

I gave her a short lesson on how people's actions reflect what is in their heart. Samantha's heart is hurting. I told my daughter that she didn't need to take what Samantha did or said personally.

She went silent for a moment and then said to me, "I have a happy heart, Mom."

"Yes, you do," I replied.

Then she asked me, "How's it I have a happy heart and Samantha's is unhappy?"

I let the question sit out there in quiet space for a moment. I could see her thinking about it, and I knew that somewhere in the question she held her own answer.

"I know how I have a happy heart."

"How?"

"I signed up for it."

"What d'you mean, you signed up for it?"

"Before I came down to Earth, I signed up for a happy heart."

The question we can ask ourselves as we enter the Wheel (or undertake any endeavor) is, "What am I signing up for?" What do you want from this experience (the Wheel, this relationship, this day)? What are you signing up for, for the rest of your life?

What you sign up for will direct your experience and impact the conditions you find yourself in. Clearly the conditions surrounding the bully's life also influenced the state of her heart and her behavior. Likely she had been bullied at home. And yet, we all know people who rise above the worst of conditions and live an inspired life. We probably can't change the bully at school (or at work), but we can maintain an awareness and commitment to what we signed up for. I imagine that when our life passes before our eyes at the time of our death, what we see is what we signed up for—all our intentions and agreements.

In the initiatory journey, the main battle of the spiritual pilgrim is with the *inner* bully, the places where we are mean to ourselves. If one is uninitiated, this cruelty is then brought out into our environment through our actions; we pollute and litter our world with our mental and emotional waste. So we start with ourselves and, as a result, the world around us begins to wake up too. In some Buddhist traditions, *Jina*s are considered "the conquerors." Jinas have conquered habitual and negative states and experience the inner light of their true essence. They have broken through the layers of social conditioning. They have exeperienced spiritual intiation through the transformation of their minds.

BEING KEPT IN YOUR PLACE:
THE ILLUSION OF CULT TIME

The only true insights that result in personal initiation transpire from distancing ourselves from all that conditions us to our social environment—challenging that which "keeps us in our place," as Parker Palmer wrote. (This is the purpose of being carried off into the bush in many traditional practices of initiation.) We must confront ourselves in the great solitary woods, *on our own.* If we want to release the imprisoned splendor within, we must break through all that makes us small, holds us back, and keeps us in cult time.

Most of us expend quite a bit of our energy in cult time. Initiation breaks us free from the various "cults" that exist in the mainstream culture—the cults of medicine, of religion, of education, of politics, and the cult of family history. Ultimately you break through the cult of personal habitual thoughts, perceptions, and behaviors. This is the challenge of those on a spiritual pilgrimage—to battle the enemies within cult time and move more and more into freedom through personal initiation and into "real" time, natural time. *To give in to a life of routine and cult time is to give up on the authentic self and to the possibility of helping enlighten and strengthen our communities.*

Any time we follow others' dogma, rules, or ideas, without discernment, we are in cult time. Any time we are on automatic pilot and acting from our habitual states and are caught up in thinking and projecting such habitual thoughts outward and not inviting direct experience, we are in cult time. In cult time we feel an underlying disconnect, a lack of belonging, so we search for this connection outside ourselves and come to depend on outside confirmation to make us feel better.

When someone else directs our choices (instead of our own intuition and wisdom doing so) we are living in cult time. Many people find that their work is in cult time. But it is not the work or conditions themselves so much but what you end up agreeing to within these conditions that makes it cult time. William, who was working the Wheel and was entering the South, said, "I keep my job for the health insurance. It's a job, but it's not a vocation. But I need the insurance, and so I feel I have to keep this job." He could quit his job if he made a conscious decision to end his agreement to work in order to have health insurance. And he could refuse to participate in cult time while at work, transforming his environment. For example, he could experience his work environment as a place to practice his spiritual principles or to strengthen his intention.

In the Buddhist and Toltec traditions, students are often told to take jobs that help them lose their self-absorption. The challenging environment is understood as a means to deepen one's spiritual commitments. The point is that it is not the environment and its conditions that determine our experience but the agreements and intentions we hold. If William were more focused on his own personal intentions and their sustaining agreements, he would not be in agreement with cult time at work.

Oftentimes we reach the doorway to Initiation when we have exhausted all the habitual ways of living a certain aspect of our life. Cult time activities do not result in a truly satisfied life but one drained of essence. It is this exhaustion that often leads into a new way of being; we listen to the exhaustion (the depression, the anxiety, the boredom, the illness, the breathlessness), and find the doorway out of cult time.

It can be challenging to break with cult time, because we can't always rely on getting out of a marriage, or quitting a job, or moving as a way of transforming or uplifting our experiences. Most likely we have to transform the inner life we have created for ourselves. In other words, keep the job and lose the negative agreements.

Thou hast only to follow the wall far enough and there will be a door in it.

MARGUERITE DE ANGELI, *THE DOOR IN THE WALL*

✹ An Exploration into Presence

Give yourself a week to practice this exercise, which encourages you to become more aware of yourself (your feelings, beliefs, agreements) in any given moment. You start here with an investigation into who you truly are and what you genuinely want. "This exercise cracked me open and helped me realize the story lines and agreements I was living," said Barb, who was in the South.

During the day practice taking nice deep breaths into your belly. Imagine that when you breathe, you breathe from the belly and, as you expand out on the out-breath, picture space around you opening up. And from this spaciousness you can ask these questions . . .

- "What am I *thinking* right now?" Then take note of what is getting your attention.
- "What am I *feeling* right now?" Notice the different, *feeling* sensations that are present at this moment. They can include emotions, intuitive feelings, or bodily sensations. You may notice how these may relate to your thoughts at the given time.
- Then ask, "*What do I want?*" Keep breathing and ask, "*What do I want right now?*" Breathe into the belly and create space around this question.

You may carry a pocket journal with you as you practice creating more space for yourself, writing down what you notice as you do this exercise. Let this practice take you where it wants to take you. Initially you will likely gain some valuable insights. Later, with these insights, you may have awareness around thought patterns and feeling sensations that accompany certain experiences. Or it may become apparent that you don't really know what you want. This will prompt you to continue to determine what it is you do want; your pain story will also begin revealing itself through such inquiry.

This practice also prepares you in the setting of your initiatory intention. Here in the South we set our intentions like we are planting seeds in the earth. Fortunately, the seed and soil around us know what to do.

2

IN THE SOUTH

Getting on the Horse of Intention

Morning has broken
Like the first morning,
Blackbird has spoken
Like the first bird.
Praise for the singing!
Praise for the morning!
Praise for them, springing
From the first Word.

ELEANOR FARJEON,
"A MORNING SONG,"
IN *THE CHILDREN'S BELLS*

ENTER THE ALAYA VIGYAN OF YOUR SOUL

We have to take personal responsibility for uplifting our lives.

CHÖGYAM TRUNGPA, SHAMBHALA:
THE SACRED PATH OF THE WARRIOR

Osho, Indian philosopher and existentialist, refers to the subconscious by the Sanskrit phrase *alaya vigyan,* or "storehouse consciousness." This is the "basement" where we keep throwing all that we want to do and experience but instead ignore because of social conditioning. Our soul's aspirations are there in the lower hidden places of our psyche. In the South we enter these places inside ourselves where we keep all this stored.

There are many entrances to this place, and the key to unlocking the secrets of alaya vigyan includes spiritual journaling, meditation, encounters with nature, listening to sacred sounds or reading sacred text, as well as intentional ritual. Throughout this chapter we offer several techniques to enter the alaya vigyan of your inner home and retrieve an initiatory intention.

Conscious Evolution

The intention behind each action determines its effect. Our intentions and our actions affect not only us but also others. If we believe that every intention and action evolves as we progress on our spiritual journey, then if we act consciously we evolve consciously, but if we act unconsciously we involve unconsciously.

ALFRED HUANG,
THE DEFINITIVE GUIDE TO THE I CHING

One should ride the horse of awakening mind.

THE FOURTEENTH DALAI LAMA,
MADISON, WISCONSIN, JULY 2008

As we get on the horse and take the ride through the Wheel, we choose to *evolve consciously* instead of "involve unconsciously."

The symbol of the South is that of the spiritual pilgrim riding the horse of intention, of an awakened mind. This pilgrim is you. The Wheel

~~doesn't matter what flavor of spiritual pilgrim you are—a Christian, Sufi, Buddhist, Pagan, Toltec, or secular, to name a few.~~ Spiritual initiation relies on you choosing your own spiritual path and committing to an engaged, ethical, and inspired life. At this point in the Wheel, you set the intention of a spiritual pilgrim, and you choose to direct your experience of initiation. You are alone in the bush, and looking around yourself you wonder, "What am I going to get from this journey? What calls for initiation in my life?"

This is not about searching for who you are and what you want to do in your life (although these can become clear as you move through the Wheel). Initiation brings forth what is already within you. Nature points to this fundamental truth—you don't have to go in search of who you are and why you are here. Everything in nature knows what to do with its life. Within an acorn lives the oak tree; within a given seed waits the full-bloomed plant. Within the robin's egg is the robin. (You won't find a chicken popping out of a robin's egg!) *Fake, but a fitting fake.*

Nothing is exempt from this natural law. However, we humans tend to exempt ourselves from this natural law (by what we believe and agree to) and feel pushed to go in search of who and what we are. Often, we find ourselves in a great deal of pain in our search for ourselves. Because this natural law applies to every sentient being, all we have to do is remove the obstacles and distractions to this inherent truth.

Start here, then, right now. As Steven Pressfield says in *The War of Art:* none of us are born as passive generic blobs waiting for the world to stamp its imprint on us. Instead we show up possessing already a highly refined and individuated soul.

Another way of thinking of it is this: We're not born with unlimited choices. We can't be anything we want to be.

We come into this world with a specific, personal destiny. We have a job to do, a calling to enact, a self to become. We are who we are from the cradle, and we're stuck with it. Our job in this lifetime is not to shape ourselves into some ideal we imagine we ought to be, but to find out who we already are and become it.

We need the energy, courage, and commitment, however, to push through the layers of resistance to experience initiation. But you don't need to consider all possibilities—instead practice the means within the Wheel that opens the true inner doors. As you push through these hard layers, you will bring forth what is already within you, and much of your suffering will cease. A spiritual pilgrim practices inner discipline, calling on the courage and willingness to move through the entire Wheel, using everything in life to open the doors and release the inner light.

Up until now random and habitual choices resulted in random, habitual results. The resultant suffering has likely brought us to our knees and to the entrance of the Wheel. But we must consciously choose to step into the Wheel. The pain from our habitual states may bring us here, but to be within the Wheel we have already broken agreements with some of our patterns. What brought us to the Wheel is not what will get us through it.

Making Intentional Choices

Intentional choices generate intentional, conscious results. Our intentions move us through a myriad of circumstances. Each action, as mentioned before, is motivated by our beliefs, agreements, and intentions (hidden and conscious). *We aspire from within;* our intentions both create and call to us. Our entire psychosocial system matches up with our intentions. Intentions recognize the law of causality—of cause and effect. Happiness and suffering alike both come from their own conditions. Instead of meeting a situation with a habitual response (being *unconsciously involved*), we will choose how to respond with *conscious intention*.

Most people use up a lot of energy simply getting from place to place (not getting on the horse of awakening). Crafting and setting intentions gives you back energy lost in running about (and sometimes in place). Conscious intentions give us the horse to sit on. They give us the energy to break through the "armor" that holds our true nature in; they give us the ability to express our inherent wisdom and creativity. Both the rider and the horse represent the power of *guided* and compassionate energy through the use of conscious agreements and intentions.

People often seek help from therapists or spiritual teachers because they feel depleted, fatigued, and discouraged by their life and the choices they have made and continue to make. Getting on the horse retrieves lost energy, energy lost to past agreements and distorted, unconscious intentions. We can actually look at the results of our actions to know what intentions we are carrying around in our heart. Later on in our journey, through different sectors of the Wheel, we will identify principles as being our reins, directing our horse (life) where we choose it to go.

✳ Name Your Soul's Aspirations

This first journaling exercise takes you into the alaya vigyan. You may want to read through this chapter once and then go through it a second time to craft your intention.

Begin by journaling about what you want for yourself and in your life. You have already practiced bringing more presence into your daily experience on page 22. Here, write out the words, *"What I want . . ."* and fill up at least one page by completing this sentence. Instead of stopping to think, rewrite the words *"What I want . . ."* Don't let your pen stop moving, and don't stop to consider, just write. This bypasses the thinking mind and gets to the subconscious, the alaya vigyan.

Next in this journaling exercise, take one entry from your list above and circle the wish that either repeats itself or sticks out as the most important one. Choose the one that, if you were to express this desire fully in your life, a lot of your other wants would fall into place as well. Write out a description of this one aspiration. Do your best to write it down in one succinct sentence. (Be careful not to mistake goals or affirmations for intentions.)

The words we carry and use are potent tools of creation. A goal or affirmation holds a different vibration and result than an intention. Too often we use goals to beat ourselves up, using some ideal we are trying to achieve as the bat. The ideal becomes a standard of measurement to compare ourselves against—too often we see how we are *not* this idea of ourselves.

An intention, on the other hand, can be more readily and easily aligned with a broader plan for your life. Instead of your goal being, "I am going to lose twenty pounds," your intention might be, "I live a physically, mentally, and spiritually active life." Or, more simply, "I live an active life." This implies that, among other things, because you are active, you are less likely to be overweight.

In Donald Altman's work on mindful eating (*Meal by Meal*), he suggests letting go of the goal and giving in to the experience. He too recognizes that goals often bring forth more resistance and fear. Letting go of goals can be letting go of harsh expectations we hold over ourselves: "You too can let go of any goal beforehand and fully enjoy the experience—independent of judging yourself or others." In Buddhist practice this translates as the ability to give up our attachments and how we think our lives should be, and instead to give in to what is actually happening in the moment. Intentions are designed to let you live each moment in alignment with your broader spiritual and creative aspirations.

Intentions are action-oriented and, as such, energize and empower us. Living and acting from intentions is an optimal use of your energy and personal power. At any given moment you are either in alignment with your intention or out of alignment. When you are out of alignment, you are likely engaged in something that is robbing you of energy and making it difficult to initiate your intention. Your initiation intention will direct your experience in the Wheel; your experience in the Wheel will transform your life.

☀ Intentions Come from Our Soul's Aspirations

Next, take your wish and design a full intention, using verbs and action words. Use affirmative, active words that bring you into the moment. Make sure to leave out words that actually point to a difficulty such as anxiety or doubt. Instead use words that express freedom from the given issue or difficulty. For example, instead of "I live my life free of anxiety," have it be "I live freely, trusting my choices."

Other examples might include:

I express . . . beauty and harmony in all my thoughts and actions.
I bravely create my truth.

I awaken . . .
I realize . . .
I act . . .
I attain . . .
I appreciate . . .

You want your intention to be one concise sentence that is easy to retrieve. Create an intention that will initiate you into a more engaged life. Once an initiatory intention is set, it will begin to uplift your entire life. Intentions are more than affirmations. Affirmations are typically "I am" statements, such as "I am beautiful, I am . . ." Too often what happens is that we express a particular affirmation ("I am beautiful"), *while feeling and thinking its opposite* ("I am ugly"). The affirmations often don't ring true with the inner world of the individual.

While attending a recent teaching, I saw a woman with a T-shirt proclaiming on the front, "No HATING within twenty feet." At first the only word I saw was "HATING." My eyes and mind were drawn to that word and her accompanying frown. Not until she got close enough (within twenty feet) could I read the finer print.

Too frequently, affirmations may lack an action component and become somewhat narcissistic in quality (too focused on an homage to self to the exclusion of altruistic action). Our intentions must reach out to those we live with—our families and our communities. "I live an active life," for example, clearly benefits others as well as ourselves.

With intentions we choose a verb and an action word to express our aspiration and motivation. This generates more accountability on the part of the spiritual initiate. It also encourages us to align ourselves, in the moment, with the given intention. Interestingly, even the fine print of the T-shirt of the woman mentioned above gave off a negative message in that it contained the implicit assumption that she would encounter hate and that she would need to keep these haters away from her. Affirmations may not break through the layers of assumptions and habitual thought states we carry around with us, but intentions, comprised of conscious and purposeful word choices, directly influence our experiences in a positive way.

Start with one main initiation intention that you will ride through the Wheel.

Once you develop a spiritual intention, keep it strong in your mind. Do not divorce from it. Commit to an inner deliberation to hold your intention consciously throughout the day. Be like the initiate who has entered the woods with the strong intention of independence, courage, and freedom. Once you have set an intention for your personal initiation, keep it conscious as you move through the Wheel as well. Of course, you will create other intentions in your life, but your initiation intention sets and generates this personal initiation experience.

Example intentions: "I experience appreciation from all life." Someone who felt unappreciated most of his life chose this intention. "I rejoice in the good fortune of others." This one was borrowed from the Bodhisattva's precepts. This person often felt in competition with others. "I remain empowered in all situations." "I live an abundant life, doing what I love." "I express my creativity with all life." "I act authentically because I know my truth." This particular initiate had lived in a marriage and life where he wouldn't speak up for himself. He found himself becoming less and less authentic.

An aspect of a conscious intention that makes it different from goals and affirmations is its altruistic quality. Whereas it may be very personal ("I live an abundant life doing what I love"), its very nature will uplift the lives of everyone who comes in contact with the person expressing the intention. Your intention will enliven you and those around you.

To further imprint your intention, you might want to journal about what your intention will look like, feel like, be like, when it is 100 percent true. When this intention is fully initiated, how will your life be different? How will this intention benefit others in your life? Does it have an altruistic quality to it?

LISTENING FOR YOUR INTENTION

One early summer morning I went out into the woods with a friend to do a bird survey. Mostly this is done by listening for songs, but it also involves observing what you might be fortunate enough to see. Unless an obvious call of a cardinal or ovenbird made its way to my ear, all songs sounded as if they came from one bird. My friend would say, "Oh, that's a scarlet tanager," "Oh, that's a red-eyed vireo," "Hear that? It's a sora rail." I would listen while more songs began to arise out of what had been a blended version of one or two songs. (Each song also had an intention—one bird called to another, one bird found food, one bird issued a warning, etc.)

I soon noticed I could hear more. Sounds became more distinct, unique. I could hear the diverse songs offered up to the listening ear. I felt pulled back to Earth, to my body and the moment. This listening practice healed some of the separation I felt within and without. The more I listened, the more I remembered how I belong to this world of diverse sound and beauty.

As I write this I can hear the birds sending out their late-morning songs, *full of intention.*

Because we are often distanced from the natural, wild world, we need to take some time in nature just to listen. I recommend this practice of listening meditation while you are in the South of the Wheel, while you are discerning a personal song of intention for your initiation. We need to practice new ways of noticing, other ways of listening. This reminds us that we are truly in the woods of the unknown, where we *have* to pay attention.

✸ Recognize Your Song

Spend an hour or two in the woods or prairie or somewhere in nature and *listen.* Simply record what you hear in your journal. Write down all the sounds (whether you can name them or not)—the thumping of mating grouse (or something thumping), a cardinal's song (or birds singing,) a hum of a bee, the trees, something large walking in the wood, the call of the crows flying South. . . . Retrieve as many sounds as you can. Write them all down.

Then sometime that day, or upon sunrise the next morning, write in your journal about what you don't remember. Begin with the line, "I don't remember . . ." and repeat this line as often as you need to until a stream of consciousness occurs. Instead of stopping to think, repeat the sentence, "I don't remember . . ." Keep your pen moving (as described earlier on page 27. Spontaneous words and memories will arise as you write. Collen wrote, "I don't remember my father hugging me, I don't remember a kind word from him, I don't remember what my favorite childhood food was."

Later on, when you can give yourself another half an hour, create a poem or prose from these two journal entries. Bring together the sounds you heard and what you don't remember. This exercise uses mental "muscles" that are typically ignored but help us to hear and recognize the internal stirrings of our intention.

SETTING YOUR INTENTION

To set your intention means to create a bridge between your intention and reality—making your intention more real. Give it legs. When making homemade jams, we want the jam to set so that we can store it and eat it over a year's time. It is not jam unless it sets. The setting of your intention is to take the natural ingredients of your life, create an intention, and "set" it—making it usable. Take more time to journal how your intention manifests for you. How will your life be more engaged, fulfilling, active? What will be different when this intention is fulfilled?

Take at least a week with this intention, journaling around it before you set it. How does it feel in your body when you say it aloud? A timely intention will feel energetic, spacious, and good in the body, and most likely risky. Close your eyes and say your intention a few times and pay attention to the physical and energetic sensations of the body to make sure that this intention really resonates with you.

Your intention will naturally generate the desire to move and create. And it can be used as a guidepost; at any given moment you will know whether your agreements and your actions are in alignment with this intention. Very soon we are able to discover how much of our energy is going into our spiritual and creative life and how much is not.

You don't hear me yell to test the quiet or try to shake
the wall, for I understand that the wrong sound weakens
what no sound could ever save, and I am the one
to live by the hum that shivers till the world can sing—
May my voice hover and wait for fate,

When the right note shakes everything.

WILLIAM STAFFORD, FROM THE POEM
"BELIEVER," IN *THE WAY IT IS*

❋ A Personal Ritual of Intention

Set your intention by creating a Wheel of Initiation on the ground and stepping into its center. The Wheel can be made of stones, cornmeal, flowers, tobacco, shells, or any object that creates a sacred circle. The four directions will be represented, along with a place for you to stand in the center of the Wheel. Therefore, make a circle with four sections and a space in the center. If you make it somewhat permanent, you can return to it to set future intentions. You can also use a labyrinth (considering yourself in the center of the Wheel when you reach the center of the labyrinth).

We have mowed a large spiral in our restored prairie, and when I am ready to set a new intention, I take my intention into the center of the spiral. Enter your Wheel when you have some time to journal and meditate afterward. From the center of the Wheel, face each direction, and, in this case, begin by facing the South. State your intention and make a commitment *to do whatever it takes* to fulfill this intention.

Fig. 2.1. A one-acre walking spiral/labyrinth on a restored prairie located on the author's land in Spring Green, Wisconsin.

For example, face South and say, "I (recite your personal initiation intention) . . . and I am willing to do whatever it takes to fulfill this intention." Then face the West, then North, and finally the East, stating your intention and the agreement to do whatever it takes. Of course, at this point you don't know what the "whatever" is—so it will take the courage of a spiritual hero to honestly set this intention. The "whatever" points to what is or is not in alignment with your intention. You will recognize the "whatevers" when they arise in your life. The "whatever" comes up as soon as you set your intention and throughout the Wheel and ranges from speaking up about what you want, to writing that book, to changing your vocation. Your intention keeps you inspired. Your intention will create movement, because inspiration likes action. In fact, when one is truly inspired, action is a natural outcome.

Trust comes up for those on a spiritual pilgrimage. For movement to take place, we must trust in ourselves to do whatever it takes, trust in the spirit world to help us out, and trust in the humanity of others to come through for us. Trust ultimately engages your intention—because with this trust, you continue to stay on the horse of intention. As Fools Crow states in *Wisdom and Power,* "without faith there is no power and there is no movement."

MORE TOOLS FOR STAYING ON THE HORSE OF INTENTION

At the most one could say that his Chi or personal god was good. But the Ibo people have a proverb that when a man says yes his Chi says yes also. Okonkwo said yes very strongly; so his Chi agreed. And not only his Chi but his clan too.

CHINUA ACHEBE, *THINGS FALL APART*

Some Advice about Advice

We all need the energy and commitment to move through the hard shell of our persona and ego to fulfill our initiatory aspirations. One way we give away our *chi,* our life energy, is through the giving of advice. If we always feel the need to give others feedback and keep giving our energy away in this manner, we won't have much left for ourselves or our intentions. The need to give advice keeps one focused outside oneself.

Can you go ten days without giving any feedback or advice to others or to yourself? You can begin with yourself. We tend to routinely give ourselves advice and judge our choices. So begin with bringing awareness to how often you give yourself or others advice. Then after a week of bringing awareness to this, practice taking some measures to *not* give advice. This practice of withholding advice and feedback prepares the way for a new way of being in the world, a more attentive, curious, listening stance rather than one that is always dissipating energy out. Listen to the individual's entire story without jumping in and giving feedback. Notice when you are in the mind of "giving advice" and how this feels in your psychophysical system. Also notice the energy of the other person when you give advice. Most people just want to be heard.

Instead of giving advice practice:

Listening until the person is done speaking. Only consider giving advice if they ask for it.

Asking a question. (Make certain it is not with a twist, where you are really giving advice or feedback.)

Asking yourself if what you are wanting to say is really improving the situation.

Focusing on what *you* might do differently.

Writing a response in your journal.

Listening some more.

Not giving advice or feedback will feel unnatural at times, especially when the habit to do so is strong. This tendency to share our opinion, to give feedback, is in the current of our culture. We have been socially conditioned to constantly give and receive feedback to the point where we find it difficult to consider relating in other ways. I often get the question, "How can I not give my children advice? Are they included in this practice of not giving advice?" Yes, they are. You may come to realize how many arguments are avoided when you find another way to communicate with your children, and how much more they have to say to you.

Listening is a skill we now have to relearn. In the Wheel there is an unlearning and undoing process that goes along with spiritual initiation. In this case, unlearning the habit of giving advice and feedback opens you up to more creative energy and more peaceful relationships with others.

Don't Play by the Rules

As we come to the end of the practices in the South, here is one more valuable tool for those on this spiritual pilgrimage: Practice changing rules into conscious choices and agreements. The more rules we go by, the more we are shut off from our intuitive, inherent wisdom.

The challenge for us on the initiatory journey is *to consciously renegotiate the existing laws, rules, and dogma* that we have consented to every day. Don't automatically be in agreement to shut off your discernment and intuition; this puts you on automatic pilot. The Wheel is a place where the old rules won't apply anyway—deep into our spiritual initiation, it would be dangerous to rely on someone else's rules when all around us is new. So, begin to challenge rules set around you and pay attention to what the moment requires. Am I really hungry for dinner? Would this be a good place to slow down? Do I agree with what the advisor just told us to do? Do I follow tradition with this spiritual practice, or is the situation calling me to do something else? What are the symptoms of my body telling me? What wants my attention?

When riding the horse of awakening, our intuitive sense of the present situation and what it calls forth from us is better than sitting half asleep atop a horse that may or may not agree with the rules. When you are in the bush, on your own trying to get through the dark night, no rules apply. When we take a spiritual pilgrimage to a new inner land we can't apply rules and dogma from the old homeland. This is true of the Wheel and of life. Continue safely at your own risk, awake and ready.

A Sunrise Walk through the Spiral

As I finished up this chapter on the South, I rose for a morning walk through the spiral that covers an acre on our prairie. Dawn was breaking through the darkness, and a soft rain promised to get me wet. After saying my spiritual vow, I prayed as I entered the spiral, asking to be ready to live more fully engaged, to express my intentions, and to bring forth all that was within me. A few steps in I found myself caught up in thoughts of what I *should* do that day.

Then I tripped. I stumbled not so much on the hole made by the mole but because of my preoccupation with planning for the day. I laughed about how true this is in life—how my worrisome or neurotic thoughts trip me up. I began to quietly pray for attentiveness and walked more slowly and mindfully into the spiral's center. As I reached the second circle of the spiral, I looked up into the western sky (the direction we are about to enter) and saw a rainbow, mixed in with a few thunderclouds and the blue-orange of the July sky. I took this in and practiced the sky-gazing meditation (see page 191 in the North).

When I reached the center of the spiral, I faced each direction and recommitted my intentions (as I do each morning):

I attain the body and mind of awakening through the power of my efforts.

I rejoice in the good fortune of all beings.

I realize the true nature of mind.

I act in ways that befit a Bodhisattva.

I live an active writer's life.

Let's commit and recommit to doing whatever it takes to bring our intentions fully out into the world, every day. At this moment we may not know completely what that will be—but let's be ready.

3

ENTERING THE WEST

Following the Right God Home

A Ritual to Read to Each Other

If you don't know the kind of person I am
and you don't know the kind of person you are
a pattern that others made may prevail in the world
and following the wrong god home we may miss our
   star.

For there is many a small betrayal in the mind,
a shrug that lets the fragile sequence break
sending with shouts the horrible errors of childhood
storming out to play through the broken dyke.

And as elephants parade holding each elephant's tail,
but if one wanders the circus won't find the park,
I call it cruel and maybe the root of all cruelty
to know what occurs but not recognize the fact.

And so I appeal to a voice, to something shadowy,
a remote important region in all who talk:
though we could fool each other, we should consider—
lest the parade of our mutual life get lost in the dark.

For it is important that awake people be awake,
or a breaking line may discourage them back to sleep;
the signals we give—yes or no, or maybe—
should be clear: the darkness around us is deep.

WILLIAM STAFFORD, *THE WAY IT IS*

FREEDOM FROM OUR PAIN STORIES

Everything we abandon before we can bring it to a conclusion
continues to live until it is played out, until the story is finished. All
strains will be played out.

ANDREI CODRESCU, *THE BLOOD COUNTESS*

As we ride the horse of intention through the Wheel for personal initiation and enter the West—the direction of purification, release, and recapitulation—what tends to meet us is our pain stories. *A pain story is made up of our agreements with the pain of the past.* Further into the Wheel, when entering the North, we will design our authentic, initiatory story. But to express such personal truth, we need to make space for it. We do this by transforming the pain stories that clutter our lives.

In the West we release the past, instead of carrying it on our back like a portable projector where what we see and experience *is* rerun after tired rerun. Each of us will continue to repeat our personal histories unless we are willing to do what it takes to end our agreements to the past.

When living and reliving a pain story, we *follow the wrong god home.*

You must know the person you are, as Stafford suggests, or "a pattern that others made may prevail in the world," and "following a wrong god home you may miss your star," in other words—your life. A culture lacking in accessible initiation processes results in a majority of people living out their pain stories. Fortunately, through the many spiritual and psychological traditions available to everyone, we can free ourselves from their weight.

Up until now you may have been using much of your energy (consciously and unconsciously) to perpetuate your pain stories. In these stories, you carry around assumptions about why things are the way they are and why you need what you need, as well as your assumptions about everything and everyone. Our pain stories may have originated with acerbic events, but we are the playwright of our lives (and the director and actor). Therefore the historical and conditional cause of our pain story holds no power in comparison to our ability to rewrite and re-create our lives.

We relive our pain stories until we consciously name the patterns and *agreements* inherited with the pain. By taking 100 percent responsibility for our experience, we can fully free ourselves from them. And, of course, as we free ourselves from our pain stories, we influence and uplift our communities and natural environment (which is always what a true process of initiation will do).

When in agreement with the past, we keep projecting the past onto the present. We live from the past, seeing and creating it over and over again. Many people ask, "Why does this keep happening to me?" when the questions should be, *"What do I do to contribute to this pattern again and again?"* "What can I do to interfere with this pattern and create a new story for myself?" One doesn't need a therapist to be free from the past. One needs the tools (*sometimes* afforded through therapy) that allow you to be aware of your pain story, along with a willingness to practice your life principles. (These principles will be determined by you when you enter the North section of the Wheel.)

A well-known African proverb reminds us that *the medicine for the wound is right next to the wound.* The medicine we need to heal from our pain stories is in the story and its surrounding experiences, the habitual ways that keep the pain going in our lives. You might say that there would not be a reason for initiation without the pain story. To be free of our pain stories, it will be necessary to name the pain correctly and honestly, to be "the principal witness of our own lives," as the Lojong slogan points out in Mahayana practices of Buddhism. (*Lojong* translates into "mind training.")

This suggests that you trust your take on experiences (trust your intuition), and second, keep an honest appraisal of how you are doing with your life. You have been with yourself since the beginning of time—you know where you slip up, get lazy, go into denial, and get habitual. Remember to practice *compassionate* inquiry into your pain story. It won't help to judge yourself, which will only increase the hold the story has on you. Imagine yourself as a caring counselor or spiritual teacher, listening to your own life story.

When you work with a new intention, a pain story around a particular theme may arise. For instance, a couple of years ago I wrote out a story about all the teachers in my life, and then I shared it with others in a circle. I wrote about the spiritual and secular teachers and the abusive and skillful teachers—they all came up for me as I wrote. When I was done, I was able to release the pain of this story (release the agreements that perpetuated the pain within the story) and retrieve the energy I had lost to it. Finally, with this renewed energy, I was able to create a present, authentic story around my relationships with my current teachers.

YOUR STORY UP UNTIL NOW

When we carry our history and our pain stories, they can become too heavy for us to bear alone. When we unveil our past and tell our stories, we are less alone. In the simplest way, we just need to be heard. But much opens and unravels as we go into our lives stories. Our pain stories can be released, and the story of our soul, our authentic story, becomes revealed, like a secret garden buried after years of neglect.

We are now going to begin a practice that will help you access your pain stories in order to be able to transform them. I want you to write out the story of your life, giving yourself as much time as needed to reflect upon your personal history and to write about it. Take the time to gather pictures and other items that may elicit more memories. What is your life story? Where and how does it begin? Is there a theme that threads your life together? Or are the events more chronological? This is your story—acknowledge and document it the way that you choose to. Practice writing it out as if you are going to read it and share it with others.

Exorcising the Why of It All

> *Nor again must we in all matters demand an explanation of the reason why things are what they are; in some cases, it is enough if the fact they are so is satisfactory.*

ARISTOTLE, *NICOMACHEAN ETHICS*,
TRANSLATED BY W. D. ROSS

As you open up to your personal history, you can let go of any need to know the *why* of it all. This is not an investigation into why things are the way they are—why you were hurt, why you are stuck, why you repeat this and that, why your mother didn't want you. To focus on the why results in the blame and shame game, because the *why* question really asks, who is to blame?

Instead, we need to focus on the *what* of it all. What happened? What is happening now? What is the relationship between what happened in the past and what is being repeated now? What wants to happen *now?* What led me up to this place in my life? Again, if something is charging at you in the dark of night, are you really going to waste your precious time asking *why*? The why of it all will only take you further away from the energy and resources of the moment and away from living your authentic life.

In my thirty-some years working with others on their psychological and spiritual issues, I realize that one does not have to know why someone did this or that (or even have specific memories of a precipitating event) in order to heal from the pain of the past.

Why Wonder Why?

THREE WANDERERS WERE WALKING on a path leading out from the deep woods and into the green, growing meadow and beyond. The path was long and narrow, with a diversity of terrain on each side. As they walked, they came upon a broken jar. One could see that the jar, when intact, had been ornate and beautiful. It had golden thread throughout and all the colors of the rainbow subtly burned into it. Next to the broken jar was a large rock.

The first wanderer approached the jar and the rock and immediately got angry. She demanded to know how such a thing could have happened. She asked herself, "Did the rock hit the jar or the jar the rock?" She felt she had to know, but neither rock nor jar were speaking. She stood there, angry and scared, and she didn't move.

The second wanderer looked at the jar and immediately became depressed. "Why would god let such a thing happen?" "Why did this beautiful jar have to be ruined in this way?" "Why is this here on the path?" "Why did I come across it?" "Why, why, why?" This wanderer went into a deep state of confusion and depression and also did not move.

The third wanderer saw the rock sitting next to the once-beautiful jar and simply noticed what had happened. The jar was broken. The rock was next to the jar. She realized that she didn't know the how of it because it had already happened. She didn't really care about the why of it because it wouldn't answer any of the more important questions. She just noticed that the jar was broken and what she could do. She bent down and picked up the broken shards, placing them in her pocket. She then moved the rock a bit to the side of the path and walked on. As she continued on down the path, the shards jingled in her pocket, making the sound of wind chimes.

The other two remained behind.

As you acknowledge a given story, the whys and hows of it may naturally arise. Notice these but do not spend much time with them. They will not generate movement and will likely result in you feeling victimized and stuck. Why your mother didn't love you can take up a lot of time, energy, and speculation on your part. Furthermore, the "why" is often part of someone else's story. *Why someone hurt you is within* their *story, so it remains out of your reach to do anything about it.*

But if you know the "what of it all"—that love was lacking in your life—you can take this information, use it to heal, and move on. You have the power to transform this energy like the third wanderer did with the broken jar.

THE WRITING OF YOUR LIFE STORY

Epictetus said that people are disturbed not by the events but by the meanings they make of them. Stories contain the meaning we make of our lives events.

LEWIS MEHL-MADRONA, COYOTE HEALING

Uncovering Personal Truth

In the writing and telling of your own life story, you discover personal truth and meaning.

Begin with a journal and start wherever you like. Don't feel you have to write every detail or chapter of your life. You can even write lists of turning points and then write about various times that stand out. As you remember and write, you may find yourself stuck at certain times of your life. Acknowledge these moments and keep writing.

Consider the following questions while writing your life story:

- What do you consider your first childhood memory? Take that and expand on it as if you were taking a camera and zooming its lens out to capture more of what was surrounding the main image (you).
- What other memories stand out for you? Include major turning points in your life.
- What are the repetitive dreams throughout your life pointing to? Dreams get to the more unconscious patterns that we may be expressing, ones that want our attention.
- What did it take to get to this place in your life? Write a narrative repeating the words, "What it took to get here was . . ." Instead of stopping to think, keep moving your pen and repeat the sentence, "What it took to get here was . . ." Just allow the words and images to come.

For years I carried certain memories around with me. One was a painful one from early childhood. It hung on to me like fear to a lost child. I would often have dreams about this time and related events. When I finally released this pain story through writing and narration, the pain story dissolved and the related dreams stopped. Even though I can still recall this memory, it is quite faint, and I no longer carry it on my back. It does not influence me or shadow my present experiences. Important to this discussion is that it was in the writing out and telling of the story that I was able to release the pain. (In this case I shared my pain story with a transpersonal counselor. I have released other pain stories in circles and rituals, as well as with friends and loved ones.)

If you have written and told your story already, you can either rewrite your story from the vantage point of having already told your story, or you may choose to focus on one aspect of your life story. You may also find that new pain stories arise as you write your story again. Some people choose to focus on a specific theme in their writing of another story. After having gone through the Wheel once, many find the practice of naming a pain story and working with it through the Wheel to be a meaningful and relatively quick process of personal transformation.

ANCESTRAL HEALING

Present in our stories are the stories of our ancestors. When someone comes in to see me for counseling and has a particular pain story to work through, I sense the presence of their ancestors lining up behind them. These ancestors often carried the same pain story. "Now this one" (*you*) is ready to end the agreements to the ancestral pain story, and they stand there, ready to help, and waiting for the release. *This healing through story and the initiatory journey then moves out in all directions*—it heals those ancestors lined up behind the person, the children in front, the family and peers to the side, the Mother Earth below.

This is what makes the healing of your pain stories so essential. What are some of your parents' stories or your ancestors' histories? Where do their histories and stories show up in yours? Can you feel your ancestors lining up? Can you see how freeing yourself from a given pain story frees those who come after you? Can you understand how it will impact the relationships around you now? Can you imagine those ancestors behind and above you smiling, dancing, and singing in celebration as you unburden yourself?

Karla, a young woman I was working with, told me, "I could feel all the women on my mother's side lining up behind me, wanting for me what they had given up—the freedom they had given up to addictions and fear. It stops here with me. I know this."

Listening for the Meaning in Your Life Story

If you are going to read your life story to a circle of friends, please first read the appendix, "Teachers and Groups"—to help make this a safe and dynamic experience. Otherwise find at least one trusted friend, loved one, spiritual advisor, or transpersonal counselor you can tell your life story to. As advised in the appendix, ask that they simply mirror your story and not give any suggestions or feedback. This is true for yourself as well— become your own mirror.

Listen to your story and witness all your emotions, agreements, and beauty without trying to change anything or figure anything out. In the listening, the story itself will show you what you need to know—your agreements to the past, what needs releasing, what you have lost your energy to. It will also reveal some of your authentic story, your personal spiritual inheritance.

- *What you will listen for in your own story is the agreements that keep the pain story repeating.* If you don't have any negative patterns (psychological, physical, financial, relational, spiritual) that seem to repeat over and over in your life, you are free of your pain stories and are living the fully initiated, engaged life. This is not to say that you will not have trials, however, for an awakened person is still human and must consciously keep their feet on the path.

  Through my work as a psychotherapist and facilitator of the Initiation Course, I have mirrored hundreds of life stories. In my workshops and encounters in my travels, I have mirrored many a story as well. I always discover the medicine next to the wound— within the stories we live and tell.

- *What you will listen for in your story are the times your view of yourself or the world changed.* This is where you moved from believing and expressing one agreement into another. Where once you were in agreement that you were an awesome example of creation, you began to feel small and devalued. Where in your story do you experience a shift in awareness or experience? Remember, the "why" is not important, but the "what" holds meaning for you here—what happened to cause you to shift your agreements? What were the agreements, and what did they become?

- *Every experience you have now is tied to an agreement you hold with yourself or the world.* It becomes abundantly clear that it is not the event or person "out there" that keeps you in your pain, it is the *agreement(s)* with a person or an event that causes the continued suffering. So we take our focus off of how others are doing us wrong, how the other is causing us so much grief, and we name the agreements within this dynamic. At this point, it doesn't matter whether you believe you can change the agreement or not. Just begin here by naming the agreements within your difficulties. At this juncture in the Wheel, after writing out your life stories, you are then ready to move further into your personal initiation.

MOVING FURTHER INTO THE WHEEL

The initiate becomes another man because he has had a crucial revelation of the world and life.

MIRCEA ELIADE, *RITES AND SYMBOLS OF INITIATION*

Metaphorically, you are deep in the woods, and all the things that would keep you lost and hungry—your fears, your inhibitions, your doubts about yourself and the world—are arising as you try to figure out how to survive another night in the bush. This spiritual pilgrimage has led you to a place that you are not entirely happy about having found. The inner struggle is caused by your attempts to live with the burden of the past as it drags you down into a deeper state of spiritual and emotional hunger. You know that you cannot use the old agreements and negative mind-sets that you have relied on up until now to get you out of the woods. You will go back out into the world initiated, but *you must first identify the agreements of the old pain story.* Be forewarned that they tend to hold on like a bungee cord, seeming to let you go but pulling you back into habitual ways.

It is the strength of the ego that holds on to the agreements of pain. It says to you: "This pain speaks the truth"; "If you give up this agreement, you will be destroyed"; "This is who I am." The ego doesn't want you to listen to your wisdom heart and follow a true god home. Rather it wants you to stay lost and focused on a false god rooted in the pain of the past.

Grace's Pain Story

GRACE WAS RAISED in a hostile environment, one of abuse and neglect. Her mother was depressed and narcissistic—a silent parent in light of her husband's authoritarianism; Grace's father was a controlling perfectionist.

Before entering the Wheel, Grace would begin to have insight into her pain stories through therapy or personal inquiry but would get stopped by questioning why and how could this have happened to her. And because there is no satisfactory response to "why" her father was perfectionistic and controlling, she would give up on her healing process (for awhile). But the bottom line was that she didn't want to feel so much pain, so she would always resume her inquiry and healing journey.

Her pain story includes a time where a neighborhood friend was kidnapped and murdered. Her father had made her go along with him while they looked through garbage bins in search of the girl's body. Both her parents continually held impossible or irrational expectations of Grace. She came to believe she could only win their love by being perfect, but she was never good enough.

Extreme as this example may seem, this story holds wisdom for us all. At a very young age, Grace *agreed* that one must try everything to be perfect, because this is the only thing that would keep her safe and possibly afford her some parental love. There probably wasn't a day that went by that her parents didn't point out some imperfection of hers to her, and she had to strive harder to win their approval (which was never given freely or fully). She also dealt with the trauma of a murdered friend, without receiving support from the adults in her life.

In spite of her family environment, Grace had a good heart, and with this she observed her mother's suffering, which made her unconsciously *agree* to carry her mother's pain. I call this agreement *"Carrying another's shadow."* By carrying her mother's shadow, Grace erroneously believed that she could help her mother, and once her mother was well enough, she would be able to love Grace.

Inherent in our pain stories is the meaning of our pain *and* the medicine to release ourselves from it. When Grace is deep in a pain story, she feels lost in the woods. Although she wants to be free of her suffering, *she must give up the agreements that she believes have kept her alive and safe thus far.* (The need to be perfect and the agreement to carry her mother's pain, in this case.)

Grace, having set her intention in the South, and with the willingness to do whatever it takes, will arrive at some personal truth that will allow for her initiation.

> *This farewell comes from a forgiving leaf*
> *that skipped with the others and then found*
> *a lucky storm that brought me here. Listen—*
> *hold on as long as you can, then thrust forth;*
> *make truth your home.*
>
> WILLIAM STAFFORD, FROM THE POEM "FOUR
> OAK LEAVES," IN *LEARNING TO LIVE IN
> THE WORLD: EARTH POEMS*

Naming Your Agreements

The true nature of our mind is pure like light, but it is getting caught on obstacles.

GESHE LHUNDUB SOPA

Can you name another agreement that may come from Grace's pain stories? Grace cannot allow herself to *trust* because she has to be perfect. The matter of trust comes up in most if not all pain stories. Her agreement is not to trust herself, others, or the unknown. Distrust weakens and immobilizes us, whereas trust empowers the mind. All agreements within our pain stories debilitate us, which is the reason we need to identify them.

For Grace, the paradoxical beauty of holding several painful agreements is that she can focus on transforming any one of these agreements to experience freedom from *all* of them. They are all within the other: to be able to trust, she would need to let go of the agreement of perfectionism; to be less than perfect, she would have to trust.

Those of us with strong pain stories have many good memories, but these are often tainted by some shadowy detail. The joy of graduation or the completion of some art project is ruined when a family member makes a sarcastic remark. The family reunion is pleasant until someone insists on driving home intoxicated. An element of disappointment seems to thread through each narrative portrayal. As a result we built agreements as to how we would be in the world.

Working with our lives stories and the pain story agreements within them, we come to experience a completeness that is often paradoxical. Our stories are full of paradoxical threads because our lives are full of our pain stories, our misses and disappointments. But they also make us who we are, as well as lead us to our greatest potential. We are capable of great love, courage, and compassion often *because* of our pain stories.

CULTURALLY ENDORSED PAIN STORY AGREEMENTS

As we have learned, our agreements, not the conditions of our lives, keep us in our pain stories. And although we hold many *personal* agreements that keep a pain story active, we also are in agreement with *culturally endorsed* pain stories. Below are some agreements I find to be at the core of so much unnecessary suffering. As Parker Palmer suggests, these agreements (illusions) "keep us in our place," they keep us from undertaking our own personal initiation.

The Agreement "Not to Trust"

Our culture encourages us not to trust our own truth. It seems many institutions today depend upon our being in a state of distrust. These include the pharmaceutical companies that promote drugs for every emotional and physical discomfort (we take the pill instead of listening to and trusting our bodies, or trusting other methods of healing); religious institutions that promote fear of self-knowledge and direct experience while insisting on total reliance on dogma and doctrine (as understood by the institution, not the individual); educational systems that teach us *what* to think rather than *how* to think; a news media that decides the important topics to be covered and too often serve as spin doctors; a therapeutic process that too often creates a dependency on the therapeutic relationship rather than leading the client to the inner healer; and a medical system that implies you must value what the doctor says above valuing your own experience.

Without trust there is a of lack movement in one's life. Action comes from wisdom *and* trust: trust in self, trust in humanity, trust in your personal principles, and trust in the forward movement of life.

> *Uprooting its opposite in this way, one should strive to increase one's zeal with the powers of aspiration, self-confidence, delight, letting go, dedication, and determination.*
>
> SHANTIDEVA

At this point you might want to ask yourself: Where am I holding on, where am I resistant or fearful? Where do I feel stuck? Where do I hold an aspiration but experience little or no movement? How is my mind habituated (what does it keep seeing)? There you will find an agreement not to trust. The antidote for a lack of trust is *movement*. For now, become aware of how your agreement not to trust inhibits you. Then, with this aware-ness, practice acting *as if* you do trust yourself, the world, and—in particular—the influence of your initiation intention. Such trust is a key attitude for the spiritual pilgrim.

Later on in the Wheel, you will experience more antidotes for this culturally endorsed agreement (agreeing not to trust) and learn how to move through such states as fear, anxiety, and resistance.

The Agreement to "Carry Another's Shadow"

The agreement to carry another's shadow happens any time we carry within us what we feel others *should* be doing to be better or to feel better. "If only he would stop smoking pot and get a job, his life would improve." "He needs to read this book." "He shouldn't do that." Carrying another shadow is not to be confused with compassion, which is the ability to do our internal work so that we can be present for others' suffering. In my Buddhist practice, carrying another's shadow is an example of "mistaken compassion." You carry this judgment and feedback within you as a weight—but what is the other up to? They are up to their life, making their own choices. Your carrying around their shadow does not help them.

I often suggest that people who are engaged in this internal gossip of what the other should or should not be doing say to themselves, "This is none of my business." A principle within the Lojong teachings of the Mahayana practice of Tibetan Buddhism is to "not ponder others," not to ponder their faults. When we carry their shadow by thinking what they should and should not be doing, we are actually pondering their faults.

Once someone has offended or hurt you and you have decided to forgive them, do you find yourself reminding yourself of the offense when this person rises up in your thoughts? Why carry the shadow of the past? What happens to *you* when you ponder others' faults? Let these go by saying something like, "I let this one go." Or, "This is done." You can even respond with, "I no longer agree to carry this."

Practice checking in with your thoughts to notice how much you may be pondering others' faults or going over their wrongdoings in your mind. If you're feeling depressed, angry, or unhappy, notice how much of these feelings relate to other people, how much of your accompanying thoughts are of others.

The Agreement That "Just This Once Won't Matter"

It doesn't matter if I slip up this one time. One drink, one more dessert (after I have had one already), one little lie won't count. I can get angry just this once. If we keep letting ourselves off the hook in this way, how do we expect to be sober, lose weight, or experience peace in our hearts and relationships? As far as the spiritual path goes, *small acts matter.*

There is a story of a young man who thought it wouldn't matter if he littered *just this once,* and he dropped a plastic bag off the side of his boat. When he did so, a fish got caught in it. An eagle, seeing the struggling fish, swooped down to catch the fish to feed its three young offspring waiting in their nest along the riverbank. The eagle began to choke on the plastic and flew in front of a car, which caused the car to swerve. The car hit a vehicle coming the other direction and killed both drivers. The eagle died alongside the road.

Every action, no matter how small, creates karma; there is always a chain of results from *any* action. You can meditate on the possibility of the chain of events that may take place from such small personal decisions and actions.

The flip side of this agreement is just as true. Imagine the young man choosing *not* to litter. Imagine the lives he saved, and the good karma he accumulated. Watch the story unfold as he goes home to his son, who is in third grade, and asks him to put the bag in the recycle bin. The son mentions that they are learning about recycling in their class at school. And the father says, "Yes, my father taught me to leave a place better then you found it." There are now good feelings all around. Each small step taken toward an active, engaged life moves us closer to full initiation.

The Agreement to Be "Competitive Rather Than Cooperative"

They are so caught up with the idea of acquiring still more that they make no room for anything else in their lives. In their absorption, they actually lose the dream of happiness.

THE FOURTEENTH DALAI LAMA,
ETHICS FOR THE NEW MILLENNIUM

A great companion book while going through the Wheel of Initiation is *Ethics for the New Millennium* by the Dalai Lama. Everything you need to challenge this agreement to be competitive rather than cooperative is within this book.

Once when I found myself caught up in thoughts of "being the best," I realized how much suffering this caused me and how this made "enemies" out of others with whom I saw myself in competition. Paradoxically, I found out how this agreement had left me carrying their shadows as well. So I let go of this agreement and replaced it with "*doing* my best."

This gave immeasurable energy back to me, which I used to focus on my creative projects and my spiritual practices. (In the Lojong tradition the slogan "Don't Be the Fastest" is good to practice here as well.) And the Fourth Agreement, "Do Your Best," in Don Miguel Ruiz's work on the practices of the Toltec, can be seen as a way to unburden yourself from this culturally endorsed agreement. The agreement to be competitive is also perpetuated by various institutions where competition is emphasized over cooperation, such as in team sports.

Laughing Coyote, a young initiate, said, "I left the volleyball team even though I loved the game. The coach clearly had her picks of the best players, and everyone else sat on the bench. I didn't want to spend so much time on the bench." She was doing her best, but the coach was rewarding the competitive ethic: the athletes who could score the most were the ones who were allowed to get in the game. The workplace, of course, often insists on this agreement. Imagine for a moment the amount of creativity that would emerge from a business that let go of competition and put energy into creating an environment where everyone can do their best.

Currently, we are learning how competitiveness and greed in the economic environment has caused the system to have a massive heart attack. The paradigm is shifting here because it is no longer capable of functioning by such an agreement.

The Agreement of "Perfectionism"

In this agreement we always attempt to change ourselves, to make ourselves better, so that we can come across as all put together or only bring forth something we believe to be good enough. Often this is an agreement to keep the false self facing outward. This agreement is found right next to the previous ones: to be competitive and not to trust. Perfectionism will interfere with putting ourselves out there in natural, undefended, and cooperative ways. We are less likely to speak our truth, sing in public, or share our creations because of a mind-set of perfectionism. As Joseph Campbell said (in *A Joseph Campbell Companion*), "Out of perfection nothing can be made."

Of course, a determination of what is perfect and what is not is completely subjective and familial as well as culturally set. "This is perfect and this is not" *is just a thought, an agreement* that is not based on some universal truth. When we focus our energies on perfectionism, we are in agreement with an illusion. To let go of this opens the door to what may be a messier life but a more complete one, where the focus is on *experience* rather than appearances.

> *As you proceed through life,*
> *follow your own path,*
> *birds will shit on you.*
> *Don't bother to brush it off.*
>
> JOSEPH CAMPBELL,
> *A JOSEPH CAMPBELL COMPANION*

The Agreement to Believe That "Happiness Is Outside Ourselves"

This agreement brings attention to our need to have certain externals fulfilled before we can be truly happy. Even those who have gone through the Wheel find this agreement difficult to break. Even after achieving spiritual insight, they want to know *what to do* to find their partner or how to get a better job or how to make more money. They also tend to seek spiritual validation by wanting to come into contact with certain revered people or phenomena.

When we tie our happiness or spiritual fulfillment to something outside ourselves, it is ephemeral and will ultimately disappoint us. When instead we put our energy into creating internal happiness through setting intentions, challenging beliefs, inquiring compassionately, training our minds, and living an engaged and principled life, the result is long-term. Buddhists consider how we are setting the karmic blueprint for future lives as well. As Geshe Tenzin Dorje says, "Investigating what we truly need for happiness will come down to what we are thinking."

What I know to be true is that nothing outside ourselves can heal the internal divide or bring us true and lasting happiness: not the perfect spouse, not the bestseller, not the most loving and skillful teacher. Not a best friend, not a lot of money, not the perfect vacation. This search outside ourselves only strengthens our feelings of separation as we search for our happiness in this way.

> "The kingdom of heaven will be like this: Ten bridesmaids took their lamps and went to meet the bridegroom."
>
> Of these ten bridesmaids five are prepared; their lamps are trimmed and stocked with oil. The other five are unprepared; so that when the bridegroom arrives, they have to hurry out to get oil. By the time they do this it is too late; the others are already in the wedding hall and the door is closed. The parable concludes with Jesus' words,
>
> "So stay awake, because you do not know either the day or the hour" (Matt. 25:13).
>
> JAMES A. SANFORD, THE KINGDOM WITHIN

The Agreement to "Put Life on Hold"

Because personal initiation relies on one's efforts, you could say *everything* responds to this effort. In psychological terms the false self has many reasons for putting your life on hold—it's averse to risk, the unknown, exposure, and the intimacy of the creative life. It seeks to keep you safe in the norm. In his book *The War of Art,* Steven Pressfield explores the battle between the unlived life and the life we live. "Between the two," he shows, "stands resistance." With this agreement to put your life on hold, you become one of the bridesmaids who are unprepared for the wedding.

We put our lives on hold because we have to heal first, or get into the right relationship, or have enough time or money to create our masterpiece, or find the perfect land or home that will sustain our creative life.

You get this, don't you? Clutter is often a manifestation of this agreement to put our creative life on hold. As the piles of paper, waste, and "stuff" accumulate, it gives us more and more things we have to get to before we can get to our lives. Then, the door closes and it is too late.

Roberta Enters the West

I WORKED WITH SOMEONE who entered the Wheel struggling with a weight issue that generated some serious health problems for her. She wept as she pointed to her body. It wasn't a diet that she was putting off, though—it was admitting that she could no longer live her life according to (in agreement with) what she assumed her children wanted from her. She also grieved the loss of her husband and didn't think it was okay for her to sell the family home and move into a smaller one by the water (another agreement she held). She had been putting her life off because "my kids won't understand." She felt that the internal struggle—to trust herself—meant that she might upset her children. The more she put her life on hold, the more weight she gained. Once in the Wheel, she decided to initiate change by holding a garage sale, and she began downsizing her life. She looked for that small house on the water. Not surprisingly, her body began to downsize as well.

Many people share they feel selfish when pursuing a dream or a passion. This feeling may actually point to how they are finally taking care of themselves. *If not now, when? If not you, who?* In reality, energy is being consumed by this agreement that could easily and quickly go into actually creating *movement* in your life.

They would rather be dependent in a hostile environment and combat it every day than manage their own lives. In this way they avoid having to confront their own anxieties and discomfort about activating and asserting their real selves.

JAMES F. MASTERSON, *THE SEARCH FOR THE REAL SELF*

The Agreement to "Disclaim Your Intuitive Truth"

Many people are skeptical about the power of intuition, either looking upon it as a gift that only certain people have, or believing it isn't real to begin with. How many times have you heard, "I should have listened to my gut"? Our intuition is always accessible, but over time if we don't trust it or listen to it, we lose contact with it. Intuitive wisdom is always drawn from the present moment, from listening to and trusting our experience in the moment. It is not based on making assumptions about others; rather, it is about tuning in to our mind/body awareness. Review the Exploration Into Presence exercise on page 22.

The Agreement "Not to Be Open or Vulnerable"

This is the agreement that makes enemies and causes us to want to keep our hearts closed to others and to possibilities. However, many masters such as the Christ and Quan Yin would tell us that the best protection is an open heart. An open posture, and living in an undefended manner, can actually protect us from harm. When we get into protecting ourselves, we make enemies by our need to keep some people out and let others in. We make them wrong and ourselves right. Our focus is "out there," rather than on challenging our internal assumptions and mind-sets.

This agreement is also linked to the agreement not to trust ourselves or others. This prevents us from taking necessary risks, because we fear we may fail or trip up in public. To break this agreement means to open up to the moment—moment by moment. You don't have to figure out how you are going to be in advance; simply practice arriving fully into *this* moment, *this* experience, undefended, open and receptive (as best you can). (Later on in the Wheel, we practice using our principles as our way to prepare for possible difficulty.)

The Stop Whining, "They Did Their Best" Agreement

> Compost our inner, stolen fruit
> as we forgive others the spoils of
> their trespassing.
>
> NEIL DOUGLAS-KLOTZ,
> PRAYERS OF THE COSMOS

Many of us have been trespassed upon. One place people tend to hold onto their pain story is in their agreements to their parents' trespasses. Most adult children want to forgive their parents but are confused about the personal work that is needed before real and lasting forgiveness can take place. There are many agreements we have with our parents that keep us in the past, such as the agreements to keep secrets, to being an extension of them instead of living our own lives, to parenting them (when you are still a child), to agreeing that hitting is good discipline, to agreeing to not do better in life than they did.

After someone has shared the transgressions of their parents, and this person is clearly still in a lot of pain, they often end with, "Well, my parents did their best." This may or may not be true given the particular circumstances, but it is unlikely they were doing their best as they beat you, teased and belittled you, neglected you, shunned you, or ridiculed your creative expression. When people claim that their parents did their best, I often see people repeating over and over again the original wound while maintaining their own pain story around their childhood experiences. Again, this is not about the other but about you and your agreements. This agreement often keeps the pain story active through its subtle way of discounting *your* reality. It is as if you are really saying, "They did their best, so I just have to deal with it."

We need to acknowledge with open hearts the trespasses of others, hold them accountable, forgive them for *not* doing their best, and then let the past go. It is unlikely that real forgiveness will take place while you are hooked by this agreement. You don't need to forgive someone for doing their best; you forgive them for their trespasses. So, you must call it honestly and the way it really is: cruelty of any kind is a trespass.

It may feel like betrayal to acknowledge to yourself that your parents did not do their best. This agreement often perpetuates the agreement to carry another's shadow, in that you are always aware of the other's pain and of how they are not capable of carrying it for themselves. In her book *The Drama of the Gifted Child,* Alice Miller reminds us, "When what was done to me was done for my own good, then I am expected to accept this treatment as an essential part of life and not question it." Question it, then release it and loosen this agreement that binds you to the past.

True forgiveness results in you no longer carrying your parents' shadow.

Inherent in each one of us is the capacity to be present, wise, and loving. That is how to let go and not feel responsible for another's choices or pain. That is how to know when people are *not* doing their best—because they are not acting out of these three inherent qualities. Life offers each of us the same inherent qualities of presence, wisdom, and love. And as importantly, life offers everyone the opportunities (until their death) to wake up to what is inherent inside them.

The "Need to Be Right" Agreement

This agreement is the main artery of our pain stories, because it says we have to be right about our view of the world as well as of ourselves. So, when we believe "I am a victim," or "I am not capable of being this or that," or "Life is difficult," we hold an underlying need to be right about these beliefs. This lets us off the hook, of course, and we get to just give in or give up. We get to blame our problems on others or the inevitability of life—"This is how it is."

This agreement is layered throughout all the other agreements, and once you begin to challenge and release this one, the others will loosen their grip on you. With this agreement we also make everything right or wrong. There is a tendency to seek validation for our views (wars are attributed to this agreement). We all need to be mindful of how we recruit evidence to back up our pain stories—our need to be right about the views we hold of the world and of ourselves.

A Lebanese man recently said in a radio interview, "It is so tragic how Hezbollah seems to hate Israel more than they love their own children." Holding to this agreement of being right keeps the separation strong between individuals and groups.

Begin to contemplate how this agreement comes up in your life and the lives of others. It keeps us from seeing others and ourselves honestly. Notice when you have strong opinions or habitual ways of viewing the world. Gently admit to yourself, "I have a need to be right about this." Next practice facing something you disagree with, and, being clear, say to yourself, "I don't agree to this." Focus on what you are in agreement with or not in agreement with instead of making others wrong and yourself right. Are *you* in agreement with this? That's the important question. This results in more action on your part—instead of the passive judgment "They are wrong and I am right" (which makes enemies).

Uprooting My "Need to Be Right" Agreement

SANDRA SEEMED TO GIVE the right answers in school, wore the proper clothes, and responded to the adults around her as if she spoke and understood their language. I just wanted to be her friend. But the friendship usually ended up as a trick on me. One day, when I was ten, the game she and I were playing included climbing up a tree to see who could reach the highest branch. We used a ladder from her garage to get past the wide, branchless trunk. When it was my turn, I was able to get to a very high branch. As I sat there, Sandra took away the ladder.

After hours of feeling stupid and stuck, I got down. I have no memory of how I got down.

What bothered me the most wasn't so much that she left me up in the tree but that no one else knew she frequently did these kinds of things to me. This theme (pain story) carried into my adult life—someone would come along, invite me to "play," and then leave me up in a tree. Others would not see how I had been wronged. There I sat feeling stupid, belligerent, and stuck. I had several ladders taken out from under me. Typically, just as when I was ten, it appeared that those around me knew only the other's side of things. Finally, in my thirties, when someone left me up in the tree, I focused all my energy on ending the agreement that kept this pain story alive and repeating itself in my life.

Through the silence of meditation and contemplation, I became aware of the place where my habitual agreements arose in this pain story, and it began to lose its grip on me. What kept me up in the tree is far more of an issue (and pattern) than how I got up there in the first place. *What kept me up there is wanting others to see who left me up there—the need to get validation and reassurance from others that* someone did me wrong.

Does this sound at all familiar? I could waste a significant amount of my life sitting up in a tree waiting for others to take my side (and support my view that I am right).

Unlocking the Wisdom Mind

Habitual and reactive states are like a locked door to the inner wisdom you can access when you challenge the habitual ways of relating to your life's circumstances.

Jessie's Story

JESSIE'S FATHER HAD just died, and the family was gathering the next day at their childhood home to hold a memorial service. Jessie was the youngest in the family and typically felt left out. In fact, this was a major theme in her pain story, feeling left out, last, and at times forgotten. She carried this story with her throughout her life and found it to be truer as time passed. On this day she arrived for the wake at her parents' house and found the front door locked. She knew most of her family was inside. This triggered her pain story, and she began to howl and scream. She felt furious.

She went to the garage and found that door locked too. She did not knock on the front door or ring the doorbell; instead she went around to find every door locked. She knew it! This was just more proof that she was locked out, left out, and kept out. She was so upset (and caught up in the agreement of being right about being left out) that she drove off, enraged, and later phoned the house, extremely upset. She demanded that someone come and unlock the front door. She forgot about the key hidden under a certain rock. She seemed to forget she could have knocked on the door.

In this scene we see an opportunity. When the pattern of a pain story arises (and it will), we can either strengthen the hold of our pain story and be *reactive,* or we can use this as a time to break through the pattern and break free of the agreements—or, at the very least, loosen their grip on us by noticing our mind-set when we are so entangled by negative reactions. Then we will find the key and a way into the wisdom mind. When we become aware, take a breath, and don't react habitually, we activate the wisdom mind, instead of repeating the past.

More awareness brings more wisdom. With this increased wisdom we see more opportunities to live compassionately. *We are giving ourselves more choices.* We loosen up the hold of the pain story (in this case, "I am always left out") and, with awareness, remember where the key is, or simply know to knock on the door.

May you continue to find all doors open to you, and if not, find the key or knock (someone is on the other side and will let you in).

❋ Spiritual Journaling and Compassionate Inquiry Around Agreements

Ask yourself: What am I in agreement with these days, and with whom? Start with people sitting closest to you in your "lifeboat." Within each relationship are numerous unspoken agreements. Then go out from there—are you in agreement with local ordinances, the work environment, the state's smoking laws, the war in Iraq? What agreements do you have with the strangers you encounter? What agreements do you hold about our economic and environmental future? Familiarize your mind with identifying agreements.

Review your story and identify a pain story within it. Name agreements made with parents. Name a few core agreements that keep your pain story active. Identify at least one culturally endorsed agreement that keeps your pain story active. What cultural agreements are a thread throughout your life and hold you in a pain story now?

Watch your beliefs for a week. Pay compassionate attention to what you may believe at any given moment. Be a witness to your beliefs. Pay attention and observe your thoughts. Trace a given thought and emotional state to an agreement. What is a belief that holds this agreement up? For example, in the story about my being left up in the tree, I was in agreement to "show that I was right." Some beliefs that supported this agreement were: I believed it mattered what others thought of me. I believed my so-called friend felt superior to me. I believed one of us had to be in the wrong. I believed she should get caught for being mean to me.

When we give up our agreements, the beliefs that underlie them will arise. They will tug at us and want to keep us living according to agreements made by a pain story. Through purification, release, and recapitulation—*the symbolic death*—we challenge our beliefs and are reborn to new agreements and resulting stories. This is central to the initiation process—you can't keep living by the old agreements and beliefs if what you want is freedom and happiness.

✳ Ask Yourself Often: What Am I in Agreement with at This Moment?

If you want to, you can, at any given time, use a pocket notebook to jot down agreements you identify and the results of any particular agreement. Ask yourself, "What am I in agreement with, and what do I believe (right now)?"

Stephan Enters the West

I DECIDED I WANTED to get a sense of how my agreements impacted my choices and relationships. I wondered, "Are there hidden agreements that I am not aware of but live by?" So I took a small pocket notebook with me and began to ask myself as often as I could, "What am I in agreement with right now, what do I believe?" What I found both scared me and made me laugh out loud!

At lunch I heard myself agreeing to eat whatever I want because I would work out during lunch the following day. I did something similar throughout the day—I made agreements to bargain myself out of being honest because "tomorrow or next time" I would say this, or do this, or remember that. The agreement to postpone my life, to put off so much of myself "until then," *showed up everywhere.*

I was in shock. But this did give me something to work with—I wanted to let go of that agreement to put my life on hold. Once I became aware of this agreement, there was no going back for me. And I decided to take the next step. Later I recognized one of the beliefs that this agreement supported: my belief that I really didn't have what it took to fulfill my choices. There was also something there about how I believed the future somehow held the answer.

✹ Ask Yourself from the Heart: Am I Doing My Best Right Now in This Moment?

Practice this when difficulty arises. Step by step, agree to do your best within the given situation. "Can I do better here?" Polish your own mirror by taking the focus off how others are doing or not doing and pay compassionate attention to your own agreements and choices. Further inquiry can include, "What am I protecting?" "How do my agreements create enemies?" Remember to simply open up to the question and compassionately inquire; don't go on a vigilante hunt for answers.

✹ Practice Acceptance

With your intention in mind, choose one aspect of yourself or life circumstance to accept 100 percent unconditionally. Practice a state of acceptance (no matter how awful you may perceive this condition to be). Accept feeling stupid, accept your debt, accept your excess weight, accept your jealousy, your grief, your fear, or your procrastination. Acceptance is not being in agreement with this dynamic but creating a presence, a *spaciousness*, and a boundary around it. Whatever we resist tends to freeze in our mind and body. *Acceptance generates a state of nonresistance so that you can decide about agreements made, and give them space so that real movement can take place.* This acceptance is a prerequisite to the transformation that you desire. Accept the way things are so that they can loosen their grip on you.

✹

As you enter the West you begin to abolish the old systems of beliefs and agreements—the old view is getting shaken up. This must be done for the establishment of new agreements. You cannot bring a new way in without abolishing the old. These practices are particularly set up to prepare you for the West of the Wheel, where you will undergo purification, release, and recapitulation.

> We find that by transforming our habits and dispositions, we can begin to perfect our overall state of heart and mind (kun long)—that from which all our actions spring.
>
> THE FOURTEENTH DALAI LAMA, *ETHICS FOR THE NEW MILLENNIUM*

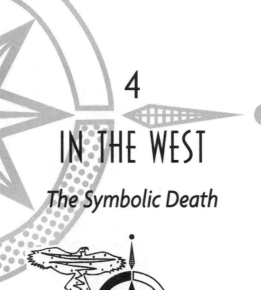

4

IN THE WEST

The Symbolic Death

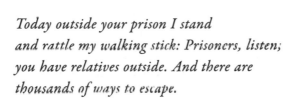

*Today outside your prison I stand
and rattle my walking stick: Prisoners, listen;
you have relatives outside. And there are
thousands of ways to escape.*

*Years ago I bent my skill to keep my
cell locked, had chains smuggled to me in pies,
and shouted my plans to the jailers;
but always new plans occurred to me,
or the new heavy locks bent hinges off,
or some stupid jailer would forget
and leave the keys.*

*Inside, I dreamed of constellations—
those feeding creatures outlined by stars,
their skeletons a darkness between jewels,
heroes that exist only where they are not.*

Thus freedom always came nibbling my thought,
just as—often, in light, on the open hills—
you can pass an antelope and not know
and look back, and then—even before you see—
there is something wrong in the grass.
And then you see.

That's the way everything in the world is waiting.

Now—these few more words, and then I'm
gone: Tell everyone just to remember
their names, and remind others, later, when we
find each other. Tell the little ones
to cry and then go to sleep, curled up
where they can. And if any of us get lost,
if any of us cannot come all the way—
remember: there will come a time when
all we have said and all we have hoped
will be all right.

There will be that form in the grass.

WILLIAM STAFFORD, FROM THE POEM "A MESSAGE
FROM THE WANDERER," IN *THE WAY IT IS*

You are now in the West, the direction of purification, release, and recapitulation; the direction of the Thunderbird who is the "lightning bolt"
of truth arriving to encourage you to live a more authentic life. Here you
will engage in practices, cognitive processes, and ceremonies that offer
you real and lasting freedom from negative states. To practice any kind of
purification, the fundamental quality needed is to generate a mind that
desires purification. Do you want to be purified of negative karma, painful agreements, fear, resistance, and habitual reactive states? Do you want
to clear the way for your true nature?

Here you will experience the symbolic death of the false self (or
aspects of it) through release. The practices contained herein will help
you get your energy back, energy that has been lost to your pain stories.

It is optimal, at this point, for you to have written at least a first draft of your life story.

PRACTICES OF PURIFICATION

Purification is any process that prepares you for a great undertaking such as an initiation. Most important is holding in one's heart-mind a wish for purification, a wish to cleanse away all that obstructs your true nature. In this chapter there are many practices of purification for you to consider.

These practices are a way to make room for deep internal work and to purify your mind of obstructions. Purification ceremonies and practices will embody the beliefs and historical customs of their given tradition. Such practices prepare the mind and body to be more receptive to spiritual states of consciousness. The one offered below helps set a positive spiritual outlook for the day. Tibetan Buddhist purification practices are called *Ngondro* and have been passed down for thousands of years.

As you move through the Wheel of Initiation, there are certain processes that need to be done in sequence to get the full effect of personal initiation. Purification (of one's mind, body, and spirit) is a preliminary for initiation, for you cannot initiate a clouded, crowded mind. Understand purification as a means to cleanse and prepare you also for the symbolic death necessary for initiation. Furthermore, as is true for all the practices in this book, the purification practices should be *ongoing*—they should be done until you reach a full state of initiation and wakefulness. They also should resonate with your chosen spiritual path.

> These rites of the Inipi (purification lodge) are very Wakan (sacred) and are used before any great undertaking for which we wish to make ourselves pure or for which we wish to gain strength; and in many winters past our men, and often our women, made the Inipi even every day, and sometimes several times a day, and from this we received much of our power.
>
> BLACK ELK, *THE SACRED PIPE*

Then the Sweat Lodge begins, utilizing the Four Elements: fire, air, water, and Earth. The Four Directions are beseeched within the warm womb (the actual sweat lodge) of Mother Earth. Fire, (Wiyo, the Sun) heats the stones; and water (Wichoni Minni, the life-giving rain), when poured onto the heated stones, produces steam. That added water is mixed with sweat—the waters of the participants—and with air. Tate Tapa, the Four Winds, carry forth the mixture of steam to the four quarters of our planet. This carrying forth of a part of ourselves out to the Four Directions tells us we are participating in a universal ceremony.

EAGLE MAN (ED MCGAA), *NATURE'S WAY*

Heat Purification

I have held sweat lodges for several years. We have a sweat lodge on our land; it is a universal sweat lodge that respects all paths to the sacred. (Sweat lodges, like labyrinths, are not difficult to construct.) Please refer to the book by Ed McGaa (Eagle Man), *Mother Earth's Spirituality,* for a detailed description of building your own sweat lodge. At a sweat lodge, people gather to enter the darkness and heat of the "womb" for purification and initiation.

Lodges come in a variety of forms and sizes, but typically hold eight to fifteen people comfortably and safely. Rocks are heated in a fire outside the lodge and brought into the lodge's center hole, where water is later poured over them. The lodge facilitator is usually the Water Pourer and is skillful at running safe lodges.*

Once the flap door is closed by the Fire Keeper (who remains right outside the entry), the lodge becomes a place of total darkness. Songs

---

*I strongly recommend that you only participate in sweats where no more than fifteen participants can be comfortably placed inside the lodge and where it is agreed that the door will be opened upon request at any time. The faciliator (Water Pourer) should routinely "check in" with each participant. I have found that this "checking in" only deepens the spiritual process because everyone feels safe enough to do deep work; they know that at their request the flap will be opened and they can leave or take breaths of cool air. Before participating in a sweat lodge or other group practices, read the appendix, "Teachers and Groups."

*Fig. 4.1. A sweat lodge made from black willow saplings
and blankets. It is used for purification practices and was
built by an initiation circle on the author's land.*

are sung, stories are told, prayer requests are made, and spirit helpers are
invited in—all with the intention of purification. During the sweat lodge
ceremony, the door is opened at anyone's request or upon the completion
of prayers and stories. Additional hot stones are then brought into the
lodge for the next round. (A round begins when we start our prayers and
stories in the dark, with the flap closed. It ends when we open the door
and let the fresh air and light in.) The intensity of the heat and darkness
assists the participants in bringing their minds to a shared point of attention, which further aids the process of purification.

After I had facilitated sweat lodges for a couple of years, I realized
that each lodge's medicine and experiences were determined by the stories shared within that particular lodge. When leading a sweat lodge in

the lodge's darkness I simply needed to ask, *"What are the stories that want telling?"* Or, *"Who has a story?"* These may include mythological stories as well as personal accounts; they contain information needed for purification of mind, body, and spirit, for those who are sharing that lodge.

In one particular lodge, seven women sat together after doing a ritual called Killing Off the False Self. For several of the women, this was their first experience in a sweat lodge. When everyone was seated comfortably on the bed of fresh cedar boughs and carpet pieces on the floor, the Fire Keeper brought in the hot stones and then closed the flap. Four stones were used for the first round, and each glowed red from within. The red glow of the rocks was the only light in the lodge.

We began our first round by "calling in" the four directions of the Initiation Wheel. We called upon the energy and intentions of each direction of the Wheel as well as the spirit helpers of each direction. We were safely held in the womb of the mother, sitting side by side, faces to the center. We set our intentions as we sat together in the warm darkness. Then I asked, "Who has a story?"

First there was silence, and then an "I do" came from a voice in the North of the lodge.

Kathy Shares Her Story

I WORK IN A COMMUNITY CENTER for international student housing. There's a day-care center in my building, and the toddler room is directly across from the reception window where I sit. When I first started working, I noticed a beautiful curly haired two-year-old girl from Cuba named Leah. Every morning I would smile and wave at Leah but would get either no response or a scowl. I just kept greeting her—"Good morning, Leah, buenos dias, Leah," each day. She would just stare back at me, with a look that read, "Who is this crazy woman bothering me?" At night I waved good-bye to her.

After a month of greeting Leah, one evening when she was going home with her mother, it was raining. Leah had a new umbrella and was wearing a bright yellow raincoat. She came running over to my window and began to tell me all about her umbrella and the rain outside and her plans for the night with her mom. I was surprised and thrilled that after all this time Leah had shared a part of herself with me. There are still days when the scowl comes out, but at some point every day, Leah will wave, blow me a kiss, or smile at me. Each day there is a moment where we are happy to see each other.

The storyteller or Water Pourer may then offer up a meaning within the story. Others often respond, and then there is more silence, more steam, and more purification.

"Small, consistent acts matter" became a theme in this lodge.

We opened the door, brought in the remainder of the rocks, and began the second round. The darkness in the lodge was deep, and we could feel the support of being in the mother's womb. We could all feel some release of what holds us back and keeps us in our pain stories. We were undergoing a purification to get rid of the false self. Again I asked, "What stories want to be told?" The rocks were heating up, and every time someone shared a story or a prayer, I would pour water on the rocks, creating more heat and steam, more purification and wisdom, more room for initiation. Several times a voice would come from the darkness, "I have a story . . ."

We would listen and the water would be poured and the steam from the stones released. We all held a strong resolve to be free of the false self.

Such a process of purification and healing can be intense but must always be respectful of each participant; it must be physically safe. People have different levels of tolerance for the heat and steam created inside the lodge. Remember, it is the responsibility of the Water Pourer to frequently check in with everyone in the lodge. Also remember that at any time a participant can request for the door to be opened.

The final story came from a voice sitting in the West, in the *Catku,* of the lodge. In Lakota teachings this is the "hot spot" in the lodge, the ceremonial place traditionally across from the entrance. This is true of our sweat lodge: the entrance is in the East and the hot spot is in the West. The West contains the energy of thunder and the Thunder Beings, the element of movement necessary for purification that leads to personal initiation. The thunder of the West can shake up and release the false self and all that holds us back.

You are now in the West within the Wheel of Initiation, the Catku, the hot spot.

Meeghan's Story/The Lodge's Catku

TODAY I WALKED THE SPIRAL (in the prairie) for the first time; this lodge is also my first sweat lodge. As I walked I became aware that I was leaving the old view of myself behind and, step by step, walking into my true self. My true self is the one who will run a triathlon in the spring, will open up to love from others, will let every day be new. A few times I would reach a curve in the spiral and think, "This must be the last one," but then there was another corner to take and circle to walk. I realized then that I have what it takes to turn the next corner even when I am uncertain how much is left to go. I will keep taking the next corner, the next step. I felt myself shedding the old me, the self that would get discouraged and be hard on myself. I have what it takes to keep going and to choose an active life. The energy that rose up from inside me was powerful, and I am changed.

To fully benefit from any transformative or healing ceremony, participants must have the ability to focus their attention; purification helps clear our minds and bring them to one-pointed focus. *Tawacin warjjila* in Lakota is translated as the "single-mindedness of intention and thought" of people in a ceremony. Being able to focus on the intention of the ceremony will increase its benefits. Again, safety is a bottom-line prerequisite for such purification practices because if one does not feel safe, they cannot effectively focus on the inner journey. The sweat lodge is just one way to practice purification.

*Fig. 4.2. Vajrasattva holding the dorje in his right hand
and a bell in his left. He is one deity who shows up in the
West to free us from obstructions that block our true nature.*

Transformation by Vajrasattva, the Buddha of Purification

Vajrasattva, the Buddha of purification, is the Buddha that sits in the West of the Wheel of Initiation. He symbolizes for me the archetype of transformation arrived at through purification, confession, and release. Vajrasattva holds the dorje/vajra in his right hand and in front of his heart. (The dorje holds symbolic significance of thunderbolt wisdom achieved through spiritual practice.) The thunderbolt is represented in many traditions as the symbolic tool that helps you break through the inner trash and get to the true nature of your mind—a mind that is open and not weighed down by the past.

A tenet of Buddhism is that negative karma can get heavier when one does not engage in regular purification practices. I witness this all the time—a student either chooses to strengthen their suffering or weaken it. They increase it when they don't experience what I call "enlightened regret," which is insight into their behavior and a willingness to do things differently. Or, they make excuses and keep the problem outside themselves (it was another person's fault or solely conditional). Or, they feel an "*un*enlightened regret," which is really a rumination on and judgment of themselves, conditions, others, or something from their past.

Fasting is one such means to purify mind, body, and soul. From a spiritual perspective, it can be about abstaining from negative habitual states that keep the pain story going, or fasting from agreements (and their resultant actions). Abstaining from certain foods or alcohol can be an effective means of purification as well. You can commit to this process yourself or use a practice within your own chosen spiritual tradition.

Nyung Nay: *Journey to the Inner Lodge*

To Know the Dark

> *To go in the dark with a light is to know the light.*
> *To know the dark, go dark. Go without sight,*
> *And find that the dark, too, blooms and sings,*
> *And is traveled by dark feet and dark wings.*

WENDELL BERRY, "TO KNOW THE DARK," FROM *THE SELECTED POEMS OF WENDELL BERRY, 1957–1982*

Nyung Nay is considered one of the more acclaimed purification practices of the Tibetan Buddhist tradition. It is a practice that intends to purify one's interior "defilements" and the exterior physical environment filled with pollutants. I stumbled upon this purification practice in a way similar to how I discovered my first sweat lodge back in 1982: it called to me, so I went—although I was not entirely sure what I was getting myself into.

This naïveté is what made the ritual all the more unnerving and powerful for me. I made the mistake of sitting in the second row, behind the monks and nuns. At least I could have hidden in back! It didn't take long for me to discover the thickness of the obstructions that clouded my mind. Nyung Nay includes hours of chanting and long sessions of full-body prostrations, as well as a fast from all food and conversation: all acts of purification. By that point, I'd done meditation retreats that were a lot longer. "How difficult could this three-day fasting ritual be?" I thought.

When I began to meditate, I felt a deep anger rising up within me. Then I found myself pondering various accounts I had read of the experiences of Buddhist masters who, when meditating in this manner, saw rainbow bodies and light coming from the eyes of Buddha statues. There were also accounts of spontaneous awakenings. I compared these states to my state of being in my own personal hell, and I just wanted something tangible like this to happen, something that would prove that I was having a genuine spiritual experience.

I knew enough not to give up (although I wanted to), and I held on to the Bodhisattva vow to do this work to benefit others (although I didn't feel how it could). I knew enough to realize that all my obstructions were internal.

At one point, a nun pulled me aside (breaking noble silence*) to ask me to "prostrate straight" (rather than crooked, because I was pulling everyone off; we were in a small, crowded temple). My anger turned into arrogance. But I kept practicing, and because I kept practicing, the result was purification. In fact, I believe this purification was so transformative that, like a ripple beginning in the middle of a pond, the effects rippled out into my life for years. The most important lesson was to finish what I started, "to know the dark," and to keep to the agreement to fast, chant, and prostrate, and to do this to benefit others. This commitment to finish what was started will often arise in any initiation process. When it does, one must push through the hot (and darkest) spot, the Catku.

During the sunrise session on our final morning, Geshe Lhundub Sopa, the Abbot of Deer Park who had facilitated this retreat, ended the retreat with a long meditation on loving-kindness and a blessing from the

---

*Noble silence is the shared willingness to not speak or engage others in conversation. In the Vipassana tradition it further means not to engage others even through eye contact.

guru. He reminded us to connect with the intrinsic value of love and wisdom within. It was a banquet for a hungry heart.

> *And if any of us get lost,*
> *if any of us cannot come all the way—*
> *remember: there will come a time when*
> *all we have said and all we have hoped*
> *will be all right.*
>
> *There will be that form in the grass.*
>
> WILLIAM STAFFORD, FROM THE POEM
> "A MESSAGE FROM THE WANDERER,"
> IN *THE WAY IT IS*

Confession as a Purification Practice

Because life itself is the template in which initiation takes place, the opportunity for purification can occur naturally. When we find ourselves regretting some choice or action, we have an opportunity for purification. We can take this as a time to consciously change some pattern that would later cause us more regret.

How can we clear the inner path of obstruction if we do not acknowledge what causes us to repeat negative patterns? Regret in this sense is not going over the past and pondering how you wish you had done this or that. Instead it is *a state of awareness that you acted in a way that was not productive.* In this case, you open up to the regret and bring awareness to it. What do you wish you had done differently? Can you isolate the behaviors and agreements that tend to bring you regret? Confession can be done right on the spot.

Rather than hiding our mistakes from ourselves, we get honest with ourselves. When we acknowledge regrets, we are less likely to continue to deceive ourselves. And fortunately, we are less likely to repeat the actions that brought the regret on! Think of this as polishing your own mirror, the inner mirror. The surface of the mirror needs to be polished for it to reflect clearly. Just so, our obscurations have to be "cleansed" to allow us to "see" more clearly; then we can *act* from this clarity.

For confession to be felt, it needs to come from the heart and from an intention of compassion and love for yourself and others. Your motivation needs to be one of love. This aspiration alone—the wish for others to benefit from your confession—is, on its own, a compelling means of purification. If you are unsure how you are hurting yourself or others, ask a loved one or trusted friend for their input.

Whatever sin I have committed unknowingly or caused others to commit in this or other lives in the beginningless cycle of existence, and in which I have rejoiced due to being oppressed by the deception of delusion—that transgression I have seen, and I earnestly confess it.

SHANTIDEVA

Being sincere in your confession is key to experiencing successful purification. Without this sincerity, you will likely only increase the strength of the false self and its related suffering. This means, don't just go through the motions of confession.

Confession is best known as being a major tenet of Catholicism, but it is found as a purification technique in most traditions, including Buddhism, Shintoism, Judaism, and Sufism. During Yom Kippur, the Day of Atonement, for example, one atones for events of the past year by fasting and purification practices and confession (Hebrew word *vidui*). As I understand it, this atonement is experienced as an inner dialogue between the individual and god and is a way to come to terms with anything that obstructs your inner light. The fasting and purification that is undertaken during Yom Kippur is an acknowledgment to the universe that you are serious about your spiritual life. According to this tradition, after a successful Day of Atonement, you are written in the Book of Life for one more year. How true this can be! Purification allows you to show up for your life (at least for another year).

What confessional practices have in common is the need to bring yourself to purification on a regular basis, whether it be a daily or yearly practice. It is not who or what you confess to but *what* you confess about. A tree can be a very good confessional vehicle. Go to a tree and confess your "sins." (A sin is anything that obstructs your true nature or causes others or yourself harm.) Let it all out. The tree won't judge you or even tell you what to do— she will simply absorb and help transform your transgressions.

Another important element of confession is the resolution not to act in the same negative way again. In the late 1980s, I was at a Zen monastery for a weekend to still my mind and get a sense of that particular practice of Buddhism. I was in the kitchen where the resident monk and a couple of students were preparing a meal when I caught the tail end of a conversation between a monk and a student, as follows:

"It's better I make it clear to you I will not do that again," said the monk, "than only to apologize for what I did. Saying I am sorry can just make it easy for me to behave the same way again." The monk looked directly at the student and said, "So, I will not do that again."

This encounter showed me the importance of putting energy and intention into not repeating the transgression. Too many times I have witnessed how apologies can be part of a given habitual pattern (the person apologizes but has no real aspirations of changing their behavior).

The five aspects of confession (found in most traditions) include *sincerity,* a *regret* (of wrongdoing), a *resolution* not to act in the same way again, taking *action* as an antidote to the "transgressions" committed, and holding a strong *aspiration* to behave in a more conscious manner when similar circumstances arise. The action taken can be internal, like praying for others, or some outward action like planting a tree, donating money, or helping others in some way.

BEWARE: BE *AWARE* OF EMOTIONAL STATES

As we do this work, various emotional states will arise. Transformational work is disruptive and emotional. Let these emotions rise up without repressing them or acting on them. (I refer you to chapter 5, a discussion of the North, for specific meditation practices if you feel the need to meditate around them.) In some cases, the purification of negative emotional states such as anger, jealousy, and resentment may be warranted. As you perform one of the ceremonies or practices, hold the desire to be free of this particular emotional state as your purification intention.

When emotional states arise, pretend you are sitting in a sweat lodge or at a Nyung Nay retreat and hold the intention to let it move through you so as to increase your purification. Experience it as part of your purification. Be willing to sit in the hot spot. Do this instead of following the story line of the given emotion. If I had given in to the emotional wave that arose during my Nyung Nay fasting ritual, I would not have made it through to the end. I would have given up, because my emotional states of anger and arrogance, mixed with moments of defeat, were telling me to give up. I allowed for these emotional states within the context of the weekend ritual and held my seat in the hot spot.

All purification rituals and practices intend to bring forth some humility on our part in order for us to become less self-absorbed. When we become less self-absorbed, we have made room for more insight. And with this insight, we move closer toward personal initiation.

BRINGING AWARENESS TO THE EMOTIONS

For a long time I practiced loving-kindness, compassion, and tolerance when I thought others had wronged me somehow. When others were unkind to me, I would engage the path of the Bodhisattva as best I could at the time. And in most ways my practice was good. However, I (unskillfully) repressed some of my emotions. In Buddhist practice this is actually a way to suppress karma and let it arise again—and it did. I came to realize I was angry with certain people for various "stuff." While I had been practicing compassionate living, I had suppressed some *emotional* content of various experiences. I thought I was being a skillful practitioner—instead I was generating more pain and karma.

The moment I realized the emotional content of pain I was presently experiencing—*anger,* in this case—I experienced a great release. I practiced confession around the times my anger had hurt myself, or others. I resolved not to suppress or carry this around with me anymore. I experienced regret and some immediate purification.

The point is to let the given emotion arise without strengthening it or suppressing it. It is not about getting angry with others, but bringing awareness to the emotion and watching it—bearing witness to your emotions. Letting it be but not giving it more "story line," not building upon it. I learned the various dimensions of this emotional state, which in this case was anger; "should" came up a lot. There was a flavor of feeling ignored or misunderstood. What I quickly discovered is that these *are just experiences,* and bringing awareness to them lets me realize that I am not these emotions; they are not *me.*

Bring awareness to the emotion and the thoughts around a given emotion, and you too will discover that you cannot get all caught up in it. Sit with the emotion but do not react to it. When I brought awareness to my anger, I could not get into being angry. I could, however, let it rise and show itself. Such emotional states are like a crying baby (that has been fed and changed)—who just wants some love and attention, space to cry, and to be held. It doesn't want you to shake it, run around in a panic, or even "do" anything. Ignoring can be fatal.

After practicing awareness with this particular emotion, relax into *presence*—into just being in the moment. Breathe, and notice the "now-ness" of experience. Then, consciously *let it go. Choose to move on.*

As stated earlier, in Buddhist perspective, negative karma can get heavier and heavier when one does not practice regular purification practices. At the very least we can all feel the heaviness of carrying such dense emotions as resentment, anger, or disappointment within our psychophysical bodies. Many traditions offer daily purification rituals as well as ones that are preliminary to psychological and spiritual work. This makes good sense to me. Whether or not negative karma is accumulative, it can only be a good thing to purify oneself as a practice for getting ready for the day.

Daily Practices of Purification

1. Circumambulation (walking clockwise) in a sacred manner around a sacred object such as a stupa or medicine wheel is a universal method of purification. You can find a stupa at your local Buddhist center (or you can make a pilgrimage to a site such as Deer Park in Oregon, Wisconsin, to circumambulate its stupa and visit the beautiful temple). Bighorn Medicine Wheel in Lovell, Wyoming, is another great destination spot. It sits atop a jagged peak and is believed to be

at least seven hundred years old; it is open to the public. There are about twenty known medicine wheels throughout the United States (all of which make great pilgrimages).

You can create your own spiral or stupa to walk. Many mornings at sunrise I circumambulate into the spiral that sits in our prairie and circle clockwise into its center around a mandala and prayer poles. Walking a labyrinth, doing a walking meditation, or even circumambulating a special tree can be a way to purify yourself and prepare you for the day. When walking, choose a mantra or prayer from your own tradition to recite, or simply walk mindfully, asking for a cleansing.

The journey within the Wheel is circular in this way—you enter in the South and go clockwise through the directions. You are circumambulating as you read this book—you are on a sacred journey through the Wheel.

2. Chanting sacred sounds and names is another means of purification. One of my teachers, A'cha'rya Jina'neshvar (James Powell), uses *kiirtana* to initiate transformation and healing in his students. He teaches that chanting and conscious breathing will not only purify but potentially raise your energy to an even more refined level of harmony. Chanting is also a fundamental means of recapitulation— a means to retrieve your energy. As A'cha'rya Jina'neshvar says, "A practice with immediate results is the chanting of *Kiirtana* (sacred names) right before meditation. This chanting purifies the mind, drawing it in toward the inner being. This chanting of *Kiirtana* is a very good way to cleanse the mind of limiting emotions such as fear and anger."

And we have these words of wisdom from Shrii Shrii A'nandamu'rti, A'cha'rya Jina'neshvar's teacher:

Whatever worldly difficulties might obstruct your path, the best positive or auxiliary force is kiirtana (chanting sacred names). Kiirtana helps a devotee to accelerate the speed toward the hub of the Universe. Kiirtana will help you in all circumstances; if any mental trouble arises, Kiirtana will help you. . . . It is the best medicine for all physical, psychic, and spiritual ailments. It will bring about not only improvement in worldly life but success in the psychic and spiritual spheres. Kiirtana will help you in all circumstances, in all possible ways. . . . By kiirtana you become as pure as if you have taken a "holy dip in the Ganges." . . . By kiirtana you will always feel that you are not an insignificant creature, you are not inferior or low. Kiirtana will always remind you that you are the affectionate children of the Supreme.

3. The *Ahhh* breath purification sound is another means of purification. This sound is the sound of life. It is the sound we make when we are born and take our first breath, and it is the last sound we make as we exhale our last breath, *Ah*. Begin with three nice deep breaths into the belly. Breathe in through the nose and exhale through the mouth. Then on the fourth one take a nice deep breath in (again through the nose), and on the out breath make the sound of *Ahhh*. When taking a deep breath, imagine opening your mind and body. Imagine *breathing in* the purification of the luminous blue sky, and breathing out all stale energy. Do at least three of these in the morning upon arising.

4. Praying with rosaries or malas, and/or the recitation of prayers or mantras as you use beads to count is a simple method of purification. A short Vajrassattva mantra would be: OM VAJRA SATTVA HUM. The translation of this mantra is, "O Vajrasattva, with your help may I bring about purification and transformation." Vajrassattva is used to call forth the internal and external help needed for purification and transformation, but you could replace it with your own deity or spiritual master: OM JESUS SATTVA HUM. OM TARA SATTVA HUM. Commit to saying this mantra ten times a morning to begin with or choose a purification mantra or prayer from your own spiritual tradition.

5. Prostrations can also be used for purification. Prostrations are a way to "bow down" to that which represents our inherent goodness and beauty. We bow down to those who remind us of our basic humanity.

This is an act of surrendering and vulnerability, and it helps purify us of arrogance and self-importance. It helps free us from self-absorption. In Victor Sanchez's teachings of the Toltec Path, he underlines the Toltec practice of losing one's self-importance. The energy and attention we put into all acts of self-importance actually keep us caught in a cycle of negative habitual patterns. This is because we feel the need to "prove ourselves" over and over again, because self-importance is such a fleeting and externally based dynamic.

Prostration then frees us from this stance of self-importance, letting go of a bit of the ego each time we bow. It helps us move past the layers of resistance that arise as we progress through the Wheel. We can prostate on a daily basis, freeing ourselves by making three prostrations to the rising sun or to our root guru or our spiritual teacher. Each tradition holds a style of prostration, and you may borrow from one that suits you. Most important is what you hold in your heart as you bow. Hold a strong desire to clean yourself of obstructions, bowing down in gratitude and humility to your spiritual source, your teacher, and your spiritual community. I prostrate to the three jewels of Buddhism (the Buddha, the Dharma, and the Sangha), and to my root guru, Padmasambhava. I have a friend who prostrates to the rising and setting sun. At sunrise she prepares herself for the day; at sunset she lets go of all the negativity from the day.

Prostrations connect us with our own sanity. As a gesture of respect, love, and gratitude to those who show us our basic goodness, we bow down and prostrate. Prostrations serve as a way to overcome resistance and surrender our deeply entrenched neuroses and habits. Each time we bow, we offer ourselves: our confusion, our inability to love, our hardness and selfish ways.

PEMA CHÖDRÖN, *NO TIME TO LOSE*

6. Another way of purification is to practice fasting. Fast from a particular habit for twenty-four hours. Just for a day, offer up a habit as a means to purify and transform your life.

Craven Gives Up a Habit

FOR THIRTY DAYS I woke up and said, "I am fasting from the habit of watching reruns, just for today." Then night would come, and it would get difficult. So for that one night I would not watch reruns. For the first ten days I found myself watching something as long as it wasn't reruns. Then I found myself reading and not turning on the television at all. As a result of this I started spending more time with my partner. By the thirtieth day I was purified of some heavy stuff and truly transformed. And my relationship of thirteen years was transformed too.

Purification

At the start of spring I open a trench
in the ground. I put into it
the winter's accumulation of paper,
pages I do not want to read
again, useless words, fragments,
errors. And I put into it
the contents of the outhouse:
light of the sun, growth of the ground,
finished with one of their journeys.
To the sky, to the wind, then,
and to the faithful trees, I confess
my sins: that I have not been happy enough,
considering my good luck;
have listened to too much noise;
have been inattentive to wonders;
have lusted after praise.
And then upon the gathered refuse
of mind and body, I close the trench,
folding shut again the dark,

the deathless earth. Beneath that seal
the old escapes into the new.

WENDELL BERRY, "A PURIFICATION,"
FROM *THE COLLECTED POEMS OF*
WENDELL BERRY, 1957–1982

PRACTICES OF RELEASE

Just as we used practices of purification to help us break our agreements to the past, we will also use practices of release, as follows.

Utilizing Thunder Beings to Release the Past

Thunder Beings are the central archetypes of the West in the Wheel of Initiation—they reside in the psyche and come out in the form of gods and goddesses and methods to free us from our egos and mental attachments. They sit behind us in the Catku of our inner lodge and both support us and fight with our agreements that keep our pain stories going. Symbolically, the West is where the Thunder Beings confront our ego attachments, heat things up for us, and help us release the inner light. For me, Vajrasattva, the Buddha of Purification, is a Thunder Being. This archetypal symbol comes out in nearly every tradition, some representation of thundering energy that has the ability to break through illusions and false concepts.

Only with the puissant forces needed to break through the illusions can we release the inner light. Imagine that your true nature is held captive by beasts such as ignorance, anger, judgment, fear, jealousy, and erroneous assumptions. Therefore an equally powerful energy must help you destroy the grip that these beasts have on you. You will find this destroyer (thunder) energy in spiritual practices around the world (thunderbolts or *dorje*s, Thunderbirds).

In short, he does the opposite of what life obliges man to do—and he does this in order to free himself from the multifarious conditionings that constitute the whole of profane existence, and to make his way at last to an unconditioned plane, a plane of absolute freedom. But he cannot reach such a situation, comparable to that of the Gods, except by dying to unenlightened life, to profane existence.

MIRCEA ELIADE, *RITES AND SYMBOLS OF INITIATION*

The vajra or dorje in Tibetan Buddhism is the symbolic tool of the thunderbolt, that which is capable of destroying illusions, mental obstructions, and projections (among its many other symbolic qualities).

Fig. 4.3. A Tibetan dorje or vajra is a Buddhist ritual object and symbol representing a thunderbolt quality of enlightened wisdom. It is a tool used to help the spiritual pilgrim break through states of resistance.

Thunderbolts typically symbolize the connection between destruction and creation. Thunderbolts are the weapons of the gods (Shiva, Vishnu, Zeus, for example) and represent the transforming influence of destruction. First comes thunder and then come the needed rains (of insight, wisdom, compassion, and beneficial influences). In shamanic practices, the Thunderbird is often the guide for the practitioner's journey into the upper worlds. In the Wheel of Initiation the Thunderbird flies with a lightning bolt on her body in the direction of the West. In Christianity thunder symbolizes the voice of god as a divine threat of annihilation or revelation (Job 36:29–33). And in the ancient Chinese oracle of the I Ching, the attribute of Thunder (Zhen) is movement. The Thunder Being of Muslims is named Jibrail, the giver of revelation.

This is where the false self begins to die and lose its grip on your heart and mind. The old ways simply do not work within the new paradigm you are creating. Your deals with the past are broken here. It is in this breaking that you come to realize your abilities as a spiritual traveler. There is

*Fig. 4.4. A Thunderbird image, derived from petrogylphs.
The Thunderbird represents the Thunderbeings that show up
in the West of the Wheel of Initiation to free us
from our negative mind-sets.*

no initiation without a symbolic death. Symbolic death of the old is where we experience transformation. Transformative death is a letting go of our habitual existence and attachments, and therefore we are made fresh and rejuvenated by our insights and the movement made through our commitment to our intentions.

Jon's Initiation into the West:
We Experience the
Most Heat When the Thunder Beings Arrive

I FIND IT SO HARD to truly feel good about some people's successes, mostly those who have betrayed me in some way. This is my Catku, my hot spot right now. Instead of being happy for them when they do well, I find myself feeling satisfied in their misfortunes. My mind seems to draw me into this and hold on to me. To sit through the hot spot means for me to not agree to ponder others' faults in this way and to end my agreement to hold someone captive in my thoughts. I realize this agreement causes me more suffering than it does them, and yet its grip is strong.

As you sit in the internal hot spot created by the Thunder Beings, your outside world is also getting hotter. What are the Thunder Beings stirring up for you? Can you sit through the heat and discomfort that brings the desired purification and initiation? What story wants to be told? The heat is coming from some old agreement that you are both holding on to and challenging. What are these agreements that tend to hold you back?

Calling Forth the Inner Kali

Kali is the Hindu goddess of transformation. She holds the archetypal power to help us let go of our illusions and projections. Part of you will not survive the pilgrimage through the Wheel; aspects of your ego must be sacrificed and released for initiation.

What needs releasing within you (the past, agreements to the pain story, habitual reactive states, old beliefs) will be apparent now, as you sit in the West, the Catku of your journey. Through purification we get release. During the purification of the fasting ritual, I was also releasing immeasurable ties to the past. I was releasing my agreement to need an outward spiritual experience for validation. I was releasing the agreement that I needed an outward reason to continue the practice.

In my studies of ecopsychology, depth psychology, and Buddhism, I see a process that bridges the natural world with the psychological and spiritual. In nature, destruction and creativity go together. We cannot deny the necessary destructive force needed for transformation. When we make everything always pretty and presentable and ignore the destructive force inherent in the natural world and in the creative process, Kali goes underground. You cannot create an oak tree without breaking through the shell of the acorn. *The internal Kali, the destroyer of the false self, will act from your unconscious if you do not engage her consciously.* This is where illness may arise, as well as addictions, anxiety, depression, pain in the body, destructive emotions like rage, relationship difficulties, and nightmares. These are all gifts from the Kali that resides in your unconscious.

Kali wears a necklace of severed heads and a skirt of severed arms. The heads are smiling because they have been freed from their illusions, from the negative influences of the ego. Kali's ultimate act of compassion is the destruction she wreaks that frees you from your prison, your pain story. This is not a pretty sight and is the reason why her image is often disturbing. She holds a head in one of her left hands and a broken sword that cuts through illusion in one of her right hands. She is the Hindus' Thunder Being.

When you encounter Kali, be ready to confront a deal breaker, to sever a deal with your false self. Her name translates as "dark" and "time," perhaps the best company for those of us in the dark of the internal sweat lodge. The West is the place of release and liberation, and the archetypes that represent the power to help us achieve such freedom are truly the compassionate ones. You have invoked the fierce compassion of Kali, or your own personal Thunder Being, by arriving in the West. Honor her and break a bond you have with the false self and your pain story.

Invoking a Deal Breaker

What's a deal breaker? It is a specific agreement that helps you break free from the pain of the past. It is a core deal you have with your pain story or your false self. Typically, it's around the particular intention you are working with at the time, meaning that it breaks your deal with the past and more strongly binds you to your intention. It can be understood as the apotheosis of your initiation. A transformation is taking place. A part of your ego is crumbling as a result of an increase in your consciousness. Your sense of reality is changing.

This break allows you to continue with your spiritual initiation. When you are at this point, the Thunder Beings are really active—something in your core is being shaken up. You are aware that if you keep doing life the same old way, you will keep getting the same old result. Because the break is real (manifested internally and externally by transforming agreements), this feels risky, scary, and uncertain. And it *is* risky, scary, and uncertain. You are stepping into the great mystery. But you must take that step and make an *outward* action that mirrors the inner awareness and shift in agreements. Remember how thunder also represents movement and taking action.

As Laurel, in the West, tells us: "All my life I have had to figure things out. In fact, I expend quite a bit of time trying to figure things out—somehow believing that will make the difference. All it has actually done is keep me in my head, searching for reasons rather than just experiencing life. My deal breaker is not agreeing to the fact that I have to figure everything out first."

And here is what Rachel, also in the West, has to say about her deal breaker:

My deal breaker? Letting go of my distrust. Distrust was my lifeboat. Or so I believed. It kept me from danger. But what I discovered through my story is that most, if not all, my decisions were led by a sense of distrust. Distrust in the other, in myself, in the world, in god. And big surprise—I kept getting validation of this distrust. So it all came crashing down on me. I couldn't ignore the realization that I was generating my pain story over and over again. Julie pointed out that my Thunder Being had shown up. The more I held onto the distrust, the more migraines I had. I was feeling as if I couldn't continue with the Wheel. This distrust caused me, as well as others, to always feel defensive. I wanted to blame everything on outside circumstances and people. But if I wanted to live, to experience initiation, I knew I had to break this deal. I remembered my agreement to be willing to do whatever it takes. And this was it.

No one can really be told they are in the Catku. You must feel the heat for yourself and trust your own wisdom. What is important here is to understand that it is inevitable that deal breakers will arise, and you will be given the opportunity to release the past.

Let's hear what Evan, while in his Catku, had to say about this: "I kept asking Julie, Is *this* my deal breaker? And she kept coming back with, 'The answer is in the question.' She gave the example of someone repeatedly asking, 'Do you think I am an alcoholic? Do you?' The need to even ask the question is revealing something."

You too will know when the Thunder Beings have shown up.

Making a Symbolic Sacrifice

Releasing the past can be done through a symbolic sacrifice, a renunciation, or a dismantling of the false self. In many traditions, animal myths demonstrate the sacrifice inherent in spiritual initiation. In these myths, when animals seek to claim or reclaim fire or light, they have to make a sacrifice of themselves. This is true of the rainbow crow in the Lenape legend, whose task was to retrieve fire for her community. It had been a very colorful bird but turned black from being burned, and its song became rough from the smoke inhaled by the fire, while at the same time the resplendence of the crow's rainbow color shimmers through after its transformative sacrifice.

Interestingly enough, these stories are often stories of "theft." The animals often had to steal the fire or light to bring it back. What or who do you need to steal your light back from? What agreements hold your inner light captive or the fire of your creativity hidden?

Dismantling the Pain Story

We become what we don't dismantle.

KEN MCLEOD, *WAKE UP TO YOUR LIFE*

Through this understanding of your agreements, you can come to release your attachments to your pain stories and their resulting patterns. The techniques I offer here to help you dismantle your pain stories and free yourself from the false self are found in cognitive-behavioral sciences, rational-emotive therapies, Buddhist practices, depth psychology, and other psychospiritual wisdom that points to the power of the mind and its transformative qualities. All wisdom teachings show that everything is experienced through our mind, our thoughts, our perspective, and our perception. You could say that our mind flavors everything it sees and experiences. Therefore, transforming our mind is the fundamental key to transforming any and every aspect of our lives.

We are totally inhibited by our own mind-set and inner difficulties, even though what we want is happiness.

GESHE TENZIN DORJE, DEER PARK, WISCONSIN, SEPTEMBER 2009

TRAINING THE MIND TO OBSERVE

The mind, fortunately, is trainable. We can learn to locate the culprit of our suffering through mindfulness of our cognitive processes and the emotions and behaviors that result. We can teach the mind to focus on such inner qualities as compassion, tolerance, and patience. How then is it we feel so pushed around by our emotional states and outside experiences? Observe your mind and experiences in the following way and then decide who is driving your bus. Is it your circumstances, your emotions, or your thoughts (mind-set)?

Borrowing from the cognitive-behavioral model, we start with a *situation* (a friend's funeral), then we identify a *thought,* a mental response ("She had a good life; I will miss her, but her suffering from cancer is over"). Next, we notice an *emotional response* based on the cognitive response ("I feel sad and relieved; I feel grateful our paths crossed"). And then we have the resulting *behavior and experience* ("I celebrate her life").

In the following model we witness how two people can have the same original situation but a completely different response and experience. Both Kevin and Joe had a flat tire on their way to an important meeting (*situation*). Kevin's thoughts were, "I am going to be late. This always happens to me. I have to get to this on time or I am screwed. This is awful." He felt angry, victimized, rushed, and defeated (the *emotional response*). He ended up getting more and more upset and arrived fifteen minutes late, still upset and not ready to present his material (*resulting behavior and complete experience*).

On the other hand, when Joe got a flat tire, he thought, "Good thing I have a spare ready. Glad it's me and not my wife. I can do this quickly." He felt okay and relieved. When he got to the meeting, he was calm and only ten minutes late; he was ready to present his material. He gave a great presentation and used the analogy of the flat tire as a metaphor for how being prepared makes life simpler because "flats happen."

Use this awareness technique to understand one of your pain stories and its corresponding beliefs and agreements. Begin with a *painful situation* in your life story (my father belittled me), to which you have a *thought response* (I came to believe I was worthless); and you *create agreements* (I must change myself to please my father, others) to the *emotional content* (feeling inadequate, feeling shame), to the *behavior/actions* (always trying to please others).

We can't change the past. But we will keep repeating it if we continue to live by the beliefs and agreements set in response to past events. Notice also that the original belief and agreement really *aren't your fault*. There is no need to add to the pain by shaming yourself. Your original thought response is understandable when you consider it in the context of your story. Be kind as you dismantle these beliefs and agreements. Most of our habitual beliefs and agreements are linked to an original belief that helped us survive or interpret a difficult situation.

Henry's Experience with Right and Wrong

FOR ME THE NEED to make those around me "wrong" as they abused drugs and alcohol, destroyed property, and neglected ethical practices was what allowed me to survive my adolescence. Telling my story and doing this work in the Wheel helped me realize that once I stepped out through the door of my family home and was on my own, this belief could have been left at the door. But I carried it around with me for decades, habitually using it as a means to protect myself. It became a personal myth that I perpetuated. Others were either in the right or in the wrong.

If you find it difficult to identify a given belief, start with awareness around a particular emotion, such as anger, fear, or jealousy, because every emotion is accompanied by a thought pattern or belief. Then trace the emotion to a historical experience in your pain story and go through the same process as above. Do your best to identify an agreement that you still hold about yourself or the world that keeps you suffering.

Closing the Door on Distractions

> *He who travels on this path (of error or destruction) is one who is distracted, who is ruled by his senses, and who lives for himself rather than for his people.*
>
> BLACK ELK, THE SACRED PIPE, RECORDED
> AND EDITED BY JOSEPH EPES BROWN

> *When we get caught up in distractions, more suffering results.*
>
> GESHE TENZIN DORJE

Black Elk and Geshe Dorje point to how there is much that attempts to *distract* us from our spiritual path and from living in integrity and truth. (The list is long!) Like resistance, distractions will keep arising—it gets down to whether we remain in agreement with these distractions. Black Elk spoke of "closing the door on that distraction," which means closing the door on all that distracts us from our spiritual development and inherent goodness.

This kind of "closing" is transformative. There are obvious distractions like alcohol or television or living in the virtual life of Facebook. But there are the less apparent ones that are psychological, such as needing approval, attachment to drama, gossiping, and the like. For instance, when I closed the door on "drama," I was no longer in agreement with those who dramatize their life. I no longer agreed to be caught up in their dramas. For me this created a much safer and saner world.

When you close a door on a given distraction by no longer being in agreement with it, then you no longer actually participate in it. But you must become conscious of what is distracting you from your spiritual and creative life. Focus on your initiation intention and ask yourself, "What is distracting me from my initiation intention?"

Kathryn Closes the Door

THIS SOUNDS ALMOST strange to say, but I closed the door on depression. I no longer agreed that everything in my life was going to be seen through the lens of *depression. Yes, I sometimes experience deep sadness, and at times I am walking through life slowly. But to define myself as "depressed" doesn't help me. While in the Initiation Course, I decided to no longer agree to see myself as depressed, thus pulling everyone else into this agreement. The circle supported me with this, and three years later I no longer view myself, or my world, through depressed lenses. I closed the door on depression.*

Now, some will read this and say that not being in agreement is simply a state of denial—well, yes and no. When you understand that an agreement is an *energetic contract*, one that once we sign we invest ourselves in, denying it may be the only way to end it. In some cases it is the agreement and the agreement alone that keeps the particular experience active. When we no longer agree to something and consciously hold ourselves accountable to this correction of mind, our relationship to this phenomenon—be it depression, be it alcohol, be it an abusive relationship—cannot hold the same power over us. The energy is no longer going into the contract, so the agreement dissolves. Then the behaviors and experiences change.

What uses up your energy and distracts you away from your initiation intention? *What consistently interferes with your spiritual evolution?* Our egos (our defenders of the false self) can be strong and intense—and boss us around. Geshe Tenzin Dorje suggests that we bring the spiritual practice *to* our distractions. In this way we do not get "caught up" in them. For example, eating when done habitually can be a distraction. When we eat mindfully, bringing awareness to our behavior, we transform the distraction into an opportunity to practice our spiritual knowledge. In both methods of dealing with distractions we open the way for realization and transformation as we go deeper into our spiritual initiation.

Step by conscious step we are freeing ourselves from our pain stories.

✷ Break the Defenses and Dismantle Agreements

To get to the root of our suffering, we need to be able to break through the ego's defenses of our pain story and all its beliefs, assumptions, and agreements. Spiritual practice fundamentally dictates that we recognize our own afflictive mental states and continuously commit to correcting them. Here is a simple (yet not easy) process of getting to the root of our habitual and painful states. Once at the root, use this process to dismantle the false self, one agreement at a time. This technique is borrowed from rational-emotive therapy and Buddhist mind transformation techniques. Write it out in your journal, do it with a counselor, a spiritual guide, or in your initiation circle. Initiation circles or counselors can hold sacred space for you as you do this internal work on your own (see the appendix, "Teachers and Groups").

Name a belief or a habitual (repetitive) thought that you have, such as:

- It matters what others think of me.
- My husband doesn't appreciate me.
- I don't trust _____ (fill in the blank).
- I have to be right about this one.
- My boss is a tyrant.
- I'm always overlooked.
- I have to be in a relationship to be happy.
- They are doing this to hurt me.

If you need help coming up with a painful belief, refer to your life story and your life experiences. Reread your story if it helps. Record it and play it back to yourself. Such inquiry helps distance you from the negative states.

Next, expand upon it.

- It matters what others think of me. Therefore I put energy into how I look and present myself. I take a lot of time going over in my mind how I think I look to others.
- My partner doesn't appreciate me. Even when I do my part around the house, he never says thank you. I just feel like giving up and not doing anything for him.

Then take this belief and either write it out in your journal or on a board of some kind if in a group.

For instance: "It matters a great deal what others think of me." Then respond with, "Okay. So what?" Write this response in your journal or have someone say it out loud for you.

Continue bringing up whatever natural defenses you have around this belief. Keep bringing to the light all the thoughts you hold that defend this belief and keep responding with, "Okay. So what?"

"But others may have the wrong idea of me if I don't care about what I do." "Okay. So what?"

"Well, I don't want that."
"Okay. So what?"

"I want every one to see how wonderful I am."
"Okay. So what?"

"I will be alone if I don't care."
"Okay. So what?"

"I don't want to be alone."
"Okay. So what?"

"I hate being alone. I can't be alone."
"Okay. So what?"

"I don't want to be alone. *Being alone is bad.*" (Core belief)

In doing this exercise, you will reach the root of the root of the defense. You will see how it just keeps circling down to a core belief (*being alone is bad*) and how much defensive posturing goes into keeping this belief going. In so doing, you will hear *all* the agreements you hold that defend this belief.

For example, the woman above agrees that she will end up alone if she doesn't worry about how she appears to others. Her core belief, "Being alone is bad," is sustained by her agreement to be invested in outward appearances. To undermine the core belief, she could end any one of the supporting agreements.

You may also reach a dead end. You may reach the state where you really experience a shift into, "Okay. So what?" This may be a moment where you see this for what it is—a belief that drives your experience and leads to various behaviors and choices, all of which strengthen each other. With this awareness and shift, you have the ability to let go of this belief and its supporting agreements and understand it for the habitual projection it is.

Even when the belief appears to be controlled by something outside ourselves, like "My mother doesn't appreciate me" or "My boss is a bully," the dismantling of the defenses makes it clear that you are suffering because you choose to carry this idea around with you, not because it might be true.

✳ The Origin of Thought

Now, take the core thought, such as "It is bad to be alone," and ask yourself, "What happens to this belief when I no longer agree to it?" Or what happens to this dynamic, this belief of "I can't be alone," after you die? Does this belief, this dynamic, have a life independent of you? Where does this thought now (in the moment of you having the thought) originate? Where does this thought in the moment arise? Does it come from your body, your brain, or your heart? Does it have an independent existence outside you? Will it continue to be true (for you) when you no longer agree to it? Will it still matter when you are no longer carrying it?

No, it will not. When you die, this belief dies with you. When you no longer agree to this belief, it will no longer have your energy in it. In the initiatory process, when you die to a belief or end an agreement, all that binds you to that belief also passes away. This passing away may take time, but everything that is dependent on this agreement weakens and dissolves too.

✳

Because persons and things are devoid of trueness of being self-instituting, they are affected by conditions and are capable of transformation.

THE FOURTEENTH DALAI LAMA,
HOW TO SEE YOURSELF AS YOU REALLY ARE

Isolating and Removing One Agreement

Small steps matter here too. Imagine one of your big agreements being like a tapestry. For Jon, a substantial pain-story agreement was to "stay married for the kids." He was clear that he was simply not ready to end this agreement (which meant either divorce or to be more engaged and present in the marriage). So we took a bigger look at all the finer threads that kept this agreement together.

Take a thread out from a big, core agreement and pull it all the way out. Because you may believe you cannot challenge the bigger one, focus your energy and practice on a smaller one. In this case, within this broader agreement he found agreements not to speak up for himself in this relationship, and the agreement not to pursue his passion to sing and act. He realized that a lot of different threads made up the agreement "to stay married for the kids." He made a list of about twenty-five agreements that he noticed were woven into this broader agreement. So he chose one: "I no longer agree to hide my passion for singing and acting." He brought this one all the way out and decided not to agree to hide this any more. He joined the community choir and tried out for the local play. (Be warned, pulling out one thread within the tapestry has a way of unraveling other agreements.)

Then the agreement that was next to this one got loosened up—his agreement not to rock the boat and speak up for himself. He spoke about his passion to sing. And then the one next to that one, not to talk to his wife about *her* apparent unhappiness, and the next one . . . When such an agreement is dismantled, the unraveling and outcome may surprise you. Ultimately he decided not to stay married for the kids and remained married for himself. Fear of letting go, of the petite death, mutates into fear of living. We don't take the little risks. We believe we cannot bear to let go, to love and to live.

Take one of your bigger agreements and make a list of smaller agreements that are woven into it (you are likely to come up with at least half a dozen). To make this simple, be aware of one particular big agreement for a few days—such as, "I have to have outside validation to feel good."

Laura made a list from this agreement because it felt big to her. She discovered approximately twenty more agreements that were woven into this one. They included: "not saying no," "being competitive with others," "needing to take more training before I risked going into business," "always explaining myself to others," "overbooking myself because I couldn't say no," "being tuned in to pleasing others." She decided to pull out the agreement not to say no: "I no longer agree *not* to say no. I could feel the entire tapestry shake and begin to unravel. I found myself saying no at least once a day."

✴ Create a Personal Ritual

Return to the Initiation Wheel you made for setting your intention, or make another circle on the ground. Enter the Wheel, and, beginning in the South, face that direction and state out loud the agreement you are breaking. Then, going clockwise, break this agreement in each direction. Ask for help from your spiritual source. Of course, this could be just as meaningful if you go outside and simply face each direction and announce the agreement you are breaking. Personal rituals give a means for you to create movement around your spiritual efforts and to call in your spiritual helpers. Most important, however, is what you practice in your day-to-day life.

In an initiation circle, you can go around while each person announces what they are no longer in agreement with. The power of doing this in a safe circle is that when you transform an agreement, it helps each one within your circle. For example, Laura no longer agreed to seek outside validation for her decisions. Everyone in the circle could identify with this one. She acknowledged that if she got stuck at any time and could not break this agreement, she would "do it for others in the circle."

✴

As I mentioned earlier, at one point it seemed that drama was just a part of life. I wasn't creating drama but realized how I agreed to the drama that was presented to me by others (via relationships, media, the community). Drama relies on an audience. And the thing is, we all want others to be in agreement with whatever we believe. One particular incident invited me to take a look at my agreement to others' dramatization of life's circumstances.

My decision was quick and on the spot: I no longer agreed to drama. It didn't take long for me to notice how drama then simply stopped showing up in my life. Along with this, the need to be caught up in another's story line or to take on another's shadow unraveled as well. This does not mean that the outside world became less dramatic, but that I was less moved by it. It no longer got my energy. A few months into the dismantling of this agreement, some drama erupted (and the potential for more), but I seemed impervious to it.

My energy body felt as if it was made of light, or was a slippery slope—the drama simply had no place to stick. I noticed how fearless I felt in the world, having closed the door on this distraction (agreement to drama). When not caught up in the drama (not agreeing to it or responding to it more consciously), I became freer to express my compassion and wisdom and be more fully present, both for myself and for the person enacting the drama.

When I no longer agreed to drama, along with it went the agreement to take other people's perceptions so personally. And more began to unravel from there—opening me more and more to my true nature, and consequently to the true nature of others as well. We can't hold on to the old beliefs and agreements and expect to release the inner light. The old paradigm is taking up too much space and leaving too little room for the light to emerge. Such inner work resonates with the natural cycle of life-death-life, the cycle of initiation and rebirth. The old must die to let new life be born.

CONFRONTING RESISTANCE

The paradox seems to be, as Socrates demonstrated long ago, that the truly free individual is free only to the extent of his own self-mastery.

STEVEN PRESSFIELD, THE WAR OF ART

Resistance can be what we move against, work with, or push through as we live our lives and move through personal initiation. In this way resistance is like a god—offering itself up to us every day as a means to remind us, "Stay awake," "Keep moving," "Enjoy," "*Participate.*" I imagine a fully realized human being may not need this brand of god but can act, live, and express without needing anything to move against. And indeed, spiritual initiation gives you more energy and self so that when resistance arises (in all its various forms), you move through it with greater determination.

Understood in this way, resistance becomes a pointer to where we need movement in our lives. The moment you entered the Wheel, resistance arose in some form or another. And now, here in the West—the direction of purification and recapitulation—resistance will surely show its godly head. If you are truly engaged in your life and in your spiritual practice, resistance is a given.

> *Resistance cannot be seen, touched, heard, or smelled. But it can be felt. We experience it as an energy field radiating from a work-in-potential. It's a repelling force. It's negative. Its aim is to shove us away, distract us, prevent us from doing our work.*
>
> STEVEN PRESSFIELD, *THE WAR OF ART*

An easy way to name what you may be resisting is to look at your agreements. Your agreements to the past are what your resistance builds on and works with to keep you stuck. They prevent you from completing that painting, writing that book, joining that club, meeting that person, taking that walk, practicing that song, writing that poem, starting that business, moving to another state, or trying a new dish at a restaurant. Resistance is like the omnipotent and omnipresent god—she is everywhere.

> *Resistance is not a peripheral opponent. Resistance arises from within. It is self-generated and self-perpetuated. Resistance is the enemy within.*
>
> STEVEN PRESSFIELD, *THE WAR OF ART*

Every time you postpone, you are in resistance. Every time you knowingly act against your intentions, you are in resistance. Every time you overeat, watch too much television, play too many video games, overdo at a job you dislike (or give too much of yourself to something you detest), spend lost time on the computer (or Internet), complain, get overwhelmed, give up on a creative project, feel jealous, compete to beat someone else instead of simply doing your best, accumulate a lot of trinkets, don't throw out or recycle useless stuff, or blame your life on outside circumstances, you are in resistance.

In the initiation pilgrimage, resistance comes up in response to your setting your intention. Ultimately, either your intention or your resistance will thrive and take root in your life. If you are not moving on your initiatory intention, then you are encountering some form of resistance. In Meeghan's story above, each corner she encountered in the spiral was seen either as an opportunity or a point of resistance. *She simply kept walking.* That's it; whenever resistance arises, just keep moving.

Anything that generates movement (physical, emotional, psychological, or spiritual) results in another successful battle won with resistance. You cannot be in resistance while you are in motion. One of my favorite books of all time, and one I quote a lot from in this book, happens to be on this very subject: Steven Pressfield's *The War of Art.* It is not, however, a comfortable read, if what you want is another excuse to postpone your life.

A familiar last stand of resistance is the excuse to put off your life and aspirations until you are "healed" or "enlightened," get that Ph.D., are in that perfect relationship, or get more training (a culturally endorsed agreement mentioned earlier). But there is not a "there" to get to first. This is the place, *right now, here,* with whatever you have available to you now. This is the entry point, or the reentry point. Go!

The Door Out

THERE ONCE WAS A WOMAN who had been imprisoned for years. She had forgotten what she had done, but felt she surely must be bad to find herself in such a dark and lonely place. In her cell there was one window a few feet above her head.

Each day around noon the sun would come through the window and give her about an hour of warmth and light. She would pull herself up and hold her face in the sunlight as long as possible and then drop down into the darkness when the sun was gone. Each day a guard would come in and feed her one meal. He would not greet her, and she assumed she was not to speak to him. She lived for each meal and for her one hour of sunlight. Had she looked around the cell when the light was coming through the window, she would have seen that there was no lock on the door and that she was free to go at any time.

PRACTICES OF RECAPITULATION

Initiation recapitulates the sacred history of the world. And through this recapitulation, the whole world is sanctified anew.

MIRCEA ELIADE, *RITES AND SYMBOLS OF INITIATION*

The moment you entered the Wheel of Initiation, you began to recapitulate your own sacred history, your own true nature. Your sacred history includes the stories and experiences that represent your true nature and your connection to the sacred, natural world. Your *pain* story includes the wounds inflicted upon you, whereas your *sacred* story includes the strengths and inherent gifts you used to survive these ordeals.

In the writing and telling of your story, you retrieve parts of your true nature lost to pain-story agreements. *Recapitulation is any process that retrieves and restores parts of our true self that were stolen, harmed, or injured in our personal history.* In shamanic practices, this would be called *soul retrieval.*

In his life's work and books, Victor Sanchez offers deliberate processes that free one's true nature from the damage of the past through recapitulation. As he says in his book, *The Toltec Path of Recapitulation,* "In terms of energy it could be said that recapitulation is the series of energetic procedures that restore our field of energy from the damage of the past." Whereas I agree that we can at times use a skillful shaman, counselor, or spiritual teacher to help us recapitulate or retrieve lost parts of ourselves, they are only assistants. You don't have to travel any long distance to get a healing from that renowned shaman or healer—such internal work can be done on your own and right where you live.

In recapitulation we are renewed and regenerated. We then direct this retrieved energy from our "lost soul pieces" to where we choose. You will feel more energized and whole as you focus your attention and redirect your energy and thoughts. As the initiate Nathan tells us: "All I know is that my old pain story lost its grip on me as I moved through the Wheel. And the further I went, the more of "me" I retrieved. When I began, I carried lot of pain in my head and body. My deal breaker had something to do with not living my father's life. . . . I lost a lot of myself to that one! In breaking that agreement alone I would say I got back years of energy, years of myself."

Letting Go of What No Longer Serves You

The practice below is adapted from various Toltec practices on recapitulation, yogic breathing, and shamanic methods. For more in-depth theory and practices on recapitulation and other Toltec practices, there are several great teachers and authors to choose from. These include Victor Sanchez, Ray Dodd, and Don Miguel Ruiz.

> *Recapitulation is the natural process of energetic restoration of our energetic body from the damages that come from the past. This natural act is done by our body. It consists of bodily remembering and reliving the meaningful events of our lives in order to perform a healing process to recover the state of energetic completeness and balance that we had when we were born.*
>
> VICTOR SANCHEZ, *THE TOLTEC PATH OF RECAPITULATION*

"Reliving the meaningful" events is not about going over and over the past, but about enriching our lives through intentional and conscious narrative practices such as those offered through the Wheel of Initiation, narrative therapies, yogic practices, and Toltec recapitulation.

Other practices of recapitulation include sacred storytelling (to others, to spirit, through your journal), transpersonal breathwork, mindfulness meditation, purification practices, ending agreements, taking time in nature, and loving-kindness practices. A true spiritual pilgrimage will naturally result in recapitulation.

The Toltec tradition recognizes that we are energy as well as physical beings. Therefore, any time there is an interaction between you and another person, there is also an energy exchange. Imagine that you are not only exchanging thoughts and emotions with others, but that you are also sharing and exchanging energy. In fact, in my training on psychic development, energy is understood as always speaking the truth. Someone, for example, may be saying "Yes," but their energy says "No." In this case, the "No" speaks the truth. As a result, there is always energy exchanged from which patterns can ensue. For me this means that if we don't take time to heal energetic patterns through various practices of recapitulation, our transformation will be incomplete or false.

Every agreement has an energy cord between you and whatever or whomever you are in agreement with. If it is an uplifting agreement, there is no need for recapitulation, but if it is a negative or destructive agreement, there is a need to end the agreement and dissolve the cord. (An energy cord can be visualized as a rope, an umbilical cord, or a tube that connects you and the other and has energy running back and forth between you.)

Practicing Compassionate Recapitulation

The following practice, which can be done in a group or on your own, will take about fifteen minutes, but with practice you may get it down to a five-minute session. It is a process of clearing out the past, where you have made agreements to give your energy (self) away. You are likely repeating the emotional and behavioral patterns of these agreements (through the repetition of your pain story). And each time you do this, you lose more of your vital energy. These are hooked places. When we react habitually to life's circumstances, we are in fact responding to the past instead of the present. Getting back our own energy helps us live our lives more fully in the moment.

This exercise is a compassionate way to view where you have lost your energy. When you seek to reclaim it, you must do so from a place of witnessing and of compassion. This exercise is also about claiming negative energy we sent out to others.

It acknowledges that we can heal our own wounds best. Again, we don't blame others for our difficulties, but take this opportunity to heal and transform our lives. This helps clear the negative agreements, the history and places that bind us to that which no longer serves us. This practice is both meditative and contemplative.

✷ Getting Your Energy Back

First look for an agreement and its energetic/emotional pattern, such as feeling invisible or unappreciated. You can choose an emotion such as feeling judged, anxious, fearful, insecure, hostile, regretful, angry, dramatic, or resentful (to name a few). This is a place where hindering emotions have arisen in your life and where there seems to be a pattern.

This recapitulation exercise (as all recapitulation processes found in the Wheel) begins with *intention*. Know and remain aware of your intention throughout the process. What do you want to get your energy back from? Notice the question is not *whom* do you want to get your energy back from but *what*. In soul retrieval practices, there is often a person you get your soul back from (an uncle who abused you, for instance), but here it is the *dynamic agreement* that one keeps losing energy to, and that is where retrieval needs to take place ("I keep feeling abused or threatened"). Even where it is clear that you are getting your energy back from a certain person, focus on the *agreement* and its emotional/energy content.

As Annette tells us: "A woman threatened me indirectly on the phone. For an instant I felt panic. Then I heard myself say, "Hey, wait a minute, I don't agree to this! I don't agree to feeling threatened." I quickly got off the phone and began recapitulation with all the times I had agreed to feel threatened. Even though this woman's face arose often in this session, I let her go and focused on getting my energy back from feeling threatened."

The transformation in the above example occurred both in the moment she practiced recapitulation and in the future; it broke her ongoing agreement to feel threatened. She later told me how breaking this agreement gave her her life back (her sacred story).

✸ Specific Steps of Recapitulation

• Sit with both feet on the ground or lie on the floor.

• *Be clear what your recapitulation intention is.* Name the emotional dynamic or agreement you intend to get your energy back from. "I am getting my energy back from all the times I have felt panic. I have lost a lot of energy, actually years, to this—and it is time to not be a walking panic button."

• *Breathe deeply into your belly.*

• *Close your eyes and* feel *your body, whether you are in a chair or lying on the ground.* Feel supported by the chair or floor.

• *Take at least three deep breaths.* Inhale through the nose and exhale through the mouth. (If you cannot breathe through the nose, inhale and exhale through your mouth.) In yogic breathing, inhaling through the nose and exhaling through the mouth is a style of recapitulation breathwork. The in-breath through the nose brings in fresh energy, while exhaling through the mouth moves stale energy out of the body.

• *Identify where you would like your reclaimed energy to go.* Where do you want your reclaimed energy to go? What do you want it to energize? Be very clear about this, otherwise it will go right back to supporting the old energetic patterns and agreements. Give it a new channel. This is a technique of mind training also. Either way, you end up with your focus on something good that will uplift your life. You can direct this anywhere that you feel a revitalization is warranted. Redirect it to your heart for love, to a friendship, a child, or to your creative impulses and projects.

• *Make a cord.* Imagine a cord between your third chakra (deep in your solar plexus) to the energy of the rising sun, the creative principle of the sun, and the initiatory energy of the East. This is a way to focus and bring in energy, from an outside source of creativity and life. Imagine this cord going from your solar plexus to the rising sun. Remain present in your body. You may also choose to connect to your deity (God, Jesus, Buddha, et al.). Imagine your deity in front of you and open a channel from your third chakra to their third chakra.

• *Review the particulars.* Review the times and places wherein you agreed to that particular dynamic (fear or invisibility, for example). Continue to breathe into your belly.

You may travel back years or moments. Track your negative emotion or dynamic and notice what happened when you gave yourself to this particular dynamic agreement (fear, drama). As you recall this, don't create more of the story line or get into the particular event all over again. Simply alight on a particular time, reflect for a moment, and then move on to another time you lost your energy to the specific dynamic. Continue to remain conscious of your connection to the rising sun or deity and hold your intention clearly in mind (what you are getting your energy back from). Do this all from a *witnessing place.* Hold this witnessing presence for yourself; hold space for yourself as you travel and get your energy back.

• *Continue to breathe into your belly.* Know that on the out-breath you are releasing everything that no longer serves you. Know too that on the in-breath you are breathing in all the energy that has been lost to this agreement. Breathe your energy into your body and breathe out all that no longer serves you. Breathe in your energy lost; breathe out all that no longer serves you. Notice where this agreement or negative dynamic wants to return or remain active. (Some energies and agreements are very seductive.) You may find yourself working with a specific person, but even in this case, focus on the energy and agreement. You have lost your energy and soul parts to the agreement that binds you to each other, not to the person himself or herself. Breathe into your belly. Remember your intention: to claim your energy back from your agreement and breathe your energy into your body and breathe out all that no longer serves you. Keep tracking and clearing the energy of your agreement. Remember too where you are now directing this energy.

• *Restate your recapitulation intention.* Do this as you come to the end of this session, and take another minute to breathe your energy into your body and breathe out all that no longer serves you. Then, take three more deep breaths into the belly and begin to complete this time of clearing and claiming your energy. Bring awareness to your body sitting or lying here now. And then let the connection between you and the rising sun dissolve. Restate your intention.

- *When you're ready, open your eyes.*

Practice this recapitulation exercise for at least ten nights in a row prior to retiring for bed. Based on your life story, choose a dynamic that is prevalent in your pain story. Or choose an agreement that interferes with your initiation intention. Keep doing this recapitulation around this particular agreement or wound until it has dissolved and/or you notice a renewal of energy. You will know that it has dissolved when the particular issue does not arise for you, or when and if it does show up in your environment, it does not hook you.

Here is Ava's account of this exercise: "When I call this energy back that had been lost to loneliness, I send it to all the places that feel invisible in me and all the places that do not feel appreciated. This way I can be in a place to claim this energy for myself and not depend on others for it. Then when I feel invisible, or someone doesn't see me (or recognize me), and I feel that loneliness rising up inside me, I don't respond from such a wounded place but from a place of wholeness and love."

Caroline Recapitulates

ABOUT HALFWAY THROUGH the Wheel, I heard Julie say for the hundredth time, "There are no rules; there are only agreements." And then she asked me, "Who decides which beliefs you are in agreement with?" I was trying to end an unhealthy long-term relationship, but my pain-story agreement was, "I move on and he shatters." I believed up until then that if I were to move on, he would fall apart. The only thing left for me to do was recapitulation.

Thus I came up with a new agreement. "My moving on (from this relationship) has nothing to do with Steve." I was letting this unhealthy relationship go, as well as all the agreements that kept me in it.

Here is a recap of my dialogue with Julie on this issue:

Julie asked, "Are you sure you are done with this relationship?"

I replied, "I'm done."

Julie: "Then it's done. There is nothing more to be gone over or do. I'm excited about what you are going to do with this space in your life!"

I became a bit resistant. "What about this weekend?"

Julie: "Is there anything there (at his house) you need?"

Me: "No."

Julie: "Then are you done?"

Me: "I'm afraid of being done."

Julie: "Focus on recapitulation. Get your energy back. Put energy into the new agreement. Don't focus on him and the old agreement."

Me: "I'm afraid of winter . . . but I know if I reclaim my energy . . . I know I won't get so depressed."

Julie: "Anytime anything comes up around the fear of 'being done' is cause to do recapitulation and claim your energy back."

I did finally move on from this relationship, and it took about six months of releasing, recapitulation, and some forgiveness too. But I have myself back now, and I have moved on.

Forgiveness—Let Go to Move On

Forgiveness is a powerful means of recapitulation.

There is the story of a rabbi who was seen praying with a smile on his face. The odd thing was that he was in a concentration camp. A fellow prisoner approached him and asked how he could get so much happiness from praying when they found themselves in such a horrific circumstance. The rabbi looked into his friend's eyes and said, "I am saying prayers of gratitude that I am not a Nazi guard."

Forgiveness comes up here in the West because it takes some internal work before real forgiveness can take place. We can forgive when and because we have done enough internal work to clear the way for forgiveness. If you just say, "I forgive Barb for hurting me," and have not gone through a real passage of forgiveness, then it is much more likely that you've suppressed some hurt feelings and your anger. Ideally you have gained quite a bit of insight around what needs forgiving through the writing and telling of your life story, as well as through the transformation of some beliefs and agreements. You have also practiced purification and release and are ready to recapitulate lost energy from someone or something you have held a grudge toward. *There is a sacred timing to forgiveness.* It comes after purification, clarity, and various emotional releases.

When we don't forgive, we hold up a wall between us and the world. The inability to forgive doesn't protect us, as some might believe, it just keeps us tight, angry, and shut off from others. Forgiveness can be understood as a final letting go of the pain stories we hold *of others*. A state of nonforgiveness means you are likely carrying someone else's shadow. *You are carrying the shadow of their transgression.* Forgiveness is a way to no longer burden yourself with another person's shadow.

Forgiveness is also an expression of our oneness. Be like the rabbi in the story above and release yourself from the transgressor. By no longer carrying another's shadow or by ending such agreements as pondering others' faults, we stop perpetuating pain about ourselves and others. Today you are living out the choices made yesterday. If you really want to transform your life, make new choices.

And choose to forgive.

In the late 1980s I designed and authored a book entitled *Hidden Victims: An Eight-Stage Healing Process for Families and Friends of the Mentally Ill.* Coupled with this, I was hired by a local mental health clinic to set up a program wherein I worked with families of those who had serious mental illnesses as well as healthcare professionals who dealt with the mentally ill. Stage six of the eight-stage process is, "I forgive and release others who I believe have harmed me." Even though there were five other stages preceding it, the sixth stage brought up the most challenges for family members and the helping professionals. Either family members felt that they *had* forgiven others, or that forgiveness was simply not possible. There were some acts that were deemed "unforgivable." It soon became clear to me that the practitioners of the eight-stage process needed a lot more guidance on forgiveness.

The director of the program was quite resistant to the word *forgiveness* because it conjured up all sorts of religious propaganda for her. This may be true for you too—forgiveness may have come too easily and not be authentic. There may be a few people or events that you deem unforgivable, or the idea of forgiveness simply brings up too many negative religious values. But forgiveness is not about approving transgressions, it is about moving on from them. An unforgiving posture can keep you imprisoned in the past and weighed down by the shadow of others.

A Teaching Story

TWO MONKS WERE TRAVELING by foot back to the monastery after a day of working in the village. As they approached a creek, they saw a beautiful woman standing next to it. Their vows included not gazing upon or touching a woman. When they arrived at the creek, they saw that she could not cross the creek, as it was deep and her dress long and heavy. The younger of the two monks nodded at the woman as he crossed the creek.

The elder monk, however, offered to carry the young, beautiful woman across the water and did so without any trouble. He set her down on the other side, and he and the other monk walked on. About a mile down the road, the younger monk, who was getting more and more agitated, asked the elder monk, "How could you carry that woman across the creek? We are not even to gaze upon or touch a woman!"

The elder monk smiled and said, "I left her at the creek, while you are still carrying her."

Who or what are you still carrying? What needs releasing through forgiveness? What do you need to leave in the past through forgiveness? Through my Buddhist practice I view others' transgressions against me as an opportunity for more happiness because it offers me a chance to practice compassion and forgiveness. And through this practice of forgiveness, my compassion and love are strengthened.

So like a treasure found at home,
Enriching me without fatigue
All enemies are helpless in my Bodhisattva work
And therefore they should be a joy to me.

SHANTIDEVA

✳ A Practice of Forgiveness

Much like the above recapitulation exercise, give yourself about fifteen minutes to do a first round of forgiveness. Name whom you are going to forgive and what you are going to forgive them for. This is your recapitulation intention. Then go through the recapitulation breathwork to get your energy back from the named transgression.

Let's say someone abused you. You will be retrieving energy lost to abuse. After you have done the breathing and the accompanying recapitulation process (following the Specific Steps of Recapitulation exercise found on pages 110–12, imagine the transgressor standing in front of you. Know that you have now gotten your energy back from the transgression. Take a moment to communicate disappointment or other feelings or thoughts to this person. Allow for the emotions that are likely to arise. Then, state clearly (to this person) that you forgive them for _____ (fill in the blank). Say something to this effect: "Your actions no longer hold any power over me. I forgive you. I release you." Then dissolve the image of the person and end your forgiveness session. (You may end up doing this practice once or several times.)

In this method of forgiveness, we use breathwork and compassion to free ourselves. When emotions arise during the session, commit to continue breathing through the emotion until your session is complete.

In the future, when this transgression or the person comes to mind, simply say to yourself, "I have released you." "I forgave you." "We are done." Some people say, "I no longer agree to carry your shadow."

If we don't negate our habitual patterns, we can never fully appreciate the world.

CHÖGYAM TRUNGPA, SHAMBHALA: THE SACRED PATH OF THE WARRIOR

The Breath of Transformation

In the ancient tradition of the Toltec as well as in yogic, Buddhist, and Sufi practices, there are two primary elements that are recognized as having the power to break any hindering energetic pattern: the breath and love (compassion). Use these two together in a practice, and you can break up the energetic pattern of agreements. When caught up in some belief that causes you suffering, use this practice to break up the *energy* that holds the pattern in place. For more on such practices, check out the many books by Don Migel Ruiz and Victor Sanchez.

❋ Toltec Breath Exercise to Break Agreements

Give yourself five minutes for this breath session. This exercise is best done sitting down, with your spine straight and feet uncrossed on the floor.

Bring to mind a hindering agreement or belief. Just flash on a given agreement or belief that you feel particularly stuck on.

Then bring to mind the vibration of love. Hold the intention of love in your mind and imagine sending it out through your entire body. Every cell, molecule, and atom is filled with the intention of love. This takes just a few moments.

Then, while thinking on love, begin to do a fast and deep breath through the mouth for two minutes only (stop immediately if you feel dizzy or uncomfortable). When you are done, simply sit and meditate on the breath and the energy body for a few minutes.

Continue to do this Toltec breath practice daily until you no longer feel that this negative agreement is true. Again, this shift is noticed either internally (this agreement doesn't come up for you, it doesn't feel true anymore), or, when the conditions of the agreement seem to arise in your environment you do not get hooked by them. The value of this exercise is that it works on the energetic pattern of a strongly held belief while your other practices work to transform thought.

You made certain agreements when entering the Wheel. These conscious agreements allow you to have your inner revolution safely. Stuff gets lit up—that is the point. What shows up as trouble is a pointer to where we are stuck, where the revolution needs to take place. This is good. Because we are in agreement to be 100 percent responsible for our experiences, we will be conscious of and responsible for what gets brought up internally (knowing that the outside will mirror the inner revolution).

This internal revolution is revealing to you the way to the inner sacred land of the three jewels of wisdom, compassion, and presence. This is not the time to give up but to progress forward on your initiatory pilgrimage. The old way may still be holding on, but the treasures of the new way are calling you.

> It is the nature of the mind to become addicted to certain ways of seeing things.
>
> LAMA ZOPA RINPOCHE, *TRANSFORMING PROBLEMS INTO HAPPINESS*

THE OUTCOME OF YOUR PRACTICES: AN INNER REVOLUTION

A revolution, by definition, means something old is abolished and the new established. When you successfully transform your mind through various spiritual, psychological, and ethical practices, you will experience an inner revolution. The West is the dawn of the revolution, where you are either going to continue thinking, believing, and doing what you always did, or you are going to experience initiation through an internal revolution. At this stage of the inner revolution, the battle between the old paradigm and the new takes place.

These two paradigms are fighting it out within you—there will be blood. We can resist a revolution, but we cannot stop it. This is a natural part of the cycle of life, just as one season is abolished so the next can come in. We can resist the changing season, but we cannot stop it. If there is suffering, resistance to change is likely the culprit, not the revolution itself.

> Without contraries is no progression.
>
> WILLIAM BLAKE, *THE MARRIAGE OF HEAVEN AND HELL*

Perhaps the best story that points to my own movement through the West is my encounter with His Holiness the Dalai Lama in 1995. He was visiting Deer Park Buddhist Center near Madison, Wisconsin, and offering teachings and empowerments. Those who donated some money to the Tibetan cause and to Deer Park got to attend a small reception for His Holiness. I attended this reception at the local Unitarian Church with about two hundred other people. We milled around in the sanctuary of the church as we awaited his arrival, drinking tea and nibbling on tiny cakes. I could feel the emotions rising up in the room and in myself. We all seemed to want something from His Holiness.

Finally he arrived, and a path was cleared for him to make his way to the podium. By sheer luck I found myself right beside the path where His Holiness would pass! Here was my chance to be near him. Then I felt a light push from behind. Everyone was crowding toward the path. The man behind me was holding flowers to give to His Holiness. This man earnestly reached past me with his gift, thrusting the flowers in front of my face.

As the man shouted out "Your Holiness! Your Holiness!" and held his flowers out toward the approaching Dalai Lama, I remembered what this was all about. It was about taking every opportunity that arises to express generosity and love. It was *not* about getting recognition from the Dalai Lama. (I no longer agreed to this.) So I stepped back and let the man behind me be in front and nearer to His Holiness.

As I stood behind the man with flowers, His Holiness walked by. As he did, he reached out his arm past the man with flowers, squeezed my shoulder and smiled at me. I felt so much love in that moment, so much gratitude. We listened then as His Holiness talked about helping the Tibetan people, and about the need to be good to one another. When he was ready to leave, we had to make another path for him. I ended up on the other side of the path, again right on the edge. I stood there, happy to be close to him again and filled with appreciation. Then a woman behind me began to cry out and push me: "Your Holiness, your Holiness . . ." She really wanted to be near him. So, again I backed away and let her stand in front of me. And once again, as His Holiness walked by, he reached around the woman and squeezed my shoulder and smiled at me.

What a lesson I learned! What a blessing I received. And it wasn't about His Holiness acknowledging me. *It was about practice.* I learned, hands-on, that when we offer love and generosity, that is what we receive in return. Loving-kindness does not go unreciprocated. I also learned that there will be times when it may appear as if we are giving up something (our spot in line), but really we are opening up to something greater.

> *When you wake to the dream of now*
> *from night and its other dream,*
> *you carry day out of the dark*
> *like a flame.*
>
> WILLIAM STAFFORD, FROM
> THE POEM "THE DREAM OF NOW,"
> IN *LEARNING TO LIVE IN THE WORLD*

5

ENTERING THE NORTH

Tat Tvam Asi

> *Sacred or secular, what is the difference? If every atom inside our bodies was once a star, then it is all sacred and all secular at the same time.*
>
> GRETEL EHRLICH, POET AND NOVELIST, SOURCE UNKNOWN

You listened to the call (in the South), experienced symbolic death (in the West), and now you are about to enter the North—the direction of unity and oneness. Just as purification comes up in all spiritual practices of initiation, so does unification with the divine—healing the internal and external separation between our selves and the rest of life. While in the North of the Wheel, we strengthen our trust in this spiritual reality of unity through meeting up with our root guru, setting our principles, working with the shadow-self, and cultivating attention. Each practice in the North brings us closer to the realization of oneness and readies us further for initiation.

ORIGINAL SIN

> *As long as we live in the misperception of being a separate entity, we encounter frustration, confusion, difficulties, and turmoil.*
>
> KEN MCLEOD, WAKE UP TO YOUR LIFE

Initiation will always be about healing the places we feel separate from everything else, to heal us from our misperceptions of separateness. Until the day we fully occupy the center of the Wheel, which is the still point, we will continue moving inward, following our soul's call to unity. Anytime, anywhere confusion and suffering arise, there is a need for personal recognition of the Tao (of Truth, of the luminous void, of dependent arising, of Brahman or the inner light). Initiation recognizes that we heal the divide through a personal pilgrimage inward and onward.

Many spiritual traditions point to the big lie, the agreement that keeps us scared, doubtful, and lonely—the belief that we are somehow separate from the rest of life, that we are outsiders and do not intimately belong within the web of existence. The original sin in the Garden of Eden story was when Adam and Eve bit the apple, which caused them to see themselves as *separate from god*. Prior to eating the apple, they had simply experienced the beauty and simplicity of *belonging* in the Garden of Eden. Once they bit into the apple, they became aware of feeling *separate*.

This is the paradox of consciousness—we become more aware, and, with this awareness, our feelings of separation become known to us. However (and this is where the paradox lies), through the transformation of our consciousness the truth is revealed to us: we are not separate. When Adam and Eve felt their *differences,* they felt a need to cover up with fig leaves. When we experience ourselves as separate from our inherent qualities of love, wisdom, and presence, from natural phenomena, from each other, and from ourselves, we tend to "cover up" with the false self.

To help heal the separation, ask yourself, "Who or what do I feel separated from?" Take the time throughout the day to notice feelings of separation or isolation. Look into times when you feel lonely, anxious, worried, depressed, confused, argumentative, misunderstood, and frustrated—there you will find the separation. What flavor does your separation take on? What are the thoughts, beliefs, and agreements built into these feelings of separation? (Use the practices offered in the South for this.) Because all our separations originate in the mind through our perceptions, we hold the power to transform and heal all that separates us. Thought transformation is the central tool of those attaining personal initiation and is an ongoing practice until the full realization that we are not separate (through continued personal initiation) is accomplished.

After gaining insight into where you feel separate, link these feelings to a belief and agreement that you hold about the other, about yourself, or about the world. Let's say you feel separate from others at work. You notice a lot of anxiety when you think about your work environment. Do you focus on how those at work are taking advantage of you? Or do you notice how often your supervisor doesn't appreciate you? Can you see where you are projecting beliefs onto others and strengthening a sense of separation through your agreements?

No matter what the circumstances, we *are* all in this together. Therefore being in alignment with the agreements that we belong to one another and that everything arises dependent on everything else will help heal any divide.

I will tell you a story that demonstrates my own experience with this realization of oneness.

"I Am That"—*The Story of the Pipe*

Several years ago I decided to attend teachings on Lakota traditions and healing practices by a nonnative teacher. This teacher strictly followed his interpretation of the traditional practices that had been passed on to him from his Lakota teachers. He made it clear that if we did not follow the traditions as laid out, we would be in spiritual if not physical danger, as well as cause damage to others. He was a brilliant man with a lot of dogma. Coincidentally, at about the same time a friend gifted me with a traditional peace pipe. I understood that the pipe was viewed as a living, breathing being, a sacred object to the Lakota, and thus I paid particular attention to what the neighboring native community said about who should and should not have a pipe. I kept it safe in my meditation room wrapped in deer hide. There it sat for nearly a year.

This nonnative teacher found out that I had been given the pipe, and on the final day of a weekend retreat, in front of several others, he scolded me for owning it, arguing that only certain people should handle and own objects that were considered sacred. He believed that I shouldn't keep the pipe my friend had given me. He went on to say that even if we "stumbled" upon a sacred object in a field or elsewhere, we should not touch it. (He, however, could own and touch sacred objects.)

I disagreed with him. That night I went home concerned by what he had said. He warned that contact with sacred objects would be harmful to the person or the object. This reminded me of the time a Southern Baptist minister told me I was going to hell because I disagreed with his sermon. I was seventeen and had read and studied the New Testament on my own. I told the minister I thought Jesus's message was one of forgiveness, love, and tolerance, not warnings of sin and damnation. He too scolded me in public and told me, "You, young lady, are going to hell!"

This time I was in my early forties, and, while I knew that the teacher's approach was not correct, I felt disappointed nonetheless. I went to sleep with this discontent. At 3:00 a.m., dreams and thoughts awakened me. As dawn arose in the sky, three crows perched themselves right outside my bedroom window, just a few feet away, cawing and cawing (this hasn't happened before or since).

They continued to caw until I got up and wrote down what had come to me in my dream, which was, *We are each the pipe.* Each of us carries the sacred within us. We are all "that" which is sacred. I wrote many pages on what came to me that night. It became clear that one must bring together, in a creative tension, the traditions of the past and the intuitive wisdom born in the moment. Rigidly adhering to dogmatic principles is what endangers the true nature of the practitioner and spiritual seeker. It became clear to me that I wanted to honor the tradition of the pipe and give it away in a sacred manner. I also knew I was done receiving teachings from that particular teacher.

That same day I went to my office, which overlooks the Wisconsin River. As I prepared for my first client, a crow showed up right outside my window (this hasn't happened before or since) and sat and cawed at me from the railing of the deck, just a few feet away. I felt the presence of a Wisdom Keeper, a spirit or an energy that was checking up on me, making sure I knew to trust my insights. I acknowledged the crow and it flew off.

Later in the week I took the pipe to our hill. On the top of it stands an old oak tree and a red cedar. I decided to sit up there with these two trees, to pray and listen to what would be best to do with the pipe. On my way up, another tree called to me. This tree, a young white oak, had an opening in its South base. The opening went deep into the tree. I knew to put the pipe in the tree. When I gave the tree the pipe, I said, "If you want this pipe to be used, you will need to give it back." That day and often afterward I would walk up to the tree and pray. I would say aloud, "I am the pipe, I breathe in the prayers, I carry the sacred stories within me, I breathe out the prayers. I am the sacred pipe. We are all that, we are each a sacred pipe."

One day about six months later, my husband, daughter, and I decided to walk the property together. When we passed the Pipe Tree, there on the ground sat the pipe.

"Look," I said. "The tree has given back the pipe!" I also intuitively knew who the pipe was for. Eagle Woman, Lois, was completing her personal initiation and was heading to a yearly Native American ceremony of the Sun Dance to honor her heritage. This three- to four-day ceremony is a dance with religious importance for the spiritual and physical vigor of those who attend and their families. This pipe was hers. (As it turns out, of course, she had been praying for a pipe to be given to her.)

My husband, a biologist, responded, "A raccoon moved it out of the tree."

I told him about what I had said to the tree. "I told the tree to give me back the pipe if it was to be used!"

He smiled and told me he had just visited an effigy mound where an elder from the Fox Sauk Tribe shared the history of the mounds. To wit: "My elders told me that the ancestors built these mounds. No, spirit of the ancestors built these mounds. No, *Spirit built these mounds.*"

In my case, Raccoon brought out the pipe. No, spirit of raccoon brought out the pipe. *No, Spirit brought out the pipe.*

When we know that everything is sacred, that every tree is the tree of life, that everyone is the pipe, that *Tat Tvam Asi* (a Sanskrit sentence that means "Thou art that"), then we will always behave as if we are walking among the holy and on the sacred. Here, while entering the North, we loosen the lie that we are separate from all that is sacred. We make contact with our own holiness (and recognize it as such). *Mitakuye oyas'in* in Lakota is translated as "All my Relations," pointing to how we are all related to (and dependent on) everything that is alive.

These verses and mantras are in alignment with the agreement that we shared upon entering the Wheel—we belong to one another. We are all part of the Tao (unifying principle) and Brahman (ultimate reality). *Ehyeh* in Hebrew is a name for god and translates into "I am," or "I shall be." To simply recite the name of god can have the effect of announcing, "I am that." In the yogic tradition "I am that" is the SO HAM mantra, believed to be seven thousand years old and passed down from the historical Shiva. In Tibetan Buddhist practice the HUNG mantra, which is considered a seed syllable of wisdom, for me represents the wisdom of our oneness and innate wisdom. Each of these mantras holds the vibrational reality of belonging.

All that separates us from knowing "I am that" is an illusion, a lie. My realization of "I am the pipe" came to me before I knew anything about the mantra "I am that." This is important to share, because this type of spiritual insight and encounter happens to us all. The reality of "I am that" is present in your life, *right now.*

Because the purpose of the Wheel is to hold an organic template for your personal initiation, you can find the mantra or meditation practice of your own that resonates with this principle of *Tat Tvam Asi,* of universal oneness. Bringing to mind the symbolic story of being in the woods and now entering the North of your initiation, begin to look around you. What felt separate and maybe even "against you" becomes what heals the internal divide.

So Hum
Puraka
Inhale
Let breath caress flame
Life into light;

Whispered
Secrets to
Soul

Rechaka
Exhale
Release treasures held
Light to the world
Sacred
Oneness to
All

Feel it
The rhythm
The pulse
Of our day

Expanding
Old hearts
Crack-crack-cracking
New ground

Sing along
Dance
Raise arms, eyes, and chin
Grow big as the ocean
Marry the moon

Listen
To pauses
To silence
To rest
Be small as a grain
On a beach of black sand

This is all there is
All

Tat Tvam Asi

Inspire
Expire

We holy, we
Breathe

Prudence Tippins, poet,
teacher, 2008 Initiation Circle

Here is a simple practice from one of my teachers, A'cha'rya Jina'neshvar (James Powell).

✸ I Am More Than My Body

Close your eyes. Take a moment and notice your breath, the natural flow of the inhalation and exhalation. Now, from that place where you are witnessing your breath, notice the experience of your body—its sensations, its form. Appreciate for a few moments all that your body does for you. As you are aware of your body, silently say to yourself, "I have a body, but I am more than my body." Repeat this a number of times and really feel how the "I-feeling" is more than the body.

Now be aware of your emotional body, noticing how the range of your emotions colors your life. Appreciate the varieties of emotions you experience and what they do for you. And now say to yourself silently, "I have emotions, but I"—and really feel the consciousness of "I"—"am more than my emotions." Repeat this until you feel the meaning of the "I" as being more than the emotions.

Now be aware of your mental body, and appreciate its ability to solve problems and help you navigate your life. Now say to yourself, "I have a mind, but I am more than my mind." Again, repeat and experience the I-feeling as being deeper and greater than the thinking mind. Thoughts will come into your awareness, but just simply note them and return to that I-feeling. You can even say to yourself, "I am more than these thoughts."

After some experience of this I-feeling, affirm to yourself, "I AM." Do this a few times and then affirm, "I AM PURE BEING." "I AM THAT."

Stay with this for a while. Whenever you become aware of the mind drift-
ing, gently pull it back to the affirmation, remembering to experience the
affirmation. If you like, you can coordinate the affirmation with your breath,
such as "I AM" on the inhalation and "THAT" on the exhalation. If you
have a mantra, experience the vibration and consciousness of your mantra
from this place of "I AM-ness." Continue until you are ready to come out
of your inner being; then, after your eyes are open, look at the sacredness of
THAT, which is all around you, with new eyes.

Next we will discuss the importance of finding the guru or gurus who
will guide you as you move forward through the Wheel and your life.

GURU YOGA (OR BECOME "THAT")

Guru yoga can be understood as a prayer of invocation. Here you pray to
god or some deity. The Sufis say, *There are as many paths to god as there
are breaths. Every path is an ideal, and everyone has an ideal.* It is from our
own personal point of view that god is known. In guru meditation, you
supply the characterization of the god or deity that you resonate with.

It would be difficult to live in this world without an ideal—a sense of
purpose and truth and a reason to live. In guru meditation, we pray and
focus on a deity as if we see him or her before us. This brings our ideal
into view. Even when one's ideal (or god, or deity) is simply the Light or
Truth, one aligns oneself to that truth, and later reminds oneself of the
essence of this personal truth. Through the root guru (which we will discuss shortly), we seek (and find) the manifestation of truth in *all* things.
We learn to see our root guru everywhere. By the time we have arrived in
the North, we have perceptually cleared the way for our deity.

What I have found is that one's selection in guru yoga, and in
particular the selection of one's root guru, uncovers what that individual
needs to develop within himself or herself. Whereas our root guru will
remain the same throughout our lives, our guru yoga can change, because
what we need to bring forth in ourselves changes throughout our lives.
Thus you may find yourself doing guru yoga with Quan Yin or with

Green Tara this month (because these are the qualities you most need to bring forth in yourself), but next month you may have an entirely different diety for guru yoga.

In the initiatory journey, there is much that is struggling to be born, to be released from within. We need to align ourselves with the gurus, deities, animals, and living teachers that are realized expressions of what is not yet fully expressed in our own lives but have been realized in these beings. We need to invoke what they represent to us.

Invocation means to invite and live with the qualities that you desire to embody, to experience them as having legitimacy and meaning—as valuable and real as any relationship. Such qualities as presence, wisdom, and compassion are inherent in each of us but may be imprisoned by habitual states, hindering emotions, and amplifying pain stories. Invocation can let us own our inherent qualities, and, in owning them, open up to joy.

> *What most of us need, almost more than anything, is the courage and humility really to ask for help, from the depths of our hearts: to ask for the compassion of the enlightened beings, to ask for purification and healing, to ask for the power to understand the meaning of our suffering and transform it; at a relative level to ask for the growth in our lives of clarity, of peace, of discernment, and to ask for the realization of the absolute nature of mind that comes from merging with the deathless wisdom mind of the master."*
>
> SOGYAL RINPOCHE, *THE TIBETAN BOOK OF LIVING AND DYING*

Calling forth your spiritual allies and deities during meditation and connecting with them in a visualization process is an ancient way to generate the realization of oneness. Choose a deity or ally that represents the vibration and aspirations that you want to emanate and that are in alignment with your spiritual practices and principles. Your spiritual source can be a deceased master or a living one.

Any energy or entity that you call forth through meditation or prayer becomes a protector of sorts, because you are "carrying" the qualities of this deity with you—and what a forcible protection that can be! You become an expression of that which you meditate upon.

There are always simple means to make contact with a spiritual master or ally. To ask the simple question, "What would Jesus or the Buddha do?" in a particular situation is to align yourself with these spiritual masters. I often visualize Padmasambhava, my root guru, going before me and preparing my way when I am headed into a possibly difficult or challenging situation.

☀ Guru Meditation Practice*

A simple practice of guru yoga includes *invocation* (which we have already touched on, but will discuss in greater detail here), *merging* with the guru/deity through the use of a mantra or chant, receiving the *empowerment* (blessing of the deity or spiritual ally), and then *becoming one* with the master or being.

✳ Invoke

"From the depths of your heart, in the sky in front of you, invoke the embodiment of the truth in the person of your master, a saint or an enlightened being," says Sogyal Rinpoche. Make the request from your heart and ask for its help. Trust that the being you call is in front of you. Pray for this being to fill you up with love and compassion and any of the other qualities that you know this being holds for you. This, of course, connects you with all these inherent qualities within yourself. I typically make the request that Padmasambhava help me realize my true nature and open my mind and heart to the true nature of others. This is the time you make your request to the deity.

✳ Merge

In this step you merge with the energy of the deity through reciting a mantra that carries the energy of your given master or being. Or you can use a universal sound of *OM AH, HUNG* (which sounds like "hoong"), or some other chant that you can sing to the deity. Experience this chant or mantra as the sound that represents this given spiritual being. The sound becomes

---

*Adapted and quoted from Sogyal Rinpoche's *The Tibetan Book of Living and Dying*.

the deity, and at the same time calls the deity to you. I chant the mantra of Padmasambhava, OM AH HUNG BENZA GURU PEMA SIDDHI HUNG.

✳ Empower

At this time, you imagine the deity sending you his or her energy in the form of rays of light coming from their body. The deity's light and energy enter you and move throughout your entire being. You are being empowered with their qualities; they take root in your psychophysical and spiritual body and mind. Sogyal Rinpoche refers to this as "sowing in you the seeds of enlightenment." Here you let the being empower you with all its qualities so that these awaken in you. At the very least, your mind is being filled with the *ideal* of this being and his or her qualities.

✳ Become One

Let the being completely merge and mingle with you so that there is no separation between your master or ally and yourself. Feel free to sit in this energy for a while. See and feel that you are the guru or deity. There is no separation between you and the divine. Touch your own inherent sacred, enlightened self. Through guru meditation you sanction the mantra, "I am that."

ADOPTING A ROOT GURU

I love the term *root* guru because it suggests the importance of getting to and nourishing the root system of our true nature. Choosing your own root guru or deity or spiritual ally is what is called for here. In my Buddhist practice, discovering your root guru is fundamental. Once you choose a root guru or ally, you have them as your companion for life. The best root guru is someone who has actually lived and practiced what you are trying to achieve.

The adoption of a root guru will help you in all things and can even assist you in dying. Keep this relationship a constant if you want to get all you can from him or her. Jumping around from root guru to root guru makes it difficult, if not impossible, for the deity to nourish and guide you. Consistency is an attribute of the North. Whatever we keep showing up for shows up for us. We have been in the woods awhile now. As long as we don't go running about here and there, our spiritual helpers know where to find us.

This is a union, so take this commitment to heart and know that the deity does too. If you do not yet have a root guru, naming him or her can be part of your spiritual initiation. Address this root guru in all your prayers. Make certain you have a natural affinity for this deity before choosing him or her. Often the root guru will find you through your dreams, synchronistic encounters, books, or teachings. The moment I saw my first image of Padmasambhava, I knew he was my root guru, and it seemed as if I had been waiting for him to show up.

Cindy Chooses a Root Guru

I'VE BEEN REALLY COOKING the task of finding my root guru. I know she's the one with me, in my dreams and visions, but I haven't been sure who "she" really is. Now I know. As Julie suggested, it felt as if she chose me. I call her Honu. It's the Hawaiian name for the deity in Sea Turtle form. After reading about Tara and Quan Yin, I was connecting to the essence of these stories, but not any of the pictures. Finally I realized Honu is the same as Mother Earth, Artemis, Tara, and Quan Yin. Hawaiians believe that the ancestors become Guardians—amakuas—and take animal forms to help us. When I sat next to a native Hawaiian on the plane and told him about my turtle experience, he said that Honu is my amakua. She's so real for me. I'm very happy she found me. I feel her in me and with me.

Honu
Mother Earth-Tara-Quan Yin-Pele-Artemis

I call on you

Please teach me your strength, wisdom, patience, and
* compassion.*

*Honu when I swam with you in Hawaii I felt honored.
You turned that cove into a cathedral. Your gentle
touch lightened our sadness—it made us laugh and
remember.*

*In my dream you knew all of me and loved me so.
You told me I was beautiful. I awoke with tears of
gratitude.*

*In my visions you've shown me how to fly, how heaven
and earth are connected in us.*

*I have felt your touch in all the gentle hands and hearts
who've helped me in my life.*

*I have felt you in me as I held my babies and knew
exactly how to love them.*

*Walking I have felt you in Nature. You fill my heart
with peace and comfort, hope and joy.*

I feel your rhythm in me, in my ebb and flow.

I am so grateful you have chosen me.

CINDY, POET AND NURSE, ENTERING THE NORTH

Tsukai, *"It Hurts Good"*

If separation is the collective wound, then habitual states are the universal form of prescribed medication. *We tend to maintain our habitual states of relating to our lives so as to not feel the separation.* But not feeling the division prevents us from healing it.

Our culture perpetuates a cult of habit and comfort junkies—we are seduced by television, video games, fast food, prescribed drugs for mild ailments (among other things)—all of which allow us to become more and more comfortable in our habitual states and less willing to be uncomfortable. In this familiarity with comfort, we become less and less active physically, mentally, and spiritually.

In Thai massage and in my yoga practice, there is an immediate reward when feeling some discomfort from tender spots in the body. In Japanese Shiatsu, this "tender spot" is called *tsukai,* literally translated as, "it hurts good." Massage therapists look for this spot. These tender spots want your attention and are treated with some pressure and movement. Instead of being distracted away from the discomfort, we are encouraged to notice these tender spots and breathe into them.

We also hold emotional and psychological tender spots, places we can choose to resist or choose instead to breathe into, to work with. We can see our emotional places, our tender spots, as our tsukai—places to bring attention and movement. We must move through the tsukai to heal the wound.

There is a danger that traditional spiritual and religious practices will become so automatic that they no longer help the practitioner heal the divide. Mechanical rituals and practices will keep us feeling lonely and separated because we won't feel the tsukai. If we don't engage our souls when we habitually kneel and pray or chant a mantra, we will not notice the discomfort of the separation, so we won't know where to apply the breath and movement. When practicing a particular technique or ritual, slow down, use the breath to bring yourself into it, and remain conscious of any underlying discomfort. Be the witness as well as the participant.

People know there is a way to have this spiritual development take place, but the Church is not helping us do it, because it's talking about metaphorical events as if they were historical facts.

JOSEPH CAMPBELL, *A JOSEPH CAMPBELL COMPANION*

WHAT WANTS IN?

Yes, we will feel all sorts of emotions while bringing awareness to our tsukai; but something beautiful, something real, wants to come in from beneath this tenderness and these habitual states. Our habits and beliefs hold the pain in place, while breath and movement release the pain so that our intrinsic nature may emerge. So instead of resisting the tender spots, get curious about what wants in. What will fill the space that this habit (this agreement) takes up? Ask yourself, *"What would come into this space if I didn't do the habitual thing?"*

Begin to breathe into smaller habits with this question, and notice how much space is opened up, and how much actually comes into that open space. Many myths portray a monster protecting a hidden treasure. We discover that, in our pilgrimage into the cave where the treasure lies, there are also many bones left at the foot of the beast, only inches away from the riches. Knowing a treasure lies waiting can motivate us to move through the discomfort and pain (the monster) and get to our inner treasure.

Don't give in to the resistance or fear the monster. *Don't become the heap of bones a few feet from the riches.*

Don't give up.

Sometimes we want to be happy or enlightened so badly that we deny the more shadowy aspects of ourselves. We repress the idea that we aren't as kind or as evolved as we would like to believe we are. We think we have our ego in check. We forget that we are, after all, human, and that having limits, and egos, is part of our humanity. You are deep into the woods now, entering the North of your initiatory process, and here an encounter with your shadow is likely.

THE DANCE OF THE SHADOW

The shadow is a tight passage, a narrow door, whose painful constriction no one is spared who goes down to the deep well.

CARL JUNG, *THE ARCHETYPES AND THE COLLECTIVE UNCONSCIOUS*

Our spiritual lives are a two-sided leaf. One side absorbs the light, the other side sits in the shadow (holds the shadow). The shadow side includes our vulnerabilities and aspects of ourselves that we often keep hidden. The shadow may reside in the underside of us, but this doesn't mean it need be unknown. The shadow is just part of being alive, a natural phenomenon, and it is best not ignored or feared. The shadow comes from our pain stories and our ego's clinging, as well as our humanity. One of my teachers would say to me now and again (and it was usually around a time of progress), "You still hold a few blind spots." I took that to mean that I still had a few aspects of myself hidden in the shadow.

The gift of the shadow is to know it is there and to work with it. Let it nourish you like the underside of a leaf. (Without the underside of the leaf transporting water, the leaf would dry up from too much sun.) For example, many people today have in their shadow a narcissist's thread of "It's all about me." Or put another way, we are not interested in much that doesn't have to do with us, doesn't reflect us or directly involve or benefit us. This is one reason we find the altruistic aspiration in so many spiritual practices. We wouldn't need this practice if there were no shadow side to us. So it is not about ridding ourselves of this narcissistic characteristic (although that would be grand), but to keep it conscious and use our spiritual principles to challenge and transform the more shadowy aspects of ourselves.

In the *Bodhicaryāvatāra*, Shantideva points to the internal enemies as the only real enemies: "Enemies such as craving and hatred are without arms, legs, and so on. They are neither courageous nor wise. How is it they have enslaved me? Stationed in my mind, they ruin me."

We carry these internal enemies with us, and we tend to let them do what they want. They cause problems in our lives because we allow them to remain hidden in our shadow and guide our actions as the internal bully. Even in the eighth century, Shantideva understood that the greatest enemies are our mental afflictions, such as jealousy, anger, resentment, and greed. He goes on to explain that these internal enemies are not part of our true nature, therefore we can become free of them. He points out, as other masters do, that these afflictions, these internal enemies, are supported by our assumptions (our agreements). Part of the antidote is awareness and wisdom (bringing the assumptions to light) and the perseverance to stay with the process of initiation and awakening.

Whatever we don't claim as our own, we project onto others. The more we project this shadow outward, the more we experience difficulty with people and situations because we keep encountering our own projections. All these difficult encounters, from the view of spiritual initiation, are encounters with our own shadow. But without the shadow, there is no initiation. This is not about killing the shadow (or stealing it, as in the story of Peter Pan) but about befriending it and integrating it, letting it be part of the conscious dance. Integrating the shadow is a way to spiritual wholeness and initiation.

The false self thrives on a repressed or denied shadow-self. The false self will destroy, con, and manipulate from the repressed shadow. It will lie to you. It will project. Our true self, on the other hand, remains conscious of the shadow and integrates it into the expression of the whole self.

The shadow can appear as an external antagonist, but when it is brought to awareness and owned as part of our internal world, it becomes the protagonist of our authentic stories. *This is one of the primary tools needed on a spiritual pilgrimage—to own one's projections, to know that our "battles" are internal, not external.* Everything in the outer world mirrors what needs our attention in our inner world.

I find shadow stories in Tibetan historical tales of monks who confront various repressed issues, such as anger or doubt. The monk claims no longer to have anger, and then comes a knock on the door. He invites the stranger into his dwelling, where the stranger immediately begins to wreak havoc. Initially, the monk is calm, saying to himself, "My, my, how patient and kind I am." But then the visitor goes too far, and the monk finds himself shouting and screaming at the stranger, who smiles and says, "Gotcha!"

The monk realizes *repressed* anger is not *freedom from* anger. It is about inviting the shadow in for tea—not locking our doors on the shadow. I am always careful when I find myself thinking, "Oh, I'm done with that issue," because soon after I may hear that knock on the door!

Wherever you find difficulty in your life, you will find the shadow. The shadow aspects, not recognized, often become what we use to keep us separate from reality, from our spiritual source, and from our humanity. The loneliness and discontent, so strong throughout these times, seem to invite the wounds of the shadow. As we enter the North, we help heal the divide within and without through the integration of the shadow.

Let's listen to Marie's story about this:

Marie's Experience with Anger

I KEPT FINDING MYSELF getting jealous and angry with a particular student. She kept getting all the teacher's time. Here I was in a class about nonviolent communication, *and I felt so hostile toward this other person. I felt worse for having these feelings. Then Julie asked what part of myself I felt hostile toward. She also reminded me to give myself some kudos for being aware of these feelings and not acting on them. I quickly realized that I suppressed the part of me wanting love, wanting recognition,* wanting to be special. *The wanting to be special was a big part of my shadow. This other student was simply my mirror. I brought this shadowy aspect out and began to do the internal work I needed to do to transform it.*

Of course, recognizing that you have a shadow is a great awareness in and of itself. Naming your particular shadow qualities, so you can bring them to light, is the work of the spiritual practitioner, and it is ongoing. Remember, the shadow doesn't just get up and go—it transmutes and evolves too, just like the light side of your being. Consider it always as part of your humanity, and bring enlightenment to it, rather then considering yourself free of it.

It Really Isn't All about You: The Collective Shadow

When entering the Wheel, we named some culturally endorsed agreements, all of which can be understood to be part of the collective and too-often-denied shadow. These culturally promoted agreements (like the need to be right) are carried in the collective shadow. Just as each of us has a shadow side, so does the culture in which we live. Cultural conditions, like capitalism, have a light side, such as that everyone gets to progress, and a shadow side, such as extreme competitiveness or narcissism that goes along with the capitalistic paradigm.

Each of us carries within us the collective shadow simply because we are part of the surrounding culture. Such pressures as being aggressively competitive, the need to be right, the need to take sides, attachments to belongings, and the fear of losing are all part of our culture's collective shadow. The dance with the collective shadow is one you were born into, without an initial choice. If you are struggling with the need to be right, for example, you may be feeling the effects of the collective shadow. To bring this to consciousness and transform it is to move against a culturally endorsed agreement.

The questions then are: Am I conscious of what these agreements are? Do I agree to them or not? And do I act on them or not? The root cause of our suffering is our strong attachment to ego; this pushes the me/us paradigm and is how the collective shadow takes hold of us. The illusion that we are independent, along with our ignorance of the fact that we "are all that," underlies this suffering.

The repressed or denied collective shadow can strip us of our humanity. We unconsciously act out the more repressed aspects of the collective shadow and find ourselves hypnotized by the communal movement around us. On the flip side, when we are seen as standing alone in our truth, often the collective shadow's response is to view us as wrong or crazy and not worth listening to. Objectification of others comes from an agreement with the collective shadow. When making the other wrong, we dehumanize them. And the need for us all to be in agreement with some collective assumption dehumanizes us. The suppressed shadow makes enemies.

To move against the collective shadow is truly a hero's journey. The continued repression of the shadow is what results in situations like Nazi Germany, not the quality of the shadow itself. Historically as well as today, the shadow element that causes the most harm on an individual and collective basis is the need to take sides. (This one is a cousin to the need to be right.) And take note that *every* group (such as *sangha*s, retreats, spiritual gatherings, and initiation circles) also holds a collective shadow—no group is exempt. The more dangerous groups either keep the shadow in the unconscious or intentionally use it to manipulate others.

The push to take sides is held in the *global* collective shadow. We are pushed to take sides in elections, in our disagreements, in war, in debates, in fights, in family conversations. This is why political campaigns sometimes get so negative—rather than presenting their views, they are trying to get the electorate to take their side. We find this tendency even in play. Most children's games are designed so that each child has to take a side, and there is usually a winner and a loser in the end. Those brilliant souls who offer up games and educational tools that remove the competitiveness are often labeled as no fun, dreamers, or unrealistic.

If you find it hard to work, play, or disagree without taking sides, this only points to how deeply seated this is in our collective shadow. The Dalai Lama advocates not taking sides with the Tibetans, not to be against the Chinese, as this approach only increases hostility, anger, and resentment. Instead he recommends listening to both the Chinese people *and* the Tibetan people and finding a way for them to live together.

We can work out our dance with the collective shadow only on an individual basis. Each of us will have opportunities to agree to take sides—*or not*. This often happens in the initiation process, where you feel yourself swimming against the current of the collective river. Part of this shadow element is that there's a pull to be part of a group (like the undertow of the river), to feel that your truth is "right." So when you feel such a pull to join a group in order to feel safe or secure in your view, be aware that this invitation may be originating from the collective shadow.

Taking sides doesn't allow us to be present for others. Instead, we are often riding the wave of argument and viewpoints. A commitment to remain aware of agreements and core beliefs will keep the shadow in view. Pay attention to times of imbalance—the shadow is likely at play. Know that spiritual pilgrimage and initiation are journeys that do not have one set arrival point and that include the light aspects of the psyche as well as the dark. Initiation includes *enlightening* even the more shadowy aspects of ourselves.

Movement toward the achievement of wholeness or completeness (or "perfection" in the sense of Jesus' use of the Greek word teleios*) is accomplished not only through the continued infusion of goodness, righteousness, and morality (striving after good), but also through the acceptance (the "owning") and conscious incorporation of one's dark and shadowy side into one's self.*

WILLIAM A. MILLER, *MAKE FRIENDS WITH YOUR SHADOW*

A SIMPLE TECHNIQUE FOR CONSCIOUS INCORPORATION OF THE SHADOW

Carl Jung warns above, "The shadow is a tight passage, a narrow door." Shadow work is work that is done by someone who is entering the North of the initiatory process. You already did some work with your shadow when you named the agreements that kept your pain story active. It is not a small task to determine how we are perpetuating our own pain stories and suffering. Being willing to do your shadow work means continuing to take 100 percent responsibility for all your experiences. (By now you have noticed how I repeat this particular agreement and commitment. Some pointers are worth such repetition. If you were in an initiation circle with me, you would hear me repeat this agreement again and again—"Be 100 percent responsible.")

One of my teachers often used to remind me of how another person's annoying characteristics wouldn't cause me such irritation (I wouldn't be personalizing it) if they didn't resonate with something inside me. To help you view your shadow side, bring to mind a friend, colleague, or someone you know. Write down all the characteristics of this person that offend or bother you. Then claim these characteristics as shadow aspects of yourself (e.g., "She talks too much and doesn't listen").

This could be a shadow aspect of how you yourself don't feel heard. You might feel that what you have to say is more important than what someone else has to say. Or it could be an exact mirror of your issue—you like to talk over other people and don't take the time to listen. "He thinks he is always right" could point to your feeling that you are right all the time. Remember, the unconscious shadow aspects of ourselves are projected onto others, so what we see in them is ourselves. Any time you are feeling caught up in pain or suffering or find yourself upset with others, there is likely a shadow quality to the dynamic. Name what it is that is bothering you about the situation or about the other, and you will meet your shadow.

Here, too, is an opportunity for transformation and initiation.

The Gift of the Troublemaker

Thus, everything is dependent on something else, and even that on which something is dependent is not autonomous.

Hence, once one knows that, one will not become angry at things, which are all like apparitions.

SHANTIDEVA

When a Troublemaker shows up in your life, you have the opportunity to let it pull you back into your pain story or use it for your initiation. The Troublemakers in our lives meet up with our internal enemies of anger, fear, doubt, assumptions, arrogance, and other afflictive emotional and mental states. What happens too often is that we mistake the outside Troublemaker for the enemy. When we do this we miss the initiatory opportunity within this difficult situation.

Once in the Wheel, everything holds the potential to assist our initiation, to bring forth the inner light. Shantideva points to how the understanding of unity, that everything is dependent, means that getting angry at things is really getting angry at an apparition, because everything we see involves projection. This translates into not being caught up in the *appearance* of things. Nothing is as it appears, because our beliefs, assumptions, agreements, and perceptions are all projected out onto the other. Or, as the Toltecs' Four Agreements point out, "Don't make assumptions" and "Don't take things personally," because these are based on our faulty perceptions.

We habitually meet our Troublemakers with assumptions about them, and we tend to take their behavior very personally. There are many conditions that caused the Troublemaker to behave in the way they did; it is unlikely to come down to just *one* reason. "Everything arises from conditions," as Shantideva reminds us in the *Bodhicaryāvatāra*. Nothing happens in a vacuum. So, challenge the assumptions, which only keep you trapped by the Troublemaker.

The Troublemaker typically addresses the place where we ourselves are the most stuck. This does not mean we are in agreement with abusive and hostile behavior or not bothered by the injustices of the world. Even the most advanced practitioners experience difficulty and witness injustices. The Dalai Lama deals with the issue of an abducted country, destruction of sacred property, abuses by the Chinese government, and the displacement of millions of his people. Yet he holds his seat, remaining engaged in life, meeting each challenge with compassion, wisdom, and presence.

He couldn't do this if he were all caught up emotionally, habitually reacting to all these wrongdoings. Instead, he focuses on what he *can* do; he does the necessary internal work so that he can benefit others. He realizes that *we can only be responsible for our side of the equation.* We can only create change from where we stand. When we are not all caught up in personalizing everything, or making assumptions, we have the energy to really make a difference in the world, to bring love and compassion where it is most needed.

The most skillful means we have in dealing with the Troublemakers that insult us, disappoint us, bully us, or get hostile or aggressive with us is to understand them as pointing to where we are caught up in a pain story. Here in the North, the Troublemaker is seen as our greatest teacher, also perhaps our greatest challenge, and our quickest means to heal the divide. As Shantideva points out in the *Bodhicaryāvatāra,* "One should always look straight at sentient beings as if drinking them in with the eyes, thinking, 'Relying on them alone, I shall attain Buddhahood'" (80:5). We get to experience *everything* as a blessing of the Buddha or Creator—as a means for our initiation. In Native American mythology, the Coyote is often portrayed as both the Troublemaker *and* the ally.

In Jessica Dawn Palmer's book *Animal Wisdom,* Coyote is depicted as holding the attributes of "trickster (*Heyoka*); wisdom keeper, creator, and bringer of fire and light." Heyoka is known to the Lokota as the one who *dreams* of the *Wakinyan* (Thunderbird) by acting in an "opposite" (paradoxical or troublesome) manner. He helps his two-legged friends by creating some trouble for them to work through. When a Troublemaker has crossed our path, it may be Coyote showing up as our troublemaking ally. The I Ching reminds us that difficulty arises to help keep our focus on our spiritual principles instead of being caught up in outside circumstances. Difficulties arise to provide us with a means to return our attention to our spiritual practice when we have strayed from it. Therefore, we learn to receive our Troublemakers as the blessing of the guru, as protecting our spiritual efforts and integrity.

Through such transformational practices, our spiritual work becomes an ethical practice benefiting even those who trouble us.

> *Whether a life situation is wonderful or not depends on the way your mind perceives and interprets it.*
>
> LAMA ZOPA RIPOCHE,
> TRANSFORMING PROBLEMS INTO HAPPINESS

MORE SKILLFUL MEANS TO DEAL WITH TROUBLEMAKERS

When you find yourself getting hooked by what others think, caught up in how they treat you (internal gossip), or find yourself carrying their shadow, say to yourself, "This is none of my business." What others think, what they do, or what their motivation is, is none of your business and only hooks you into a negative pattern of worry, judgment, and assumptions. When the Troublemaker occupies your consciousness, instead of following that story line down its rather predictable path, simply say to yourself, "This is none of my business."

As stated earlier, you can also employ such lines as, "I don't agree to this," or, "I let this go." This allows you to return your attention to the present moment. Troublemakers then are made powerless, because your attention and effort is on your spiritual practices, not on them.

Ultimately, you don't want to be the focus of anyone else's anger or negativity. So, why add to it by putting *your* thoughts, feelings, and actions into the mix? Experience the Troublemaker as someone just like yourself—someone who wants happiness, "same as me." They would not act this way if they were not suffering; they too want to heal the separation they feel inside. Can you feel compassion for that?

KARMA AND TROUBLEMAKERS

Prayer can be a forceful vehicle of release when you are feeling the tug made by a Troublemaker and the difficulties related to that. Here you understand the difficulty as rising from some past action of yours and realize that the two of you have some karma to work out. You will want to act in a way that clears the karmic debt and helps you both. This way you are not creating more karma or more pain.

At the very least, you are generating compassion on the spot, and that is better than creating more negativity. You may repeat the prayer, "May this difficulty release us both from our karmic debt." Or, "May this difficulty be an opportunity for us both to wake up to our true nature." Aspire for this difficulty to awaken and benefit you and your Troublemaker. Find a cognitive response that works for you and maintain that consciousness whenever the Troublemaker comes to mind. Once you are no longer hooked by the trouble, even if this Troublemaker knocks at your door, you will remain undisturbed and undistracted from your principles and intention.

Of course, you always have the Wheel of Initiation to use when trouble comes knocking at your door, or as in the case below, calls you on the phone.

DEALING WITH TROUBLE "ON THE SPOT"

While entering the North, some of our most difficult situations may arise. We encounter situations that push us to give up (we have been in the woods a long time now), or to give in to the illusion of separation. The North is where we begin to internalize the Wheel itself and come to realize we can enter it at will during challenging times.

My Coyote Story:
Using the Wheel When Encountering Trouble

THIS IS ONE OF MY INITIATION stories and passages. In it I will give you examples of practices of the Wheel and show you how you can enter it "on the spot" and progress through it, resulting in an initiation around any given difficult situation or thorny emotional problem.

This story begins in 1989 when I went on a weekend pilgrimage to my first sweat lodge at the base of Bear Butte Mountain in South Dakota and then on a *one-night vision quest on the mountain itself. Eagle Man, (Ed McGaa), author of several popular books, was our teacher and guide. In the sweat lodge I was given a spiritual name, Peyta Wigmnunke Winyan (Flaming Rainbow Woman), by the stones (Grandfathers). This was a very influential initiatory experience for me, as this name has resonated with many events of my life.**

On a more recent summer vacation my husband, daughter, and I went to Wyoming and planned on stopping at various sacred sites along the way. I began this trip in a difficult place emotionally, and this threatened to ruin the entire trip for me. A colleague had called me on the eve of our departure and unloaded some drama. (Coyote had shown up, and I was face to face with a Troublemaker!)

I immediately entered the Wheel to respond to this. Even as the Troublemaker was talking, I entered the South, where I set my intention to enjoy the trip (which she and her drama were threatening to derail) and to "act in ways that befit a bodhisattva." I then progressed into the West, where I released the agreement to be drawn into her story lines. I felt relief but prayed for strength and guidance (as I entered the North). As she spoke, I said to myself several times, "I do not agree with this." This encounter reminded me of all the times I have been hooked by other people's perceptions and agendas, thus challenging several culturally endorsed agreements on the spot.

This time, however, I was clear that I was no longer in agreement with the other's perceptions (which included making assumptions about others). I did not have to waste energy pondering this situation, instead I chose my intentions and spiritual principles to focus and rely upon. (For more on principles see page 197.) I will give you a warning here. Often what you will find is that when you disengage your energy from a given agreement (in this case to drama), the person on the other side of the agreement may attempt to hook you back into it. No one wants to be left

---

*Flaming Rainbow was Black Elk's white transcriber and friend. He transcribed and translated *Black Elk Speaks.*

with an empty fishing line! This is all the more reason to stay focused on your intentions and your principles. After working through the conversation in this fashion, I was able to focus on our vacation, although I was still somewhat shaken by the encounter.

Once on the road, I realized that we would only be an hour away from Bear Butte Mountain. I had not visited it since my vision quest back in the 1980s. The day we were to visit Bear Butte, we stopped at Crazy Horse Monument, where I felt an immediate letting go, because my difficulty was so small in comparison to the betrayal and suffering Crazy

WEST

Thunderings showered up and challenged my agreement to be hooked by the story lines and perceptions of others.

NORTH

I called on my root guru, I encountered Eagle Man, and I experienced "oneness."

SOUTH

I set the intention of "I act in ways that befit a Bodhisattva" and I transform several culturally endorsed agreements.

EAST

I focused on spiritual principles and visited Bear Butte Mountain with my family.

Fig. 5.1. Here the author uses the Wheel of Initiation "on the spot" when difficulty arises, describing the actions she undertook to combat difficulty in each quadrant of the Wheel.

Horse and his people had endured (more Thunderbeings of the West showing up). I thought of the suffering of the Tibetan people too, which was caused by similar betrayals.

My family and I decided to head up Bear Butte Mountain the next morning. I had my prayer ties I had made that morning in my pocket (entering the North). While inside the building at Crazy Horse, my husband came up to me and asked, "Isn't Ed McGaa Eagle Man? Isn't he the one who took you to Bear Butte?"

I had not seen Ed since our initial pilgrimage at Bear Butte (he still lived in Minneapolis). "Well, he's in the next room," my husband stated.

Here was the medicine man who had introduced me to sweat lodges and vision quests and initiated me with my first spiritual name. He had also translated the story of White Buffalo Calf Woman in my book *The Thundering Years*. I knew this to be an encounter with Spirit, and, upon this encounter, I had fully arrived in the North of the Wheel. I gave my prayer ties to Eagle Man (I would make more that night for our visit to the mountain), and I listened to him talk about how to include Black Elk's vision in my initiation book.

This encounter was a reminder of how *Spirit is working with us all the time,* wanting and willing to help us (a quality of the North). At this, I felt the influence of the Troublemaker withdraw and experienced a strong connection to all of life, including compassion for the Troublemaker. I felt a deepening of a commitment to my way of life, to the vow of the Bodhisattva, and to the Wheel of Initiation (expressions of the East). I then began the "return journey" (which follows a successful initiation) up to Bear Butte with my family.

The destiny of the world is determined less by the battles that are lost and won than by the stories it loves and believes in.

HAROLD GODDARD,
THE MEANING OF SHAKESPEARE

YOUR *AUTHENTIC* STORY:
CREATING WITH THE TAO

Who are you? someone asks. "I am the story of myself," comes the answer.

N. SCOTT MOMADAY, QUOTED IN *KEEPERS OF THE EARTH*,
BY MICHAEL J. CADUTO AND JOSEPH BRUCHAC

When we answer the question "Who am I?" (in the many forms we ask this), we are telling ourselves and others our story. This story then gains momentum and becomes others' story of you, as well as the one you keep narrating. Through our authentic story, we cocreate our lives. We get to say yes to this and no to that. *We are our stories.* The beauty of it is that we can rewrite, script, and create through the stories we weave of ourselves and the world. Here in the North, you begin to determine what you will be taking *out* of the woods with you—claiming more of your innate qualities and leaving the false self behind. N. Scott Momaday goes on to say, "In his traditional world the Native American lives in the presence of stories." I find this true within the traditional world and spiritual practices of Tibetan Buddhism as well. Stories hold the power to reveal, heal, and transform.

Scripting Scenes for Your Authentic Story

Sometimes we know we need to change, but we need more tools to rewrite our story. Just as our pain story was repeated through agreements, so is our new, authentic story. In cognitive-behavioral therapies, a great antidote for anxiety and fear is *scripting* a situation (scene) before you enter it. Using the analogy of bread baking, scripting is writing out or reading the recipe before making the bread.

In cognitive-behavioral practices, research reveals that what we hold in our minds directly influences our experiences. Buddhism has known this for thousands of years. You can make "scenes" from your authentic story (initiation intention) and write them out. You can script on a daily or weekly basis, or write a script for certain occasions. An authentic story becomes a promise to ourselves—a promise to fulfill our intentions

In your script, you will write out how a particular future scene will ideally unfold. Let's say you are attending a gathering, and you want the event to go well. You want to behave according to your spiritual intentions. Script it first. Instead of heading into the scene with your attention on your doubts, fears, or negative expectations, hold this script in your consciousness. Have something else to place your attention on. Often I take a moment in the morning to script what that day will be like, and I let it go to "rise." The day itself is the oven where the baking takes place, and the universe provides the heat.

Once a week I share my scripts with my script partner, Laurel, and she then carries this script in her consciousness too. For the past twenty-five years, I've created a yearly script and "scripting board" of how I want my year to look. On New Year's Day, my family and I create scripting boards or mandalas. These posters are images and words that resonate with how we want our year to progress. Then we have images that we can look at every day. These not only provide a reminder of our intentions but give us a means to gauge how our choices are in alignment with our scripting board or personal mandala. This is not a matter of passively making a board or writing a script and then sitting back and trusting that it all will magically come to be. This is a practice of creating through the power of intention *and* attention.

Whatever we give our attention to becomes manifest in the world. We have seen how we tend to script with our pain stories and that what we get is more pain. Now we script from our intentions and our authentic story and related agreements, and as a result, we experience more happiness.

You want your scripts to feel possible and to be possible, and you want them to be specific and uplifting as you read them. Ultimately, they benefit others, because whatever uplifts you uplifts those around you. Because the story is ongoing, you may add to your scripts as often as you want. You will, however, want to reread them routinely. And if you have a script partner, you will want to tell them to each other. You will discover that every script within your authentic story holds many agreements that sustain it. It can be quite helpful to name these agreements and carry them in your consciousness throughout the day. Bring regular attention to what you *are* in agreement with. Each day as I script, I agree to do my part to fulfill my intentions.

Once you script an initiatory story, identify agreements that support your intention and story and hold them on a conscious, accessible level. You want to be able to know *on the spot* whether you are acting from your intention and its sustaining agreements. Your emotions will help you realize whether you are in alignment with your truth, with your authentic story.

Scripts also let you know whether you are in alignment with *ultimate* truth. Relative truths (your personal truth/intentions) are naturally in alignment with absolute truths (the Tao, the natural order of the universe). Ultimate truth is always true and absolute, while relative truth is true relative to the person and situation. *Ultimate truth will always feel correct and benefit others.* That's how we know it is ultimate truth. So when your story (your truth and intentions) align with the Tao and are in the flow of the natural order of life, it will *feel* thus. This is the reason the image of the Wheel is open from the center outward. The still point of the Wheel is always open to the universe. When this connection is blocked, there is an interruption in the flow of our lives, and we feel it in our psychophysical realities.

When our lives are out of alignment with our relative and absolute truths, we will feel this disharmony through our emotions and physical experiences. When we are out of alignment, we need to check back to what story we are living by, what agreements and beliefs we are expressing in the world.

Checking In with Your Intention

Do a personal inventory as to how much of your life is actually in alignment with your present intention. Anytime throughout the day, you can check in and notice how your thoughts and actions are or are not in alignment with your intention. Life moves more smoothly and you have more energy when these are in alignment. Ask yourself, "Is what I am doing at this time in alignment with my intention?" (This is a yes or no answer.)

If no, how far off are you? If yes, how close are you? If you are continually out of alignment with your intention and therefore not fulfilling the promise of your authentic story (true nature), either a rewrite or a stronger commitment to your promise is necessary. An authentic story becomes a promise to yourself—a promise to fulfill your intentions, a promise to evolve spiritually.

Don't break the promise of your story. At the center of the Wheel of Initiation is a still point, a small dot. Nowhere in the Wheel of Initiation is the circle closed; there is always movement and possibility between the center point and the universe and the Tao. Everything is connected, open, moving within and about the Wheel. When we are feeling afraid, doubtful, ashamed, we are not feeling this unifying principle but cutting ourselves off from it somehow. Because our authentic stories come from our true nature, they are in alignment with the Wheel's still point. But be careful—this is never about shaming ourselves for any of our unhappiness. Instead we have the ability to transform our lives and our communities through what we anticipate and agree to, as told by our scripts.

So, you are now ready to step fully into the North of the Wheel. You are still in the woods, and you are still undergoing initiation, but now you have the light of your authentic story to get you out of the woods and back to the community, when it is your time to return.

> So that's what destiny is: simply the fulfillment of the potentials of the energies in your own system. The energies are committed in a certain way, and that commitment out there is coming toward you.
>
> JOSEPH CAMPBELL, A JOSEPH CAMPBELL COMPANION

FINAL PRACTICE BEFORE ENTERING THE NORTH

Early on in my mind-transformation practices, I found myself at times inundated with certain dark thoughts that just seemed to appear randomly and out of nowhere. They would show up at different times in my life and interfere with an otherwise pleasant time. They didn't seem to have any cause. Asking why they existed only generated more unhappiness on my part, so I decided to pay more attention to *when* they arose. Knowing that the problem is next to the wound, that the solution is within the question, I noticed how, if it weren't for these random dark thoughts, I would be feeling connected to my experience at the time. I would be more present. In fact, they tended to show up at times that would otherwise be particularly beautiful.

Skillful Means: You Become the Trickster

In this case you choose to become like the Heyoka, the Trickster. I have shared this practice with countless clients and students, and they report back how remarkable the results are. When negative, contrary, or dark thoughts arise in the mind, turn inwardly toward the thought as if you are about to greet it. Then do a small bow and say to it, "Thank you." Know that this particular thought or belief would not be arising if the *opposite* weren't actually true. Then notice and open up to what is *really* going on—touch the beauty of the moment. Turn your attention to your present experience.

You then become the Trickster to the negative thoughts. You free yourself of a negative perception by not letting it block your view of reality, of the present experience. Instead it pulls you more into reality, because it becomes a flag that something beautiful, something real is actually happening right now. Let's say you are enjoying a wonderful conversation with a friend, and you begin to have thoughts about what an idiot you are, or how bad you feel about your body, or something along those lines.

Then identify these thoughts as flags and turn and face them. Bowing to them in gratitude, you say, "Oh, thank you, you would not be showing up if something beautiful weren't happening." The Trickster has taken back the moment. Soon that particular flavor of negativity will stop showing up—you have tricked it into oblivion, because it no longer works to distract you from the moment or to undermine your experience.

> *Wherever I went, a new life begun,*
> *hidden in the grass, or waiting beyond the trees.*
> *There is a spirit abiding in everything.*
> WILLIAM STAFFORD, FROM THE POEM "YOU
> DON'T KNOW THE END," IN *THE WAY IT IS*

6

IN THE NORTH

Taking Hold of the Sacred Thread

There's a thread you follow. It goes among
things that change. But it doesn't change.
People wonder about what you are pursuing.
You have to explain about the thread.
But it is hard for others to see.
While you hold it you can't get lost.
Tragedies happen; people get hurt
or die; and you suffer and get old.
Nothing you do can stop time's unfolding.
You don't ever let go of the thread.

WILLIAM STAFFORD,
"THE WAY IT IS," IN *THE WAY IT IS*

How Blue Bear Held On:
An Adapted Myth Borrowed
from Various Indigenous Creation Stories

WHEN THE WORLD WAS BORN, it began to fly out into space due to the whirling winds. There wasn't anything to hold it in place. To prevent Earth from whirling out of control, the Creator put a Sacred Bear in each direction to help hold it in place. The whirling wind continued, but Earth stayed put, kept its seat, so to speak, while the Bear in each direction held on to it. And this was good.

In the North, the Creator placed the Great Blue Bear and gave her the one Sacred Thread to hold on to. Blue Bear of the North has held her seat since the birth of Earth and has never let go of the Sacred Thread. But, as in all good stories, Blue Bear was tested for her strength, endurance, and patience. Crow gathered many birds to cause a disturbing wind to encircle Blue Bear. The birds and wind made such a disturbance that Blue Bear began to doubt she could hold on. She began to blame the Crows for her difficulty and became annoyed with the Creator for giving her such a task. The Crows cawed and cawed, and the winds of disturbance howled. Earth below Blue Bear disappeared, and all she had was her end of the Sacred Thread.

But Blue Bear kept her place. She did not stir. She held on.

The Crows were relentless, and Blue Bear began to feel the wind of fear, the strongest wind of all.

But she did not move. She kept hold of the Sacred Thread. She stayed put even though the winds stirred and whirled and there seemed to be no chance of an end. Finally, the Crows got tired and left. And Blue Bear could see the great blue Earth right beneath her and the Sacred Thread connecting them. She took a deep breath, and a sigh passed over and around Earth. And once again, it was good.

Now the Great Blue Bear sits just above Earth in the North, bound by the Sacred Thread. She sits and holds on. She asks that each of us hold our place and never let go of our own Sacred Thread, though the winds may whirl and the voices disturb. Hold your seat. Don't let go of the thread. Hold on.

Every day, we are being handed the Sacred Thread. But to have a hold of the thread, we must take it from the Creator. We must sit quietly long enough (in one place) so that which we seek can find us.

The soul is like a wild animal—tough, resilient, savvy, self-sufficient, and yet exceedingly shy. If we want to see a wild animal, the last thing we should do is to go crashing through the woods, shouting for the creature to come out. But if we are willing to walk quietly into the woods, and sit silently for an hour or two at the base of a tree, the creature we are waiting for may well emerge, and out of the corner of an eye we will catch a glimpse of the precious wildness we seek.

PARKER PALMER, *THE ACTIVE LIFE*

THE SACRED LANGUAGE OF THE UNIVERSE

In the North we become the meaning-makers, and have direct experience with the divine as we cultivate the attention of a spiritual pilgrim.

Direct experience with the divine, which happens primarily through breaking free of our pain stories, is the sacred language of the universe. But how can we know when or how to attribute spiritual meaning to any of our experiences? Are there actually secret systems of the universe written in Sanskrit, Tibetan, or Hebrew, or in some special code that we need to decipher to achieve enlightenment? What is god's language? What does it mean to experience the true nature of our minds? What are the ways we can communicate with our spiritual source—or how can we bring on a direct spiritual experience? How does the divine make contact with us?

Direct experience is dependent on an *internal* shift, an awakening, a change in perspective that brings on a knowing, a real understanding of reality. You touch the place (or it touches you) where you experience oneness. Oneness comes from healing the separation within and without. Typically, a good feeling accompanies this. You change and become more open from these experiences and therefore interact in the world in a saner, more enlightened manner. To do this, you have to remove whatever clouds your view of your own true nature and the true nature of the world. As we continue to do our inner work to dismantle the pain stories and uproot the beliefs and agreements associated with them, we find ourselves having more and more direct experiences.

Religions tend to claim that there is one god and one language that god understands. But what a limit to put on such a great archetype—to make her a one-language god! If it is god we seek, it is much more likely that she loves us so much that she responds in the spiritual language and practices by which we consistently communicate. The key does not depend on one particular spiritual tradition or method; the key is in finding the mystical practices that resonate with our own authenitc stories. I personally have met many, many people who speak of meaningful experiences and encounters within their spiritual practices, and I myself have had experiences that I claim as proof of the interactive nature of the spiritual world.

What I have discovered is that whoever is willing to do the inner work and *wherever someone is consistent* in a given spiritual (ethical) or sacred practice, they meet up with the divine. Your spiritual source will be found in the practices themselves.

This consistency affords us our direct experiences. But divinity comes in many, many forms. Direct experience is really making contact with one's own compassion, beauty, inherent nature, and humanity.

However, when we keep putting our spiritual practice "out there" and *don't commit to doing the necessary internal work on a regular basis,* we remain spiritually hungry. Many people go running off to sacred sites, native rituals, healing practices, ashrams, spiritual gatherings, and new age shops in search of a spiritual experience. They want to make contact. But it is not the place or the item or the ritual (or the teacher) that affords anyone a spiritual encounter, *but what we bring to it.* As Joseph Campbell reminds us in many of his teachings, "The meaning of life is whatever you ascribe to it." The great diversity in spiritual and secular paths holds the potential for direct experience. The simple naturalist who searches for beauty in the wild of the wood and prairie will also encounter the divine, especially as the naturalist returns time and again to the outdoors.

Initiation decreases (and ultimately ends) our search for spiritual experiences. At the same time, the actuality of our direct experiences increases. You are no longer focused on searching for external experiences, you are deepening the chosen spiritual practice that naturally leads you to the divine.

> *In Lakota framework everyone is a meaning-maker, everyone must make sense of his or her experience.* Woableza *has been translated as "realization." It has always seemed to me that this word acknowledges that each person has a capacity to make meaning; that understanding is very personal, is timed by him or her, and is not predictable; and for woableza to exist, a change in the person should take place.*
>
> GERALD MOHATT, THE PRICE OF A GIFT

We are the meaning-makers, as Gerald Mohatt writes in his book *The Price of a Gift*. Every time I enter the prairie spiral or visit the Deer Park Buddhist Center in Oregon, Wisconsin, or meditate on my cushion at home, I become open to making contact with the sacred, with my spiritual source. In my case the Buddha knows where to meet me—on my meditation cushion, in the spiral, or at the temple; and he knows the language I speak—the Mahayana tradition of Tibetan Buddhism and the language of the natural world. Because Spirit loves me so much and is listening, it will communicate to me in the same way I consistently communicate through my spiritual practices.

Your Hold on the Sacred Thread

This reliability in my practice allows me a gateway into the spiritual world and is my hold on the Sacred Thread. The North is the place in the Wheel to take ownership of your given practice, if you haven't already done so. The North is the doorway to the divine and is where one gets hold of the Sacred Thread. This does not mean you won't study or read a variety of spiritual texts but that you choose one *core* practice. You choose your spiritual language. You decide how you are going to listen to the inner stirrings of your own soul. I have met countless people who attend spiritual events for a meaningful spiritual experience but neglect to follow up with a daily practice.

You might say that attending many events and purchasing lots of spiritual trinkets is like "crashing through the woods" to encounter the wild animal. You will more likely scare off what you are looking for. If you want to have the Sacred Thread handed to you, quiet down and be steady in your practice. My regular practices, given to me through the Bodhisattva path and Lojong principles within the Mahayana tradition, as well as my daily encounter with nature, makes my spiritual language clear so that when I am being contacted, I know it.

Spiritual experiences happen through the filter of our internal language and our views (perspectives). When you regularly pray to the Lakota Ancestors, for example, that is who you will receive contact from. This demonstrates both the power of the mind to create but also the grace of the universe (and the soul) to respond to us in the language we best understand. This builds our faith and our willingness to work more deeply with the aspects of our true nature and our chosen spiritual practices.

Because a valid spiritual experience is mostly *internal,* its effects are long-term. (You could understand it as lasting lifetimes.) All we experience now is based on past beliefs and agreements. By the same token, all that we agree to now will result in future experiences. We are creating our futures right now. Because this is not determined by outward events but is internal, the results of our efforts can follow us beyond this lifetime. We may leave our bodies behind, but we take our karma with us (our spiritual nature, which includes our agreements).

A valid spiritual experience is different than a religious experience (although there can be an overlap here). A religious experience often emphasizes the outward event and is often directed by a teacher, priest, or guru of sorts. Alternatively, one is often taken through a persuasive religious experience and is converted to that doctrine.

When this is the case, one is being persuaded to agree to what an experience may mean, rather than bringing their own meaning to it. This is how various psychological and religious groups recruit. In such groups you are directed what to think and experience, and a true shift in consciousness does not occur. Another danger arises when a teacher or a practitioner proclaims that his or her way is unique and that he or she alone holds some formula and special technique. Religions are often founded on one man or woman's spiritual experience, because that person and others assumes this is how the experience should look for everyone. Then what you find is a lot of followers trying to mimic someone else's experience.

Those who are dedicated practitioners follow a multitude of paths. From this, it becomes clear that, given our diversity, no single religion satisfies all humanity.

THE FOURTEENTH DALAI LAMA, *ETHICS FOR A NEW MILLENNIUM*

The Dalai Lama's point is that there are many paths to the divine. The Buddha often counseled students not to follow him but to go practice and discover the truth for themselves. A fundamental difference between religious doctrine and spiritual practice is this invitation to *find the truth for oneself* instead of having someone else dictate it. A skillful teacher will lead us to the teacher within, and to our own personal experiences with the divine. This is what makes gifted teachers so content and open—they know that the spiritual path is available to all and that it comes in a variety of forms. (See the appendix, "Teachers and Groups.")

When my grandmother was dying, I told her to take Jesus's hand. She loved the Bible and always prayed to Jesus for guidance. She was such a beautiful woman. And even though I am a practicing Buddhist, I know that Jesus was there to take her hand.

RENEE

To have an internal shift in consciousness and therefore a personal spiritual experience, one ought to remain mindful during any regular practices. For example, if my walks in the prairie were robotic and rushed and I wasn't engaged in my walk, it would not provide me with much more than some fresh air. My paying attention is what makes this walk spiritual and therefore transformative. Too often religious experience assumes that just going through the motions is enough. But it is not. This, too, is where religious and spiritual can overlap—if you bring mindfulness and presence into your religious practices, they are more likely to have transformative effects.

Henry Holds His Seat

HENRY WAS A GIFTED ARTIST and counselor who also had great difficulty finding any lasting peace in his life. He was always discovering various techniques of spiritual healing and methods of insight to try. He was a voracious reader and always wanted to discuss his latest spiritual discovery in his sessions with me. Although he had a regular morning practice of hatha yoga, he was continually engaging in different practices to "find his center" or be treated for his chronic underlying unhappiness.

Then he came to me with his latest discovery! Some code had been revealed that unlocked ancient healing secrets. (A cautionary flag arises for me when I hear words such as secret or promises in this context.) He was going to attend a rather expensive seminar to learn how to use these symbols. I suggested instead that, for thirty days, he go outside every morning at dawn and sit under a favorite tree and just listen (before he put his money down). I also suggested that he put away all his spiritual and psychological books for these thirty days, that he simply arise every morning and do his yoga and go sit quietly by the tree.

"For what reason?" he asked me.

"Great question. What's your intention in attending the training?"

"To learn how the symbols can help me. To connect more with sacred truth."

"How about you ask this question while sitting under the tree? Give yourself at least an hour each morning and get under the tree by sunrise, so that you will actually be sitting under it for some predawn time."

"Whatcha hoping that'll do?"

I wasn't about to make any promises. He had been given plenty of those by other healers, teachers, and books. All I knew for certain was that through his sincerity in questioning, he could tap in to an answer within himself. He just needed to sit in one place long enough (literally and internally). He had to stop crashing through the woods if he wanted more of his soul to emerge.

"Are you willing to find out?" I asked him.

Henry began a month of tree-squatting and took a sabbatical from reading books and attending workshops or trainings. He sat under a tree almost every day for thirty-four days. (I also recommended that he not consult with me until after his time with the tree). His consistency in his yoga practice helped him follow through on this commitment. About five weeks later, he showed up in my office. I would not be exaggerating to say that he was smiling from ear to ear.

He sat down and said, "Got it."

He basically went on to describe how the tree and he "held the code" and that he came to realize everything holds the code. He reported having a miraculous healing from his underlying unhappiness through the realization that life is a mixture of happy/unhappy and that it is all just part of god, "all part of Brahman." He told me that all his intense searching made him feel separated from the truth because the truth kept being placed "out there" somewhere. "I felt so driven to find that missing link to happiness or insight," he said. He admitted going through some very unpleasant times under the tree but also relayed that his yoga practice helped teach him to "stay with it." He decided to give up his search but continue his practice of yoga and tree sitting. That was the last time I saw Henry, but whenever he comes to mind, I see him sitting against some tree, and it brings a happy smile to my face.

So much is dependent upon our ability to listen and notice what is going on around us and within us.

Several autumns ago, I walked up to the pine tree in my backyard and asked it one question: "What is institutional violence?" The tree did not answer right away. So I sat at its roots and waited. The backyard was covered with brilliantly colored leaves, the air was fresh, and suddenly I forgot that I was waiting for an answer. The tree and I were just there, enjoying ourselves and each other. After sitting for a *long time, I turned to the tree, smiled, and said, "I no longer need an answer." Then I thanked it and awarded it the Grand Transnational Peace Prize.*

THICH NHAT HANH, *LOVE IN ACTION*

THE GREAT CONVERSATION

We can all tap in to this inner wisdom and link up to our spiritual source; we just have to find our tree! Of course, some of us might not have an actual tree readily available, but what we do have is the time of predawn and sunrise to sit quietly and listen. I was introduced to the *Great Conversation* through William Stafford's poetry. William Stafford was born in Kansas in 1914 and was author of more than fifty books. He wrote in his journal daily. As a conscientious objector during World War II, he began his unswerving ritual of writing before dawn each day. I understand now how his poetry reaches into my being and stirs up the hope and goodness that is lodged there. His words wake me up and point me in a more sane and humane direction. His ritual of getting up before dawn was a thread that we can all take hold of if we want to.

I knew that he tapped in to some universal language, one that was not bound by dogma or beliefs. I discovered that this time of predawn is known as "spiritually awake, spiritually dense," where anyone and everyone can tap in to the vibrations and intentions of an awakening world. It is still dark during this time, but the sun will soon rise, and everything natural is on the verge of stirring and awakening. Being present in this predawn time will stir what is naturally awakening inside you as well. I have heard this time called the Great Conversation because of this and because there is much to listen to. All we need to do is show up and pay attention.

❋ Experience the Great Conversation

To be part of the Great Conversation, rise an hour before dawn and find a place outside or near a window to sit and listen. Simply listen, but have your journal handy. Bring your awareness to the moment and listen to the Great Conversation that takes place in a still-dark but awakening world. Then, as the sun rises, engage in a sunrise ritual of your choosing. Ideally, follow it up with your meditation practice.

Other Great Conversations can take place while you are sitting under a tree, walking mindfully on a path, or sitting somewhere in the wild at a time the sun is about to rise or set. Even though regularity in practice provides one with direct experiences with the divine, there are also universal means of communication with the spiritual world that do not depend so much on a consistent practice.

These are times when our soul or the spiritual world is trying to make contact with us. The success of the communication will still depend upon our ability to discern meaning for ourselves. Everyone has access to symbols such as spirals and mandalas. Everyone dreams. Everyone can visit the natural world. Everyone can experience certain encounters as meaningful and synchronistic. Everyone can join in the Great Conversation.

Quite simply, there are times in life when doors are closed, people are opposing you, or you are in the dark and feel disconnected from self and others. To know how to navigate our lives in a sound and creative way during these times, we need periods of reflection and stillness—so we can "see" the thread that is being handed to us. During difficult or dark times, the thread *is* being handed to us, but we may be unaware that this is taking place.

Paying Attention

Fortunately, our soul as well as the spirit world can rely on universal languages in any situation, at any time, *if we are paying attention*. Wake up, listen, write your insights in your journal, meditate, and notice how your mind clears and your heart opens. The Great Conversation has a way of opening us up, not only to the spiritual density of that time, but also to our own humanity. This makes the task of the spiritual pilgrim quite simple—we don't have to go to someone else to make this contact for us or to have others interpret soulful or spiritual encounters. *We decide* what is meaningful for ourselves, and there we find the spiritual connection that we long for.

EIGHT EAGLES, FORTY CROWS, AND A HAWK, OH, MY!

Several years ago I was trying to make a decision about how to respond to a certain community that had invited me to their rituals and gatherings. I knew I wanted to release any association with them, yet at the same time wish them well. One aspect of their gatherings that held particular concern for me was their sense of spiritual drama and spiritual exhibitionism. They implied what one would experience in their rituals, and these implications often laden with warnings. The leader would share dreams and "visions" she had of possible dangers, while at the same time directing what others must do to fulfill some prophetic nudge she had received. I was told that the gatherings often became complicated and rule-oriented, and certain people were perceived to have special roles. Manipulating people with fear and shame was typically employed to induce people to attend.

About this same time that I had made a decision no longer to associate with them, I arrived home from picking up my daughter from school. When we got out of the car, the sky began to fill up with birds. What made this unusual was that initially there were eight eagles circling above us, and then about forty crows came out of the North to join them. Soon a red-tailed hawk was part of the mix. For what seemed like a long time (but was probably only about five to ten minutes), they all flew above us in some synchronistic ballet and then took off, heading East. This was atypical in that they were all flying together, circling at the same time and not fighting.

I was relieved that my daughter witnessed this with me; she thought it was awesome and said, "The birds just love our land and home." I asked myself what this might be pointing to. Certainly such a sight was going to get my attention—the encounter felt somewhat tied to my recent decision. Because my daughter was part of this encounter, so was her response— *birds love this land.* I love this land. This resonated with my intention to keep my spiritual practice close to home and not to get involved with groups or practices that took me away from this sacred place (within and without). Any group or practice that takes too much energy and time away from self (personal spiritual practice, creativity) or home (land, family, soul) is a good one to say no to.

When such spiritual encounters happen for me, as with the eagles and crows, I notice them, appreciate the beauty inherent in the encounter, *discern for myself what it means,* and then let it go. I am the meaning-maker of my life. I encourage you to do the same.

I consult the I Ching in the same way: I trust the message as timely and discern for myself its meaning *in the context of my life at that time.* Basically, eight eagles, forty crows, and a red-tailed hawk is bound to get my attention. What encounter has gotten your attention lately?

Here is Shannon's account of coyotes that appeared in his life recently: "What does it mean to keep having a coyote show up? I heard many coyotes howling the other night, then one ran across the road the other day, and I recently had a dream where I encountered one."

I would trust these coyote encounters, decide what they mean, and use the dream as a way to gain greater insight about one's life. In this man's dream, the coyote was trying to lead him away from one place and to another. But he was reluctant to trust a coyote and couldn't see where it was trying to lead him. After waking and considering his dream, Shannon decided that it meant for him to reconsider where he was in his life at the moment. Perhaps it was time to venture down a new path both professionally and personally. His dreams, as all dreams do, often point to the internal work that needs to be done to create movement in one's life.

Each spiritual encounter should inherently hold within it a way to benefit you and others. Such an encounter should feel uplifting and give one hope, even if the lesson accompanying it is a tough one.

> *The birds flew above us*
> *The spirit of the birds flew above us*
> Spirit flew above us
>
> *Coyote called to him*
> *The Spirit of Coyote called to him*
> Spirit called to him

I kept encountering this same spiritual teacher. One time I bumped into him at a farmers' market. Another time someone gifted me a book of his. After several encounters I decided to check him out and attended one of his teachings. This relationship has helped restore a part of me I thought was lost forever.

MARNIE

Holding a Symbolic View

In Tibetan, *gyud* means "thread"—that which joins together. Gyud is similar to the meaning of the word Tao. Translated simply, the Tao is the unifying principle within all life. You might say that everything that expresses the intrinsic nature of all phenomena is our gyud. When we experience our oneness with all life, we have hold of the sacred gyud. But to know and take hold of the thread that is being handed to us, we must be able to *see* the thread. This may not be something we can see or touch with our physical senses but something we "see" and *experience* through our spiritual and symbolic sight and language. We reap more spiritual essence from our day-to-day experiences when we see from a symbolic point of view.

Recently a man came to me who had been bitten by a brown recluse spider years back, one night when he was asleep. At the time, he felt it became a totem. It is a highly poisonous spider, but because the bite was on his ankle, the impact was minimal. At the time it bit him, he did not have the context to understand this experience as the possible initiatory process that it was. The spider, seen and experienced in the context of his life, could be understood as trying to wake him up, and as poisoning him. (That makes it initiatory—something that has the ability to both destroy and create.) For several years, he kept having encounters with the spider in his dreams and in his waking life.

This is typical of such spiritual encounters—that which wants our attention keeps repeating itself until the internal or external issue is uncovered and resolved. This man discovered, while in the North, that a spider was not so much his totem as it was the medicine he carried *within* himself. *He was Spider.* He carried the poison but also the web of life. He had the ability to weave his dream wherever he chose. He decided to use the spider as a means to wake up to his life's calling, but he wasn't sure what that was.

He realized that, as a recluse spider, he was able to bite what could kill him. In this case, the threat was something that was asleep: The spider could have easily been killed if the sleeping man had rolled on it. This got him to consider what aspects of his life were asleep and might benefit from a bite. What parts of his life called for initiation?

Because he saw himself as the spider, he understood the sleepiness as the greatest danger. He realized that he felt surrounded by sleepy people at his job and in his friendships. His job and his social life were indeed killing him.

He began by choosing not to hang out in a bar after work with friends, and he decided to eradicate alcohol and drugs from his social life. He sought several other social outlets, and, as a result, he encountered someone who knew of an ideal job (not in any way like the one he held), and he seized the opportunity and moved on.

Depending on the context, your intention, and both your pain and your authentic stories, a bite from a spider could mean something quite different than what it meant for this man. You must search out the symbolic meaning within the context of your own life. Use this meaning to move you on through the Wheel and to further initiate your intention.

Being Your Own Meaning-Maker

Here are the simple steps to being your own meaning-maker. First, examine the events of your life for their symbolic significance as well as their more prosaic explanations. Second, interpret the symbolic meaning in the context of *your life* situation; don't make assumptions based on any collective meaning. You *decide*. Finally, experience the symbolism as a *pointer*, but don't mistake the experience for the final say on the matter. Ask, "What is this encounter, this symbol, pointing to?" Use the encounter to generate movement in your life. Anything that you view as holding symbolic meaning can be used for your initiation.

Again, imagine yourself out in the woods, alone, deep into the initiatory process. You can't go running out searching for someone else to assign meaning to your experience. *The initiatory journey makes you the meaning-maker.*

★ ★ ★

You have been in the Wheel for some time now and have gone through some inner psychological work that has prepared you to trust and make meaning from such spiritual encounters. If you have tried to bypass the requisite internal work, you may miss the encounter, or you may not trust your experience. Or you are likely to interpret it through the prism of your pain story and agreements.

Synchronicity: The Tao of Spiritual Encounters

Synchronicity can provide us with confirmation that we are on the right path, as well as let us know when we are not.

JEAN SHINODA BOLEN, THE TAO OF PSYCHOLOGY

To appreciate a synchronistic encounter, you must trust yourself. This trust comes from knowing the difference between an agreement that supports your pain story and one that supports your authentic story (initiatory intention). Trusting in yourself further strengthens your trust in yourself. Trust is like a muscle; it gets stronger as you work it.

All the Eastern religions contain the underlying agreement that there is an essential tenet that connects everything to everything else. Everything arises conditionally. Because there is no real separation (except that which we project), nature and Spirit are always pointing to this natural phenomenon of interdependence. Nothing occurs in isolation; everything is interdependent. Equally so, built into every action is a reaction; for every cause there is an effect. If you want to know the cause, look at the effect. The synchronistic encounter or event is the *effect,* the cause is your prayer, question, intention, belief, or agreement that preceded it.

Basically, a synchronistic encounter is a *meaningful* coincidence. It is an acausal encounter that cannot be logically explained but is responding to some internal issue or question. As Jean Shinoda Bolen says in *The Tao of Psychology,* "Synchronistic events are the clues that point to the existence of an underlying connecting principle." Meaningful coincidences get your attention, so you don't have to go searching for them. They come to you from the Tao and are signs on your path. They will begin to show up the moment you commit to something, such as an initiatory intention.

They arise like road signs saying, "This road is a major detour; reconsider your plans." Or, "Keep going."

Either way, they are there to help you on your way. Because the natural world also relies on intrinsic timing—a cycle of creativity and rest, the waxing and waning of the moon, the rising and setting of the sun—synchronistic encounters will help you with your natural timing. There is a time to move and a time to stay put. We are in this interplay of interconnectedness and karma, and the Tao is interacting with us all the time. As we access the inner light by removing what blocks us, we also connect with all the light everywhere else. When we make contact with our inner divinity, we automatically make contact with all that is divine.

You have to have the ability to interpret these encounters symbolically *and* logically. This means that you have both a symbolic and a psychological language to work with. Pay particular attention to meaningful coincidences while in the North, both as a practice to strengthen this ability, and to receive help. Don't go on a vigilante hunt in search of these encounters—simply notice what comes up, *what gets your attention*. Notice how your dreams may be helping you interpret synchronistic encounters, as in the coyote story above. If you dream about someone and then run into him or her, what does this person represent to you? It may be that you are meant to do something with this person; it may mean that this person simply holds symbolic meaning for you. *You decide.*

When doing this, put the ego aside as best you can. Our egos will either try to make a bigger deal of it than it is or make us doubt its relevance. Connect the synchronicity to your life in a logical way, yet at the same time, try to understand its symbolic meaning. Spirit works with and through natural law. And while these synchronistic events have been going on all the time, you may only be noticing them now because of the internal work you are doing. You are practicing letting Spirit get your attention. Your view is getting more expansive.

Initiatory Oracles: The I Ching and Nature's Wisdom

Oracles are traditionally a means by which deities are consulted, insight is gained, and advice is sought. In consulting an oracle, we can affirm our connection to the Tao, to all of life, and we open up a means for our spiritual source and soul to communicate with us. We set up contact with our deity and inner teacher, inviting them to guide us.

Common oracles include the I Ching, nature (natural phenomena), and the tarot. (I recommend the Osho Zen deck.) Tibetans have the divination system of Mo, which they have consulted for centuries. Mo is used in conjunction with various tantric and meditation practices. Oracles can help you script your day, interact with the spirit world, and live from a more spiritual and ethical place. Oracles can offer you the means to live your intentions and principles. They help you notice the Tao interacting within your life.

I have worked with the I Ching since the age of sixteen; this is a meeting place for Spirit and me. My two favored oracles are both universal and accessible by all, and ones I recommend for the initiatory pilgrimage—the I Ching and nature. Choose an oracle that is dependent upon some established philosophy (the I Ching is at least three thousand years old). The Mo system, based primarily on the Kalachakra Tantra, was developed by Jamyang Namgyal Gyatso in the late 1800s. The tarot is a divinatory system that may date back to ancient Egypt, and the Osho deck borrows from Zen and transcendental practices. Nature as an oracle is found in most indigenous traditions and is typically an intricate part of most divination tools. And having been around the longest, it holds the most verifiable intelligence. If your chosen oracle is nature, there are many resources that can help you extract meaning from your encounters, such as *Nature's Way* by Ed McGaa (Eagle Man), or Jessica Dawn Palmer, *Animal Wisdom*.

Calling Forth the Sacred

A trader leaving for India was earnestly begged by an aged woman to bring back a saint's relic for her. He promised to do so, but being busy with his own affairs during his stay abroad, forgot his promise. However, as he neared home the sight of a bleached skeleton of a dog reminded him of the old woman's request.

"The dear old dame is superstitious," he said to himself. "A bit of this dog's bones will do for her." He then broke off a tooth from the dead animal's jawbone and wiped it clean. He wrapped it in a silk scarf and presented it to his unsuspecting supplicant.

"Here, Old Mother," he addressed her, "I have brought for you a most precious relic: a tooth of the great Sariputra, Buddha's favorite companion."

The old woman, beside herself with joy, thanked him profusely and with deep veneration placed it on the altar of her shrine. Each day she worshipped before it with devotion. And as time went on, she was joined by other equally fervent devotees, while the trader laughed in his sleeve, smothering his disdain for what he considered their foolishness and credulity.

However, he was astonished, along with others, to find one day rays of brilliance emanating from the altar that held the roadside picking: the object had ceased to be a mere dog's tooth; it had been transformed into a true, holy relic.

Hence the saying "Sincere prayer, worship, and supplication can make a thorn a relic of adoration."

SUDHIN N. GHOSE,
TIBETAN FOLK TALES AND FAIRY STORIES

Through visitation of and sincere devotion to a site or an object, it becomes sacred; continue to give it relevance, and sooner or later, you will have a direct experience with the divine. When I enter the prairie spiral in the morning, my deity becomes known to me. I make the place holy and sacred through my presence and by sanctifying it. If you are far from a prairie or wood, make a sacred, natural place in your home. Create a sacred place where the sun comes in, where you can see and feel it rising in the morning. Build an altar. Consult your oracle and read from your sacred text in this place. Return to this place again and again, and turn all thorns into relics of adoration.

When you can get outside, do. Time in nature quickly connects you with the Tao, the gyud, because nature is the simplest, most accessible expression of divinity. When you go for a walk and listen, when you sit with a sunset or meet the sunrise, you are participating with everything sacred, and the separation vanishes.

NATURE AS ORACLE: THE MORNING OWL

As the meaning-makers, it is not so much what shows up on our visit with nature but what we notice and observe. It is about what gets our attention and what we, in return, give our attention to.

On this morning, a small barred owl sits on a branch that stretches out over the prairie. Its head, buried in its chest, looks small and round. As I watch her, two crows appear on a nearby branch. She sits still as if not to notice them. One crow gets very close, but the branch is too small to be shared. The owl remains unmoved. Then another crow lands in the top tree branch; now there are three interested visitors. The crows begin to move in on the owl, and at one point they peck at her. After a while, the owl moves to a branch closer in to the tree trunk but still exposed to the prairie and my view. Soon, two of the crows get as close as they can, and she lifts her brown body from the branch and glides deeper into the woods. The crows follow her and then land on a high tree above, holding watch for a few minutes.

What is *not* observed today is that this owl, on another day and season, tried (and maybe succeeded) in feeding upon the eggs or babies of these crows.

This became a perfect metaphor of karma and conditional cause. The owl *appears* to be innocent—meditating and enjoying an early morning snowfall—and the crows come along simply to disturb her peace, for no apparent reason. *But the crows know.* They remember—this owl or its relative once stole one of their eggs. Karma. Conditional cause. Dependent existence. Owls are unlikely to get a peaceful morning undisturbed by crows as long as it is in their nature to rob crows' nests.

For the owl and the crow, this is all part of their nature and will be repeated many mornings over. So I use this as a teaching and ask myself,

"What am I experiencing right now in my life that started with some decision made in the past?" Because everything is dependent on everything else and nothing happens in a vacuum, how is any difficulty I am presently experiencing based on a choice I made in the past? This, of course, would be a good question for anyone to contemplate.

What other meaning may I retrieve from this encounter? I see these animals as a reflection of our cult-mind—how we just repeat and repeat certain ways of relating and do not develop our consciousness or how we relate to one another. Unlike these birds, we have a great capacity to challenge and change our ways of being in the world through the transformation of our minds and compassionate action.

Each day gives us an opportunity not to repeat a painful cycle. By consciously taking a look at the pattern, we can alter our course and therefore the outcome. This can enrich our insights. Initiation is threatened if our feet are always on concrete and our view of the sky is limited by roofs and artificial lights. Use the contemplative observation of nature and its ways as a means to provide you with feedback on your spiritual initiation. We need the night sky, the morning sunrise, and the changing of the seasons to experience and understand our personal initiations.

At this point in the North of the Wheel, it would be particularly good to spend a stretch of time in nature. Go for a walk where you consciously engage with wildlife. Spend time meditating in nature. Find a spiral or a labyrinth to walk. Sit at the base of a tree.

The Thread of Attention

The essence of the Buddha's teaching is to turn our undisciplined mind into a disciplined mind.

THE FOURTEENTH DALAI LAMA,
MADISON, WISCONSIN, MAY 2007

The Dalai Lama went on to point out in this teaching how the undisciplined mind is the root of all suffering. He speaks of spirituality as being about thought transformation: "freedom found through the discipline of the mind." In all the teachings of his that I have attended, he focuses on the "supreme vehicle," which is mindfulness: "Spiritual seekers are seeking an equanimous state of being. This mindfulness (supreme vehicle) is what helps transcend duality." It helps transcend a mind that sees and experiences separation. The Bible points to this supreme vehicle as well: "Be still and know that I am God." For me, this means to be still and know "I am that."

Sitting in the dark of the woods (of initiation) with an undisciplined mind, an inability to stay focused, makes you vulnerable to internal and external distractions and dangers. These distractions can ultimately lead you away from your intentions. *There is one practice above all others that leads to your hearing the call, listening to it, and being able to follow it because you are not distracted from it.* This tool, which I am fortunate to have been introduced to at the age of sixteen, is the practice of meditation, of cultivating attention. Through the cultivation of attention, you are generating a disciplined mind.

One morning when I was meditating (and knowing I was going to write on this topic), I noticed how everything sane, beautiful, and creative in my life is so because of my meditation practice—this practice gives me the *ability to put my attention where I choose.* This is Blue Bear's main thread, and it is mine. I can save the world and keep my seat because I have the ability to practice guiding my attention where I choose in any given moment, thus training my mind. I can keep hold of the Sacred Thread no matter what. (I do not claim that I always, in all situations, successfully use this skill, but I am quick to discover when I have let go of the thread because my world begins to spin out of control.)

This is what you must go for. Nothing else in your spiritual practice or in your psychoemotional work compares with your ability to place your heart-mind where you want it to be. Cultivating attention is really about letting go. Instead of holding onto the past, or the negative thought pattern, or the outside drama, we let it go. The Buddha in his teachings refers to this as "leaving things as they are." There is much sanity and peace in just leaving things as they are—not trying to change or control anything and everything. This teaches us to be the cause rather than the effect of our lives. We are not so bounced around by outer conditions. We are then able to transform our thoughts and the world around us.

This helps us make conscious choices that result in more favorable outcomes, because whatever we give our attention to *becomes*. Many who seek consultation with me want to know their calling or know how to follow a calling when they already know what it is. Many ask, "What stops me from following my heart and doing what I love?" Every time I receive a flier or read an ad in a magazine on an upcoming conference, there is typically a workshop on "finding your purpose."

How is it we don't know our calling? How is it we don't get down to following our bliss, as Joseph Campbell would say? How much of our money, time, and thought goes into trying to figure out what our purpose in life is? I would say that everyone knows their calling—it gets down to listening to the call and following it rather than getting lost in all the distractions. And, as we discussed earlier in this book, distractions are as boundless as stars in the universe. This is what makes this central to your personal initiation—there will be all sorts of demons showing up to scare you off your path.

Disturbing thoughts and other distractions become like wet snow on a hot highway when we are in presence. With enough warmth of awareness, the "snow" (distractions) soon dissolves. Often the metaphor of a muddy glass of water is given to illustrate the power of sitting meditation. Let a dirty glass of water sit still long enough, and the mud will settle to the bottom, leaving clear, drinkable water on top. The mind works in a similar fashion. Let it rest long enough in the mindfulness of the moment (resting in the breath), and it too will settle down. Mindfulness meditation practices are often called practices in "calm abiding."

Because there are many practices of cultivating attention, developing mindfulness, and transforming the mind through meditation, only a few will be described here. However, there are fundamental characteristics of any given meditation practice that are necessary for the practice to generate attention and help transform the mind. Use these as parameters as you find your own practice.

1. You must be actively cultivating attention through the practice, not just reciting a mantra or simply sitting on the cushion and breathing.

2. Sitting includes a practice of "letting go," an observation of impermanence. For example, you meditate on the breath, letting each one go. You practice letting go of thoughts and return to the breath or the mantra. You may also meditate on the aspects of impermanence.

3. You sit through the rising and falling of different emotional, psychological, and physical states as you return your attention to the object of your meditation (the mantra or the breath).

4. There are no preferences or attachments to certain states, such as bliss, clarity, or insights. This follows on a previous characteristic of a true practice—you are willing to let go of a preferred state and be with whatever else is arising in the moment. You open again and again to the reality of presence.

   When I was introduced and initiated into my first meditation practice at the age of sixteen (which was Transcendental Meditation), I would say it saved my life. At the group sessions that I attended, everyone seemed to be walking about in a state of bliss. Being sixteen, my normal state was more often than not a state of agitation.

   When I began meditating with a mantra, I mostly meditated by myself. What I sought was inner and outer peace. Later in life, when I was trained in Vipassana meditation, my teacher at the time, Shinzen Young, would remind us, "Don't prefer. No preference, just presence." What a wonderful tool to take with me in the world—the ability to let go of preferences! When we are attached to preferences and how things *should* be, we are no longer in calm abiding. This does not mean I don't have preferences and wants! What it means is that I have an expanded capacity to let go of what I think should be happening and embrace what is actually taking place. This allows me to respond to what is really going on rather than what I wish was going on.

5. The sitting meditation practice is understood as a means to tame the mind, to still the mind and prepare it for mind transformation

(mind training). You can't train a wild animal until you have quieted it down enough. (It's hard to catch a flying bird.)

6. You understand that all your internal issues are likely to arise on your meditation cushion and that this is also a place of transformation as you practice "holding your seat," sitting still and being attentive—keeping hold of the Sacred Thread of attention no matter what arises. So, for example, any impatience you feel during your sitting practice is an opportunity to practice calm abiding with this particular emotional state. This transforms a distracting emotional state into an opportunity to practice, as Geshe Tenzin Dorje pointed out early on.

7. Finally, your meditation practice is preceded and followed by the study of your chosen spiritual discipline. This means you are committed to a given spiritual practice and its ensuing principles.

In general, I recommend receiving instruction from a qualified teacher or attending local group meditations. However, there are many good books with accompanying CDs that can bring the practice home to you.

Establishing a Practice

Throw everything else away if you only have time for one practice and give your time to meditation. Calm the mind and contemplate spiritual principles, and the rest of your life will come into alignment with your practice. A teacher once shared this story of a Tibetan monk who was imprisoned around the time the Dalai Lama was exiled to India. This monk spent most of his adult life in prison, undergoing abuse and torture by the Chinese government. On his release, he met up with his friend the Dalai Lama.

"Each day I was quite afraid," he said.

The Dalai Lama listened.

"I was not afraid for my life. Every day I feared that I would lose my compassion for the Chinese."

Sustain the Practice

As we sit in the North, challenges to our stamina to see the journey through to the end are likely to show up. The challenges may manifest as fears, disappointments, distractions and anxieties, or anything that attempts to separate us from ourselves, from our spiritual source, and from our equanimity. Much can come up that tries to rid us of our humanity and compassion. The imprisoned monk knew that to lose his compassion was a much greater danger than the loss of his own life. His life was something the Chinese government could take any time, but his compassion, his connection to his humanity, was something he had regardless of outside circumstance and could only be given away through his consent. Sometimes sticking to the spiritual and ethical path feels like a burden because you may be surrounded by difficulties or the success of the pilgrimage seems so far off. How many hours, days, years did this monk deal with abuse while sustaining his compassion?

We can use the fears and difficulty that arise while in the North as pointers to what attempts to hold us back, to rob us of our humanity, and to keep us stuck in the illusion of separateness. We could choose to give up. So when that which tries to separate you from truth arises, you have the golden thread of attention to bring you back to your intentions, to your spiritual principles, and to the present moment. Hold the Sacred Thread of attention long enough, and you will survive the danger. Keep your attention on your practice.

At a time of difficulty, if you choose instead to act from a place of frustration and separation, you will strengthen the sense of separation. Or if you give vent to your frustration and thrash about, thus crashing through the woods, you will strengthen the habitual response and lose sight of your intention. Instead, if you choose to, sit still, keep hold of the thread, and you will save the world. *Difficult times present you with an opportunity to keep hold of the Sacred Thread, to heal your part of the separation that threatens us all.*

Any time you are feeling disconnected, defeated, afraid, or anxious, find the thread back to the moment, and be willing to do whatever it takes to keep hold of your compassion and humanity. Just for now. Just for his moment. When we do not have a meditation practice and do not bring awareness to our initiatory intentions and agreements and then find ourselves confronted again and again by abusive prison guards and Troublemakers, we *feel captive once more of negative states, and we project these outward onto our lives and the lives of others.*

Only through various practices of cultivating attention *and* transforming our thoughts can true, lasting freedom and happiness abide.

> *By knowing how to succeed in tranquil repose,*
> *one is able to obtain careful deliberation.*
> *By knowing how to obtain careful deliberation,*
> *one is able to harvest what he really wants to pursue.*
>
> SHANTIDEVA

While walking the spiral as the sun rose, a white egret circled above me, making a spiral in the sky. While she flew in the morning mist, she would frequently disappear into the white-blue morning sky. At times she and the sky were one, at times the sky was a backdrop to her flight. After a few turns above, she landed in a nearby pond. As I walked through the spiral, my mind went in and out of the present moment and I found myself eclipsed by my thoughts. I brought myself back to my walk and my meditation.

Then I noticed how these discursive thoughts arose from where my attention also arose, and that behind these thoughts was the luminosity of my mind. I experienced these thoughts momentarily as *part of the luminous mind,* and I was struck by how these discursive and sometimes disruptive thoughts also arise from the skylike nature of mind. When I was watching these thoughts, they too would at times disappear into the skylike void of my mind, like the disappearing and reappearing egret.

This experience showed me the true nature of mind: Our thoughts are like the white egret, part of the luminous void and yet distinctive also. Ultimately, however, there is no separation, not even in the mind.

THE GREAT VEHICLE: MINDFULNESS PRACTICES

The inner shrine by which God's name is hallowed can be developed only through letting go, releasing some of the clutter inside that keeps us too busy to be silent and receptive to the "still small voice."

NEIL DOUGLAS-KLOTZ, *PRAYERS OF THE COSMOS*

In the West, we released some of the inner clutter and now can more easily hear the inner voice and experience our connection to our inherent light and to reality. As we watch the mind, we see how shallow thought is, because the movement of thought lies mostly in words and conceptualizations. But at a deeper level there is a movement in our mind that can be experienced when we no longer rely on words and concepts, when we're just *experiencing presence.*

In this state, our thoughts become like the white egret and dissolve into the vastness. At this level, we experience a strong pull we could almost call a homesickness, a longing to be home, to return to the source, to be whole. It is through being still that we can experience this connection that we long for; a connection that is always present.

✳ Experience the Moment through the Breath

Simply begin with a fifteen-minute morning meditation practice of sitting and watching the breath. If you already engage in regular morning meditation, consider adding fifteen minutes to your already existing practice. Begin with fifteen minutes until you can practice up to forty minutes each morning. The point is to establish a routine of daily meditation; the most challenging part will be actually showing up and taking the time to sit and practice.

Choose a specific time each morning for meditation. Commit to show up at this time and place even if you don't believe you have time to meditate. What you will find is that once you show up and are ready, you will make the time.

Sit like a mountain, erect but naturally alert, not rigid. Your spine should be straight and not resting fully on the back of a chair. Neither should you slouch if you are on a cushion. If you can, sit on a zafu (a meditation cushion) or stool, whatever allows for an erect spine. Relax your shoulders and take a couple of deep breaths into the belly. If you like, release a few purification breaths—"*Ahhs*"—on the exhalation. Then bring your awareness to your body, *sitting*. Bring your attention to the physical sensations of the body. Relax your awareness in the body, sitting. Notice any sensations, without judgments, that may be rising and falling in the body.

Then, as you continue to breathe naturally, choose a place in the body where you can bring your attention to the breath (either the rise and fall of the belly or, more commonly, the in-and-out of the breath through the nostrils). Let this be where your attention returns, to the breath. Let the breath breathe by itself. Make no effort, just breathe. Then rest your awareness in the physical sensation of breathing. Rest your awareness there as best you can. Rest in the sensations of your body sitting, your body breathing . . . Then give your attention to just being—have a sense of your own presence. *Just sit, breathe, and be.* Let go of thought and expectations, just rest in the breath and the body sitting, rest in the moment of being.

If you find your mind wanders off, which it routinely will, bring your attention back to the present moment through the body and your breathing. Return your awareness to the physical sensations of breath, lovingly and compassionately. Try not to add to the thinking mind by judging your practice or getting down on yourself if your mind wanders off. I spend much of my time in my sitting practice returning my attention to my breath.

Use the leash of awareness to bring you back to just sitting, just breathing, just being.

Practice compassionate action on the spot with yourself by letting go of all the mental constructions, and just rest your awareness in sitting, breathing, and being . . .

When you find yourself caught up in thoughts, label them by saying silently to yourself, "Thinking, thinking," and then return to the breath. Labeling thoughts can help you realize more fully that thought is just that— thought. Otherwise you find yourself building on these thoughts and losing your experience of calm abiding. This tames and disciplines the mind, which is a strong aspiration of the North. This also prepares us to move East, into initiation.

Compassionate response to yourself as you sit in meditation is an important part of the practice. Do your best not to become impatient and annoyed with yourself if and when you are distracted by your thoughts. You may also get upset with yourself about being upset, and on and on the judgment goes . . . until you bring compassion and equanimity to it. Then, in that instant, all the layers of thoughts and feeling in the moment dissolve. Notice that!

You generate a lot of freedom and bring forth the inherent qualities of presence, wisdom, and love when you practice sitting meditation consistently enough. Many of my meditation teachers suggest that along with a daily sitting practice, we attend at least one four-day retreat and one ten-day retreat a year. When this is not possible, maintain your daily practice and try a full day here and there to help you move through the various layers of resistance and distractions that typically arise.

What I have found is that when one is halfway through a retreat experience, or halfway through the Wheel, the big distractions arise. This is when the big deal-breaker may surface, and you find yourself sitting in the Catku of your meditation practice. *Keep sitting* and move to the other side through the realization that everything passes.

One day, as I stated my Bodhisattva vow out loud at the start of my daily walk on the spiral in my prairie, I prayed to be free of the thoughts and concerns that clouded the true nature of my mind. I looked up and saw an eagle flying from the South. It arrived above the spiral and flew in a few circles, mirroring the spiral. Such sights on my walks are a true blessing and have a calming effect on me. Just as this experience arose, two small birds appeared and began to peck and swoop at the eagle. Bothered, the eagle flew off and out of sight.

This pointed to how getting caught up in internal gossip, pondering others' faults, or being distracted by worries chases off the true nature of the mind, and we lose the bigger picture. To obtain an eagle's view, we need to tame the mind through regular meditation practice so as not to be chased about by the pecking of our thoughts.

Enlightened Eating and Karma

The most important thing in spiritual practice is food: when you eat, how you eat, why you eat.

LAMA SURYA DAS, BUDDHIST MONK

Your karma is in the refrigerator.

DONALD ALTMAN, ART OF THE INNER MEAL

One morning when completing my meditation session, I had a personal insight. I realized, *"I need to bring my relationship with food into my spiritual practice."* When we eat, how we eat, why we eat, and *what* we eat are a microcosm of the relationship we have with all things. We can choose to uplift our relationship to food, thus transforming all our relationships. When I chose to contemplate my relationship to food, meditate on how to best interact with food, then make the appropriate changes in my dietary choices and behavior, I noticed an immediate lightening-up of my mind, body, and spirit.

I admit that a conscious relationship to food is quite a challenge for me. A conscious relationship to food can feel as if we are swimming against a very strong current (family and cultural agreements). We can begin with a willingness to be slightly more aware of our body and our agreements surrounding our diet.

What are your own agreements with your body and food? What are your intentions for each meal, or when you shop for groceries? Check in with your body—how is it responding to the path you have chosen? In many ways our choices make us gods, at least over our own bodies and mind. The food we choose to eat directly impacts every aspect of ourselves. As we cleanse ourselves of poor food choices (agreements), old ideas and energy patterns also break up and dissolve. Your relationship to your body and the food that you ingest may become a central focus of your meditation practice and your efforts while in the Wheel.

At one point I decided to enter the Wheel with a new initiatory intention. Even though I had other spiritual intentions, I wanted to focus on this core one. I borrowed from Shantideva teachings for the Bodhisattva and came up with: *I attain the mind and body of awakening through the power and truth of my efforts,* because I know that the power of my efforts can awaken even the most sluggish parts of my being.

Around this time I attended a teaching at Deer Park (the nearby Tibetan Buddhist Center in Wisconsin), at which Geshe Tenzin Dorje spoke about the process of waking up. He mentioned how each of us can wake up to our true nature and become enlightened in a single lifetime. In *this* lifetime. I thought about the many people—challenged with eating disorders, addictions, illnesses, or pain—who simply want freedom from their respective conditions, and how they too aspire to a healthier, more balanced state of being.

Geshe Tenzin Dorje spoke of how (from the Buddhist perspective) the karma of this life and past lives influences how easy or difficult it is to wake up to our true nature. Some of us are like gasoline and can wake up quickly with one rapid strike of a match (or a random spark). Others are like dry wood; it takes the right conditions—not too much or too little wood, and sometimes more than one match—to get us going.

Then there is a third group that he referred to as wet wood—or, worse, wet rock. As wet rock, we find it nearly impossible to catch fire. (Having said this, I once attended a sweat lodge where a rock cracked open after water was poured on it, and a flame came out of its center. So even wet rock, given the right conditions, *can* catch fire.) Geshe Tenzin Dorje mentioned that it would be helpful to acknowledge which we are— gasoline, dry wood, or wet wood/rock—to help direct our practice and encourage patience if we are wet rock.

When it comes to spiritual initiation, we can be any of these at various times. Possibly, you are gasoline in certain areas of your life (wherever you feel creative or enthused). Other aspects of yourself may be more like wet wood, such as your relationship to food and to your own physical body. To awaken our relationship with food and our bodies, we need to create inner and outer conditions that will enable *even a wet rock to catch fire.* We do this by getting honest with ourselves about our present conditions and the challenges we may face with our eating habits and our bodies. We also need to embrace a willingness to initiate more suitable conditions for an awakened state in all areas simultaneously.

A great place to begin is a simple meditation practice wherein you eat mindfully, taking the time to chew at least twenty-five times before swallowing. Ingest one small mouthful of food at a time, and rest your utensil on the table between bites. You too may set an intention at some point to encourage a more conscious relationship with your body and diet. I also suggest that you begin your morning meal by reading a passage from Donald Altman's daily meditation book, *Meal by Meal,* to enjoy a more enlightened meal and to have more practices for conscious eating.

Trekcho: *Seeing through the Appearance of Things*

Trekcho means cutting through delusion with fierce, direct thoroughness. Delusion is cut through, and the primordial purity and natural simplicity of the nature of mind is laid out.

SOGYAL RINPOCHE, THE TIBETAN BOOK
OF LIVING AND DYING

Many psychological and spiritual practices offer ways to break through the delusions made by our projections and conceptualizations (beliefs and agreements) so that we can experience reality. Delusions are those persistent beliefs and agreements that are put out by our pain stories (our false self). The practices throughout the Wheel facilitate such personal breakthroughs. Entering the familiarity of oneness or impermanence, even if for just a moment, gives you a foundation of authenticity so that you can release your pain agreements. You then have more trust in your practice because you have some personal understanding of reality. The reason meditation teachers have you sit with all that arises, is so that you can move through the duality of "me and other"—the delusion of separation—to experience oneness. But when we are busy and caught up in outer distractions or inner habitual states, we miss the opportunity to be familiar with reality—with the true nature of mind and of life.

A gateway to reality is the realization of impermanence. My first Vipassana (insight meditation) teacher, Shinzen Young, challenged us to find *one thing* that was permanent and unchanging in our lives. Vipassana is translated as "insight," or "seeing clearly." It is the direct observation of physical (breath/body sensations) and mental objects (mantras/yantras) in all aspects of impermanence (watching the breath come and go, for example). This also points to how nothing exists on its own independently; everything is connected and dependent (dependent arising). The out-breath is dependent on the in-breath as well as the body breathing, for example. Everything is constantly in flux, and everything is interdependent. Nothing arises without conditions.

Much of Shinzen Young's instructions developed ways for us to penetrate through our grasping and aversions and sit in a state of impermanence. As do many Buddhist teachers, he demonstrated how a personal understanding of the impermanent nature of things helps us release our grasping, habitual mind-set. I suggest that if you haven't already done so, you should look for something, anything, that is permanent and therefore nonchanging. Then in your own realization of impermanence, take the time to journal or contemplate the interdependence of all things. Choose any object and notice all that is involved for it to be in existence. Notice how everything is transient and exists dependent on many other objects. A wonderful teaching on this topic of meditation is the book *How to See Yourself As You Really Are* by the Dalai Lama.

Many meditation practices encourage one to meditate on impermanence or death. Because everything is changing—coming or going, expanding or contracting—being attached to any one thing can cause us a great deal of unnecessary suffering. Several meditation teachers and pain clinics teach Vipassana and mindfulness meditation practices to those in chronic pain, helping them experience the impermanence of pain as a way to alleviate its grip. Having the skillful means to let go of grasping after things that are impermanent is another way to prepare ourselves for initiation.

Apocalypse
does not point to a fiery Armageddon,
but to our ignorance and complacency
coming to an end.

JOSEPH CAMPBELL,
THE JOSEPH CAMPBELL COMPANION

Trekcho is part of the practice of Dzogchen. Dzogchen is considered the primordial (essential) state that is at the heart of all spiritual paths. It is the practice of being fully and immediately present. As is true of all of the practices discussed in this book, Dzogchen doesn't require you to convert to Buddhism or any other doctrine. Furthermore, Dzogchen shows up in most spiritual practices but by a different name. Practices of "atonement" (at-one-ment) are examples of Dzogchen. Any practice that allows you to experience the "now," immediate presence, is Dzogchen.

This practice emphasizes that because we are all Buddhas by nature, full awakening is possible within this lifetime. It is the intention of the Wheel to provide you with a continual template creating the conditions for you to become fully initiated, or even fully awake in this lifetime. I asked a friend what practice best helps her to be fully and immediately present. She told me it was the Sufi practice called Sipping in the Light. In this practice, you hold a soft focus while sitting outside and imagining that your eyes are sipping in the natural light. There are many wonderful books that teach such practices. Ideally, you will find a practice that resonates with your chosen spiritual path.

A good instructor of meditation is essential for a successful meditation practice of any kind. Lama Surya Das's book and CD, *Natural Radiance,* bring the Dzogchen practices to you. Neil Douglas-Klotz, in his book *Prayers of the Cosmos* provides many meditations to help you "sip in the light" and to become fully present. Such practices as Dzogchen and various initiatory practices, once only given to the few, are now offered to the many. We cannot have so many people living unconsciously, so habitually, on the earth and expect her, or us, to survive.

We cannot keep living from our past. We must develop a strong means to be fully present now. After all, it is in the here and now that it all happens. It is through the raising of our consciousness and living a more initiated lifestyle that we are likely to last and to thrive. And, borrowing from a Buddhist term, making the "short path" (to an awakened life) more accessible is necessary at this point in our evolution. The more of us that awaken to our natural state, the more of us that release our imprisoned light, the better all of us, and our planet, will be.

※ Open Your Eyes!

Here is a simple practice of Trekcho meditation borrowed from several Dzogchen teachings. This meditation helps us break through the veil of delusions that cloud the mind. After at least fifteen minutes of your basic sitting practice (discussed earlier), open your eyes. Hold a soft and natural gaze that is lowered; you should not be looking out at anything specifically. Opening your eyes and lowering your gaze in this manner can help pacify thoughts (and keep you awake if you are sleepy). (This is more clearly explained in Dzogchen commentaries, where we are told that there is a physical connection between the nerves of the eyes and the channel of the heart. The channel that goes from the heart to the eyes is called the *crystal kati*.) Working with our vision (our view) in this technique helps us break through conceptualizations (delusions) and "see" reality through our eyes, but also with the heart.

With open eyes, open self, open heart and mind, sit and look out into the world. Imagine opening everything up while holding a soft focus outward, not resting your gaze on any one thing in particular. Allow and open, just *looking, seeing,* and then *letting go.* Experience freedom and liberation through looking out, then seeing (connecting with), then letting go . . . not getting hooked by arising thoughts, perceptions, or emotions.

This helps you be aware of the skylike nature of the mind, as the story of the egret showed. Your thoughts are just like the egret going in and out of the luminous sky, becoming part of the sky. Practice letting everything arise in the mind too, thoughts and perceptions, then let it all go: *thinking, awareness, letting go.* When emotions arise, use the same practice: *notice* the emotional state, bring *awareness* to it, then *let it go,* moving on, gazing out, and resting in the luminosity of it all.

> Looking out, seeing (making conscious contact), letting go.
> Listening, hearing, letting go.
> Thinking, awareness to the thought, letting go.
> Feeling, connection to the emotion, letting go.

※

For further reading I recommend Sogyal Rinpoche's classic, *The Tibetan Book of Living and Dying,* as well as *Dzogchen: The Heart Essence of the Great Perfection,* by the Dalai Lama.

Here are two more meditation practices that will help you align with the rhythms of nature and the luminous mind.

❋ The Dawn of Creation Meditation

This exercise is best done outside. Face the East about fifteen minutes before the sun rises. As it rises, breathe in through your nose and out through your mouth. Breathe in the light and power of the rising sun and all the potential that it holds. As the sun rises, raise your hands and face your palms out toward the sun, as if to catch its energy. Keep raising your hands slowly until they are above your head.

You are taking in all that the sun represents—energy, light, power, the new day, beginnings, and life. You are open to the moment of creation, the dawn. The new day fills you up with all its natural potential. Keep breathing. Breathe in the light.

This would be a wonderful morning ritual to help you get in sync with the rhythms of the Earth. Natural sunlight feeds the mind, body, and soul. The study of photoperiodism reveals how animal cycles are dictated by day length and by the pattern of the sun. This dynamic can help bring us into balance with our own natural beat. Too much artificial light makes us artificial. Along with this morning ritual, at least fifteen minutes of sunlight during the day would be greatly beneficial to your well-being.

❋ Sky Gazing Meditation

This is also best done outside but can be done as part of your morning sitting meditation practice. (It is borrowed from the Buddhist practice of Dzogchen, but similar practices are also found in yogic and Sufi practices.)

Take a few moments to still the mind. Stand gazing up at the sky. Take in four deep breaths, inhaling through the nose and exhaling through the mouth. On the exhalation, make the sound *Ahhh.*

Then, after the fourth *Ahhh* breath, simply gaze up at the sky and rest in the vastness of the space and sky. On your exhale let go, releasing the stress and concerns in your mind and body. Notice how you too are part of this vast blue spaciousness and how your mind contains this skylike quality. Breathe and relax, looking out and blending your mind and view with the vast spaciousness. You are unifying with the vastness of life, gazing out with a soft focus. Don't look for anything, simply gaze out and be open. You become part of the vastness; you are mingling with it, the source, the luminous sky. Your being and the energy of the vast sky are naturally one.

This meditation helps you loosen up your attachment to objects and projections. Let go and relax into the vastness, without any expectations of what should or should not happen. Let everything pass. At some point, experience stepping more into the sacredness of now and its void. Relax into the void, the spaciousness, into the state of just being.

Give yourself five to fifteen minutes to practice this meditation.

POST-MEDITATION: CULTIVATE ATTENTION IN THE WORLD

When in post-meditation, we can apply similar practices of attention and insight to bring more sanity and peace to our day-to-day existence. Whenever there is disturbance, the sanest action in most cases will be to leave things as they are—*look, connect, and let go*. This is not to say that we shouldn't take action and intervene when we see someone suffering. We should. But we should do it from a place of mindfulness, holding an attentiveness to what really requires our help.

First, bring your attention to what is going on in the moment (rather than mixing in assumptions and a pain story), and then decide how to respond. Use the bridle of mindfulness to help you pay attention to all that is going on, to fully show up and listen. What we find is that in many cases the response is to not act. We find that paying attention and fully engaging in the moment is quite enough. We become less and less reactive and more and more peaceful with our lives and their circumstances. As we do all these practices, we come to realize more and more how we are not our experiences, and we find a new freedom in this awareness.

Now go practice.

THE FOURTEENTH DALAI LAMA
AFTER A WEEK OF TEACHINGS,
MADISON, WISCONSIN, JULY 2008

As we put into practice the exercises in the Wheel, we are also disciplining the mind. When we take our next step by moving into the East, we will be taking our more disciplined minds to the very threshold of initiation. A disciplined mind, through the cultivation of attention, is a mind that *is ready* to have great wisdom and purpose bestowed upon it.

POINTERS FOR READINESS

- Meditate daily.
- Look out, notice.
- Let go.
- Be in nature.
- Know your intention.
- Breathe.
- Listen now.
- Watch the sun rise.
- Let go of the pain story.
- Find the Truth in your practice.
- Cultivate attention.
- Listen to the Great Conversation.
- Know what you're in agreement with.
- Come home to the present moment.
- Appreciate the Troublemaker.
- Be the meaning-maker.
- Forgive/let go/move on.
- Contemplate impermanence.
- Remember we belong to each other.
- Trust and take the next step.

7

ENTERING THE EAST

Crossing the Threshold

The sacred world is connected with East, because there are always possibilities of vision in this world. East represents the dawn of wakefulness, the horizon of human consciousness where vision is constantly arising.

CHÖGYAM TRUNGPA,
SHAMBHALA: THE SACRED PATH OF THE WARRIOR

The ultimate goal of the pilgrim to Pemako is Yangsang Né, the paradise of Dorje Pagmo's innermost heart. According to Padmasambhava's prophecies, a future generation to inhabit the earth will emerge from this most sequestered of valleys—born again from the secret lotus of this "mother of all Buddhas." For some Yangsang is an Elysian haven where fruits and self-sowing crops ensure freedom from toil, and life-giving waters confer longevity and everlasting health. For others, Yangsang refers to the innermost reaches of the human heart, a field of energy without boundary or end that certain environments help reveal.

IAN BAKER, THE HEART OF THE WORLD

Plants and animals follow nature's way; no choice is necessary. Given the right conditions, it is inevitable that the acorn becomes an oak. It is just as inevitable that our true nature will be revealed. We have only to continue to create the right conditions (or certain environments, as Ian Baker mentions above).

Inevitably, it is our *choices* that allow us to access "the innermost reaches of the human heart," releasing our inner light as we continue our spiritual evolution. (The choosing of our intentions over habits, the choosing of positive agreements over negative ones.) *Correct choices generate the right conditions for initiation.* And it is our sprtual principles that we name while entering the East that always give us the best options to choose from in any given situation or challenge. Our light remains imprisoned until our principled choices crack through more layers of the false self. To enter the East is to enter the direction of personal vision and revelation where, through our trials, we move through the threshold. Courage to live a principled life will give us the mometum that will break through any remaining fear and resistance. It is the visions we hold of our selves and the world that we carry across the threshold into the new paradigm.

PRINCIPLES OF A SPIRITUAL PRACTITIONER: THE ROOT SYSTEM OF THE AUTHENTIC SELF

Nothing can bring you peace but yourself. Nothing can bring you peace but the triumph of principles.

RALPH WALDO EMERSON, SOURCE UNKNOWN

Principles help us continue to break hindering patterns and live a truly inspired life. When a habit arises and we want to change it, a "destiny decision" is being presented to us (as Joseph Campbell would say). We can decide to do the habitual thing or call forth our inherent wisdom through the application of our principles. Principles are like oars in a boat or reins on a horse; they help move us in the right direction. Principles that are in alignment with our spiritual practices, and therefore our intentions, are capable of transforming our lives "on the spot."

A principled life is led by one who chooses to bring forth what is latent in the seed. When participants go through the Wheel's yearlong Initiation Course, by the time they enter the East, they realize a need for core principles—ones that are accessible and reliable in any circumstance. Spiritual initiation cannot truly take place without committing to a set of personal, core principles. We begin to ask ourselves, *How are we going to be in the world once we have gone through spiritual initiation?*

Understand that principles give you a way to live in the world and a way to fulfill your spiritual intentions, your destiny. Principles are a means for your spiritual evolution. When you encounter difficulty, you don't have to engage with the problem or the drama. Neither do you have to get caught up in your perception of the situation. Rather, bring forth a principle and apply it. Even those times when you may forget your principles or cannot bring one to mind, your curiosity about which principle to employ may help you with the particular predicament you find yourself in. This will enlighten your perceptions and your actions. It's hard to be personally caught up in a difficulty or a drama when you focus instead on the compassionate action you could take. Your curiosity alone will help you be objective about the situation and ethically find your way through it.

Part of your journey as you go through the Wheel for the first time will be to choose some root principles (if you don't have any), ones that you agree to develop for the rest of your life. These are chosen now while entering the East, while you fully comprehend what it means to live an initiated life. This is a core practice of any spiritual pilgrimage and initiate—to practice our principles in order to benefit others. Once your core principles are established, consecutive trips through the Wheel are opportunities to apply them more vigorously and to discern which particular ones to use in any given situation. Remember my story about entering the North (page 147). I employed several of my Lojong principles from the Mahayana tradition the moment the difficulty arose, and they helped me through the problem successfully.

While investigating principles from diverse traditions and practices,

I found that they all have common elements. I present them here to help you design or claim your own root principles now.

- Authentic principles offer an altruistic and ethical means to interact in the world.
- Authentic principles are simple to understand and can be used on the spot.
- A natural process of recapitulation is activated when using a principle: You get energy back that was lost to negative agreements and bring forth your inherent wisdom and goodness.
- You take 100 percent personal responsibility for your life and use your principles to help you do so.
- Authentic principles reflect and support the reality that everything in life is dependent upon everything else (dependent arising). Therefore your principles positively affect others too.
- Authentic principles provide you with means to be less self-absorbed.
- Authentic principles help you realize the preciousness of life and teach you not to waste it. I watched a wonderful docudrama, *The Cave of the Yellow Dog,* that took place in Mongolia. It depicted nomadic life in this century. An elder was teaching a young child how precious life is. She gave the child a needle and some rice, then asked the child to drop a kernel of rice on top of the needle. After many attempts, the child was unsuccessful. The elder then said, "This is how easy it is to be born as a human being." This life is certainly a rare opportunity. Don't waste it!
- Authentic principles allow you to release the habitual patterns and transform the mind.
- Authentic principles strengthen your trust in yourself and others because they bring out the best in you.
- Authentic principles instill and strengthen your patience and perseverance on the ethical path.
- Authentic principles help develop positive karma and release negative karma due to past choices.

- Authentic principles help you deal with negative and habitual emotional states without getting hooked by them.
- Authentic principles bring forth equanimity.
- Authentic principles are life-enhancing agreements that sustain and promote your intentions.
- Authentic principles ultimately uplift your life and bring you lasting happiness.
- Authentic principles are in alignment with spiritual tradition and wisdom that has been tried and tested throughout the centuries. They have some roots in our spiritual heritage. Sacred texts can be referred to for insight when applying your principles.
- Authentic principles will transform habitual thought patterns, clearing the way for your true nature. All principles should have the capacity to transform the mind, bringing it into a more enhanced state of awakening.

My core principles are those found within the Mahayana tradition of Buddhism, the Lojong teachings. The Lojong teachings offer the practitioner seven points that have within them fifty-nine principles. Each principle (often referred to as a slogan) gives us the ability to completely transform our attitude overall as well as on the spot. Fifty-nine may sound like a lot, too many to be truly accessible. I have memorized approximately a dozen of them and work with these twelve on a regular basis. I continue to study the others and apply them. You can choose the entire fifty-nine teachings or simply chose a few to be your core principles. I find that *The Four Agreements* by Don Miguel Ruiz is a wonderfully condensed version of the Lojong teachings. The Four Agreements would be great to adopt as one's personal principles.

The Four Agreements are:

- Be impeccable with your word.
- Don't take anything personally.
- Don't make assumptions.
- Do your best.

Our spiritual principles, whether they come from the Toltec, the Buddhist, or some other spiritual tradition, are a strong expression of what we are in agreement with. When I practice a principle, I am stating to the world and to myself what I am in agreement with and what I am not in agreement with.

After you have selected your core principles, a great way to complement your practice is to choose texts or books that help you understand your principles more fully. I consider texts as maps that help keep us on the best path to the fulfillment of our intentions and principles. We are on our own but not alone—many have gone before us and applied such principles as the Four Agreements or the Lojong slogans.

Here are fourteen principles taken from the Lojong teachings for you to consider. They may become your core principles or may simply be used as guideposts while you set about choosing your own.

Train in the Preliminaries

These are described as the four reminders. I like to refer to them as the *four humbling truths*. In our daily life we:

1. Remember the preciousness of having a human life. We value everyone's life, including our own.
2. Remember impermanence and that life ends; death comes to us all. Why waste a moment?
3. Remember that whatever we do, good or bad, has a result. We are continually experiencing the results of previous choices and actions. Your life is your path.
4. Remember that self-absorption or always putting yourself before others and getting caught up in how others perceive you causes more attachment and more suffering. Always focusing on getting what you want and avoiding what you don't want won't bring lasting happiness. Your false self needs constant positive reinforcement or praise for your choices; your true nature does not rely on such ephemeral tributes.

Abandon Any Hope of Fruition

For me this means, *want what you have*. One of the deepest habitual patterns is based on our feelings of unworthiness, of not having or being enough, which makes us focus on the outcome of our efforts rather than the process. We give too much attention to what we are getting out of something rather than what we are putting into it. Give up any hope of being special or reaping personal rewards from your efforts. Focus instead on the present moment and all that is part of it. *Appreciate what you have* and you will feel the abundance of your life. In addition, this principle keeps you safe from spiritual and psychological scams that lure you in with promises of what's to come (because they have something you want).

Don't Act with a Twist

A twist is a hidden agenda that will benefit ourselves somehow. It protects our egoic, false self. A teacher of mine used to call acting with a twist the "Nice game." One acts nice to get what they want, not to benefit someone—for example, when we put down or belittle someone while making ourselves look noble and good.

So often we are encouraged to react and prove ourselves. In particular, I have noticed that e-mail communication frequently invites us to act quickly and impulsively and often with a twist. When I must communicate with e-mail, I do my best to slow down, consider what I have to say, and check to see if there is some twist that I've unwittingly embedded in the message. If not, I send out the e-mail. Also, I am reminded of the fact that I am either creating good karma by my actions, or negative karma. If I act with a twist, it is sure to boomerang back at me in the future.

Don't Be So Predictable

Don't always move toward what you favor and away from what you are uncomfortable with. This is a good reminder of how not to be so habitual—be willing to challenge your routine response to life's circumstances. Our habitual responses are so often based on assumptions. (Remember the Toltec agreement about not making assumptions.)

For me, this also means not planning or contriving a response when I have difficulty with others. Instead, allow some time to pass, which will enable a possible resolution and perhaps some surprises to unfold. Waiting opens us more fully to the possibilities inherent in a situation rather than mistakenly relying on assumptions and projections. This is also about not staying angry. Don't be so predictable as to hold a grudge against someone. Find a way to let it go.

Transform All Mishaps into the Path of Bodhi

Bodhi means "awake," and the word reminds us to use all the unwanted and unfavorable circumstances of our lives as the actual material of initiation and awakening. Nothing on our path is exempt. Everything can be used as a catalyst to help us to practice our spiritual principles and live by our intentions. This is key to getting ready for our return back to the family and community from our time in the woods (the Wheel). Our boon includes our personal principles, and this one certainly helps transform the world around us.

Always Maintain a Joyful Mind

We can remain joyful because we know every situation can be used to open our hearts even more, and to discipline and transform our minds. I love this because then nothing can take us away from our principles and our ethical path. This encourages us to be like the monk who kept his compassion while in the Chinese prison. If we see the Troublemakers as our greatest teachers, we are grateful to them. Everything can bring us joy. This is wonderful! We don't go on a spiritual pilgrimage expecting it to be like a ride on a cruise ship. As a writer, I find too that challenges I meet on my path can be used in my work, both fiction and nonfiction. This helps create a joyful mind because it is all material, all grist for the mill of the spiritual traveler or writer.

If You Can Practice When Distracted, You Are Well Trained

A difficult and challenging time must be taken as an opportunity to express in the outer world our highest inner principles.

BRIAN WALKER BROWNE, HEXAGRAM 26,
THE I CHING OR BOOK OF CHANGES

This is about cultivating attention even amid distractions, much like what Black Elk means when he speaks of "closing the door on distractions." This points to how we can practice awareness and live by our intentions even when surrounded by distractions. This resonates with the twenty-sixth hexagram in the I Ching, which I refer to in my book *I Ching for Teens* as "Practice Under Fire." Ultimately, times full of distractions are a great opportunity to develop our spiritual efforts. Life ultimately tests our abilities to hold on to our intentions and principles.

Don't Bring Things to a Painful Point

Don't humiliate other people or yourself. This can be a challenge when the outside drama is intense and feels personal. The Toltec principle of "not taking things personally" helps with this. If we don't take things personally, we are less likely to add to the drama and pain of the situation. Make friends with all your painful feelings, instead of creating a crisis on the outside. Make friends with yourself, and let the drama go. Don't build on angry feelings. Don't carry things to a point of regret.

Don't Be Happy about Someone Else's Misfortune

Don't be happy that another person or someone who has caused you pain is going through difficult times themselves. Don't point out how others are failing. Don't use someone else's pain to make yourself feel better. I once heard this phrased as, "Don't step on other's backs to prop yourself up."

Don't Ponder Others' Faults/Don't Carry Another's Shadow

Don't carry another person's shadow. Don't waste your precious time thinking about another's faults or wrongdoings. For me this also means not to compare ourselves with others. When we do this, we tend to make ourselves better or worse, creating an unnecessary separation between the other person or persons and ourselves.

What you are likely noticing by now is that principles are pointers to what we are in agreement with and what we are not in agreement with. I often frame my principles in terms of what I am in agreement with ("I agree to practice even when distracted"), or what I am not in agreement with ("I don't agree to ponder others' faults").

Be Grateful to Everyone

We can be grateful to everyone, particularly our Troublemakers, because, as we know, they show us where we are caught up in our pain stories. That reminds me of a Zen story about something that took place when the Japanese were overrunning Korea in the 1930s. Japanese soldiers entered a Korean Zen monastery and found most of the monks gone. But the abbot remained, sitting like an iron lotus in the zendo. The officer in charge drew his sword, walked up to the abbot, and said, "I could run you through without blinking an eye!" The abbot roared back, "I can be run through without blinking an eye!" The soldiers left the abbot alone.

I imagine that really happened. Our principles are often our best protection when we are in upsetting situations, as this story points out.

Of the Two Witnesses, You Decide

Trust yourself. You know what you need. You know how well you are doing. *You decide.* You decide where to put your attention and what to agree to. You know where you are tripping up and what you need to work on. This helps you when you are confronted with conflicting views, or when you are trying to discern truth from various versions given to you. You decide. This is a reminder too that you are the meaning-maker.

Don't Malign Others

Don't gossip about others. Don't listen to gossip, and don't add to it. Even in subtle ways, don't gossip or put others down. Gossip can be a way to try to feel good at someone else's expense or to falsely make a connection with someone. Ask yourself if you trust someone who gossips about others.

Be mindful of how you might be in agreement with culturally acceptable means of gossiping (office chitchat, Internet chat rooms, reading splashy magazines full of celebrity stories, etc.). One of my teachers believed this practice to be particularly important because it directly impacts one's heart.

Change Your Attitude, but Remain Natural

All this mind training is about changing your response to circumstances in your life and about befriending yourself. This change in attitude (beliefs and agreements) doesn't happen overnight; it happens gradually. Be patient and kind to yourself as you go through the transformation of your mind and life. Let it be a part of your daily way of life. Don't indulge in posturing about your efforts; let them be natural and organic.

Changing one's attitude also means not getting dramatic and showing off your spiritual experiences. Remain natural, as though they're no big deal. Enjoy the moment or the experience, and then move on.

> *Instead of always being caught up in a prison of self-absorption, look out and express gentleness to all things. Then just relax.*
>
> PEMA CHÖDRÖN,
> COMMENTARY ON THIS LOJONG PRINCIPLE,*
> CARD 24 FROM *THE COMPASSION BOX*

Don't Misinterpret

"Don't misinterpret" is ostensibly a simple slogan, but there is more to it. This is true of all spiritual principles, such as the Four Agreements, or the principles of Tao Shiatzu, or the Ten Commandments. They may be pithy one-liners that *point* to a principle, such as, "Don't make assumptions," "Don't covet your neighbor's wife," but there is more text to study to fully understand and carry them out.

For me, the "Don't misinterpret" principle is about not misinterpreting

---

*For more on these and other Lojong principles, refer to Pema Chödrön's book, CD, and card deck: *The Compassion Box: Powerful Practices from the Buddhist Tradition for Cultivating Wisdom, Fearlessness, and Compassion.*

spiritual teachings. Be careful *not to assume* what a teaching means. Find out through an established teacher, read and study the text, and continue to learn more and more about a teaching and its meaning. It is not uncommon for people to take a spiritual teaching and twist it around to meet some self-absorbed posturing rather than use it to help them awaken (or in the case of some religious or cult leaders, use it to manipulate others).

Another way to misinterpret principles is to apply them only when it benefits you—for example, "I won't make assumptions about those who don't make assumptions about me." The Lojong teachings refer to six specific teachings that might typically be misinterpreted, and they all get down to how our misinterpretations are a means to benefit ourselves and promote more self-absorption rather than helping others. A great resource for the Lojong principles is Traleg Kyabgon's book *The Practice of Lojong: Cultivating Compassion through Training the Mind.*

These Lojong principles are thousands of years old. They are attributed to the great Indian Buddhist teacher Atisha Dipankara Shrijnana, who was born in 982 CE. Atisha studied and practiced under a renowned teacher, Dharmakirti. For a long time, these slogans (first called the Atisha slogans) were kept secret and revealed only to select disciples. They have since been transmitted in several forms (by various adept teachers), and for the last couple of centuries they have been available to us. These and other established principles can be relied upon to guide us. Think of it! Humanity has been using principles such as these to awaken and to behave ethically for centuries. Jesus the Christ was certainly an example of someone who lived by a set of ethical principles, and in the end he too experienced initiation (symbolically represented by his dying on the cross and being resurrected).

You can start with the Lojong principles or identify some others from your own spiritual practice. Another option is to identify principles borrowed from your life experiences and encounters with spiritual truths, as Lisa does below. Choosing your own principles instead of borrowing them directly from a particular tradition can lend itself to a more personal spiritual initiation, as it is an expression of trust in one's own inherent wisdom. However, make sure that your principles meet the criteria given in the template for spiritual principles on page 197.

Lisa's Twelve Root Principles

IN MY 2007 INITIATION CIRCLE, when Julie asked us to determine our principles, I began to wonder if I even had any. I'd already read several of the books she'd been referring to, including The Four Agreements. *I agreed with the principles offered as examples in the initiation circle but didn't really think of them as my principles. Perhaps I had not lived with them long enough. Perhaps that didn't matter.*

When I reflected on what my principles might be, I realized that I had carried them inside me for a long time, and if I had to describe how they had come to me, I would say only that they were examples from my life that had "stuck." They were fundamentals modeled by my parents while I was growing up; constructs from my ballet teacher thirty years ago; observations I made a few years later on the way my Tai Chi instructor conveyed himself; and recognition for how I had sustained myself during some difficult times this past decade. Acknowledging all this, it was easy to list my principles and then share them with my initiation circle.

A year after I had completed the initiation course, when Julie asked me to write out an example of how I have applied each principle, I had a moment of "Oh, no! Do I really try to live by these principles?" And fortunately, an acknowledgment from my heart told me that the answer was yes, I do!

- *"My whole body is my opening" Julie taught me this, and I adopted it first as my personal initiation intention in the initiation course and used it later as a core principle. I must never forget it, for it engages me to offer and receive from my entire rainbow body rather than from my ego-constricted mind.*

  An example of how this principle works came to me early on in my initiation course. I went into the course intending to use the Wheel to help me write and publish my book. I learned immediately that the initiation course was about much bigger things . . . like the concept that God is infinitely larger than the universe and yet able to fit inside your heart. Coming into the circle each week, I was often nervous and reserved, hoping I could squeak through the evening unnoticed. On the evening of our fifth circle, Julie sang us a song about how we were "opening up in sweet surrender to the luminous love light of the One." She then asked us to sing it . . . but not as a group. We were invited to step alone into the middle of our circle and sing it solo, then remain there while the rest of the group mirrored it back. It was one of the few times throughout the initiation year where I volunteered right away, because I knew that if I waited, my nervousness would build. I sang the song, listened to the others sing it back, then quickly took my place in the circle.

At the end of the evening, Julie gave us the ensuing week's intentions, adding one for each of us that was tailored toward our personal initiation intention. My personal initiation intention was, "My Whole Body Is My Opening." To me she said, "Write a song and plan to sing it for us." She added that she'd thought the solo singing would have been difficult for me. I said nothing. I just wrote the intention down with all the others she'd given us and went home. To bed.

I was so dismayed. And pissed. To sing someone else's song solo had been hard enough, and now she wanted me to write and sing a new song! I was awake and fretting all night long, perplexed that it was taking me so long to write my book, and now she wanted me to write and sing a song. I'd never ever said I wanted to be a songwriter. I cried and cried, scheming the entire night to find a way out of this dreaded assignment. However, in addition to this intention, Julie also reminded us not to complain about things and not to give in to resistance. If in agreement, she said, follow through. So I was doomed.

But as another teacher had taught me, "The ego builds a door and the soul says, 'Come.'"

The following morning, frayed and distraught, my skin soaked with tears, I rose and went to my meditation room. I faced the southwest, the direction of Julie's home relative to mine. I closed my eyes and prayed and implored her to let me off the hook. I begged and pleaded. You could hardly have called it meditation. And while I was imploring, a most magical thing happened. The words and melody of a song came cascading from within me on an "upper class rapids" of tears. It was a

song for my sister Pam, who had been killed in a multiple-vehicle colli-
sion the previous year. I thought it a remarkable song, complete with a
message that it's okay to let our tears flow. I honestly did not think that
I could have composed it. But I did.

The next week, with eyes closed (stillness can be found in darkness),
I sang the song for my initiation circle. Sniffles and the rasping sound of
Kleenex being pulled from boxes suggested to me that the song's magic
was underway. This whole songwriting phenomenon reminded me of
the Brothers Grimm fairy tale of the Shoemaker and the Elves, where
my mind was the shoemaker . . . worried, perplexed, and weary . . .
while my heart and soul (my true nature) were the elves . . . loving and
capable . . . composing the very song I needed. My whole body was
indeed my opening.

- "I am the breath of God." *And so are you . . . and you . . . and*
  you . . . and you . . . I learned this from the God in my heart. I heal
  myself with the breath of God. Breathing into the aches and pains of
  body and life does wonders for healing. All my gaps and compromised
  regions need oxygen; breathing is the vehicle for wondrous results of
  wellness. My ballet instructor elaborated on this principle. "As long as
  you keep breathing, you can do anything," she told me, and she was oh,
  so right.

- "The Holy One is discovering itself in me." *I learned this prin-*
  ciple from my Sufi studies and Hazrat Inayat Khan. It feels tantalizingly
  good to know this. Playful, mischievous, loving, and True. I imagine the
  Holy One as an artist inside me, with the ability to create me wherever
  I go, whatever I do, and however I feel.

- "Keep your standing side still." *My ballet teacher was a gold mine*
  for concepts that were important in ballet, and I embraced them as
  principles for my life as well. In times of adversity, I vow to keep my
  standing side (the part of my body in repose) still and my heart wide
  open. When I am angry or disappointed, afraid, or anxious, I keep my
  standing side still. Whichever side of me is the strongest and most loving

and self-assured, this is the side I keep still. With my standing side still comes the passage of time and the weakening of whatever tried to throw me off balance. "Hold your seat," says my standing side. Patience. Patience.

- "Come down like a cat's paw" and "Let the weight of your body carry you down." These have to do with treading lightly and with being grounded, even when the Grand Puppeteer—my mind—tries to separate me from my divinity. Alone in a sweat lodge one night, I realized that "Come down like a cat's paw" is not just the manner in which I need to tread upon the earth but also the manner in which I need to tread upon myself. It means I need to let myself down slowly when my mind tells me I've behaved imperfectly by screwing up. It means I need to let myself down slowly when I have not lived up to my own expectations or those of another. Letting the weight of my own body carry me down (and not the weight of others) is soft, subtle, and natural, with nothing forced or strained.

  My Tai Chi instructor could move his body with molasses-like grace. "Inspiration," he said, "comes from within." If he didn't have that inspiration, he could not move that way. He worked always to let his inspiration be bigger than his resistance, and his body responded with remarkable grace. "Be an iron rod wrapped in cotton," he encouraged. He was both strong and yielding, and he could not be toppled in duelistic Tai Chi challenges.

- "Don't go away mad." My father never let us go away mad. He encouraged the entire family to discuss and hash out all difficulties and disagreements as they arose. This always worked. And still he whispers those words to me from his place in the spirit realm. "It doesn't make sense to be mad," he says. "The heart doesn't want to be mad. It wants instead to be glad." Three members of my birth family have died. Each one left quickly with no chance to say good-bye. My brother died suddenly at the age of forty-two of heart failure. A month prior to my brother's death, my younger sister, aged forty-six, told me that she was upset with the decisions I was making *with my life. Our brother's death allowed Pam to open to a place of love with me. We had loving conversations with one another. We had both learned that life is unpredictable, and it can be taken from us at any time. My brother's death was a gift in that it opened her love, so that when she died three days later en route home for his funeral, she was not angry with me. Don't go away mad.*

- *"There are no 'shoulds.'"* This was another principle Dad proffered. *My father encouraged us to follow our own truths and set our own intentions and standards, to evaluate those put forth by others and come to our own conclusions based on what feels right in our hearts. The word* should *never passes my lips without my questioning its validity.*

- *"This above all, to thine own self be true."* I got this one from *my mother, who got it from Shakespeare. I heard these words from her during my college days—a time in my life when she let me know that I would always have the means to make the right choices by looking into my heart and my truth.*

- *"Whatever goes around comes around."* This one also came from *my mother, and it taught me to accept responsibility for the choices I make. All of them. I am 100 percent responsible for my choices.*

I am grateful for my principles. They help me in difficult times, yet they are also fun, often magical, and I love how they came to me. And not only do I rely on them, I know that they rely on me. For if I fail to use them, then they will wither away, just like any of my other gifts.

Strong in our principles, we are able to see out into the world in a sacred way.

And I saw that the sacred hoop of my people was one of many hoops that made one circle, wide as daylight and as starlight, and in the center grew one mighty flowering tree to shelter all the children of one mother and one father. And I saw that it was holy."

BLACK ELK, "THE GREAT VISION," IN *BLACK ELK SPEAKS*

VISION QUESTING: PILGRIMAGE TO THE INNER REALMS OF THE SACRED MOUNTAIN

For Tibetans the key to pilgrimage is danang, the sacred vision that transfigures the environment into a pure realm of enlightened energies. Even the most miserable circumstances invite this shift in perception. . . . The ideal pilgrimage is not simply to visit sacred sites but to facilitate an inner transformation at places that challenge conventional ways of seeing. In this sense, the more destabilizing the surroundings the better.

IAN BAKER, *THE HEART OF THE WORLD*

Ian Baker points to how the supreme pilgrimage relies on an "inner transformation at places that challenge conventional ways of seeing." To have a sacred vision "that transfigures the environment into a pure realm of enlightened energies," we too must be able to "see in a sacred manner," as Black Elk does in *Black Elk Speaks*. How we look out on the world will determine what we witness and experience. In Black Elk's case, he first had to see *himself* on the central mountain before he could have his vision of the sacred way of the world. We too have to shift our ways of seeing so that we can actually see our own sacred vision of the world. Your movement through the Wheel has facilitated the inner transformation for seeing your own vision—a vision that has called to you since birth.

Sometimes the best way to wake up to our potentialities in the East is to call forth a vision. Visions are recounted in Black Elk's "The Great Vision" (in *Black Elk Speaks*), in Kahil Gibran's *The Prophet,* and throughout the Bible and Koran. Padmasambhava and many other Tibetan masters shared visions, they are also told by yogis, gurus, shamans, medicine men and women, and many spiritual teachers of today. We need our visions for individual and planetary transformation. The Dalai Lamas throughout the centuries have had many visions they shared to help guide and advise the Tibetan people. You too have visions that can help steer you on your spiritual pilgrimage.

Where there is no vision, the people perish.

PROVERBS 29:18

And when I breathed, my breath was lightening.

BLACK ELK, "THE GREAT VISION," IN *BLACK ELK SPEAKS*

Our dreams and direct experiences often hold our visions. Poetry, like that of William Stafford, holds poetic visions of the world. Visions are glimpses or full pictures of our destiny and the destiny of the world. A vision is a view of the world's true potential. Visions hold an image of what wants initiation in our lives. Like an oracle or our synchronistic encounters, they point to something that asks for our acknowledgment and *fulfillment*. Sometimes they are strictly personal; other times they hold information for others.

Whoever receives a sacred vision is the one responsible for carrying out its purpose.

At best, we can use our visions to benefit others, to help bring more love and sanity to the world. Visions, like oracles, may hold a difficult or challenging lesson, but they will always build faith and give us a reason to trust the universe. If someone else's vision depresses, shames, or frightens you, don't agree to it; let it go. In personal spiritual initiation, it is far better to have and fulfill your own vision than to attempt to fulfill someone else's. Through your journey, universal truths are revealed that will benefit those around you. A great way to bring a personal vision to others is to write a story, myth, or poem, or draw or paint a mandala. *Of course, your actions in the world will be the strongest expression of your vision.* Rest assured that those who may benefit from that particular vision will discover it. My office and home are filled with the visions of others in art, poetry, books, music, and sculpture.

As you enter the East, you have already cleared the way for a vision and for a personal understanding of it. When you understand your vision, you then have the capacity to create the conditions to *fulfill* your part of it. I believe Black Elk fulfilled his part of his vision when he told it to Flaming Rainbow and gave the world his book, *Black Elk Speaks*. When reading or hearing of another's vision, such as that of Black Elk, we discern for ourselves what it means in the context of our lives and what we can do to honor it further.

> As I rode through the rainbow door, there were cheering voices from all over the universe, and I saw the Six Grandfathers sitting in a row, with their arms held toward me and their hands, palms out; and behind them in the cloud were faces thronging, without number, of the people yet to be.
>
> BLACK ELK, "THE GREAT VISION," IN BLACK ELK SPEAKS

Personal Initiatory Visions

Personal visions have a way of appearing in many forms until we understand their true import. I myself have envisioned personal spiritual initiation for over two decades. My teen journals contain passages about initiation, and I have unknowingly written initiatory myths throughout my lifetime.

The vision (image) of the Wheel came to me through meditation, dreams, and transpersonal breath sessions. When we are carrying a vision (and I know that we all are carrying at least one), synchronistic occurrences will help us realize it. Our visions are born into the world with us and, with the right conditions, come to full fruition through us; they are the kernels of our destiny. As you make way for your inner light to shine outward, your visions will become clear. Something has been nudging at you for a long time now. What is it?

Annette's Vision

I HAD A REPEATED VISION of myself walking up a long grassy hill. The top of the hill was flat. The sky was blue, and there wasn't any wind. As I walked up the path that led to the top, I saw a circle of men and women dressed in burgundy robes.

*They were waiting for me. I came into the circle, and they all began to smile and laugh. No one spoke, but the message to me was clear—*I belonged to them and they to me. *I experienced such a feeling of oneness, of belonging. I knew I was to carry this image and my bond with these individuals throughout my life and work. This vision has encouraged me and sustained me.*

Through your visions, your personal destiny is meeting up with the destiny of the world. Thus not only does the world support your visions, but in carrying them out, you help the world fulfill hers. You will find insights into your personal visions in your myths, in your pain stories, and in your authentic stories, as well as in your synchronistic encounters and dreams. There are themes to your life—there you will find your visions.

This is the time to seek a vision, to get more depth and insight into your initiation. How will you know that what you are experiencing is a vision? You will know because it carries within it a sacred vision of the world. It is part of the larger, divine movement toward wholeness and awakening.

> *"Seeing" a spirit, either in dreams or awake, is a certain sign that one has in some sort obtained a "spiritual condition," that is, that one has transcended the profane condition of humanity.*
>
> MIRCEA ELIADE, *SHAMANISM: ARCHAIC TECHNIQUES OF ECSTASY*

Seeking a Vision through Transpersonal States

Transpersonal means "beyond the personal," beyond the limits of ego and the body. (For more on transpersonal work, see the appendix, "Teachers and Groups.") Whenever one seeks to induce a vision through a transpersonal state, a qualified teacher, partner, or circle should be present to facilitate it and hold space for you. Chanting, breathwork (Stanislav Grof's Holotropic Breathwork, rebirthing-breathing, shamanic breathing, and pranayama breathwork), shamanic journeying, Sun Dances, ecstatic dance, various yogic practices, vision questing (extended time in nature), sweat lodges, and certain practices of guided meditation enable transpersonal and altered states that can bring forth a personal vision. On many occasions, I have witnessed the transpersonal effects of sharing one's life story with others.

To call upon a vision is intentionally to create an altered state so as to receive an insight. This altered state allows you to let go of your mind and body. Whether the vision actually comes from an outside spiritual source (spirit or deity) or from your inner shrine (soul) makes no difference. A vision is a vision.

To bring forth a vision of your own, you must be the journeyer. You must be the one to take a pilgrimage to the sacred internal site. A qualified teacher and guide will hold the space for you as you travel to your internal mountain. (And in the case of Sun Dances and other sacred ceremonies, an invitation by those holding the ceremony, along with the proper preparation, is likely required.) If you receive a vision and are confused about it, discuss it with a qualified and trusted teacher or counselor. A vision cannot be understood by a clouded mind or a soul in hiding.

That which you seek also seeks you. You must simply open the door and make room in your heart and psyche, and the vision will come forth. Your vision needs you to manifest it, just as you need it. In many traditions, when a vision comes to someone, it's believed that that person's energy has left their body and traveled to a place of wisdom. It is also important to know that our experiences when in a transpersonal state are directly influenced by our intentions going in.

The pious will lack the means to open the way to the hidden lands. . . . Those who contemplate going will often fall prey to their fears and will lack the prerequisite courage. Those who do go will often be slandered by (others) who are envious of their good fortune. . . . For those who lack the auspicious circumstances to journey to these hidden lands . . . the beyul will remain no more than imagined paradises of enlightened beings; they will not manifest through contemplation and idle talk.

PADMASAMBHAVA,
"THE OUTER PASSKEY TO THE HIDDEN-LANDS,"
QUOTED IN *THE HEART OF THE WORLD* BY IAN BAKER

Whereas the *beyul* are the sacred hidden lands within remote parts of Tibet, Padmasambhava also refers to the inner beyul reached through various Tibetan tantric spiritual practices. In Ian Baker's memoir of his spiritual travels in Tibet's hidden lands, he emphasizes the corresponding internal pilgrimage that must also take place. To travel to these places, you must get beyond just talk and speculation. These inner hidden lands can be reached through the practices within the Wheel of Initiation as well as through established practices from your chosen spiritual tradition.

In the Initiation Course, I set aside at least four evenings where the group does *bindu* breath sessions. This is borrowed from Stanislav Grof's Holotropic Breathwork and yogic and shamanic breathing. I play specially chosen music, which, combined with the breathwork, induces an altered state of consciousness.

I highly recommend breathwork to bring on an initiatory vision. If you can, find a local facilitator of Stanislav Grof's Holotropic Breathwork,* a certified rebirthing-breather, or a well-trained shamanic practitioner who specializes in breathwork (such as Linda Star Wolf of the Venus Rising Institute in North Carolina). I also suggest at least one night of vision questing under the stars or following a more traditional route such as the Lakota Hanblapi, which means "seeking a vision." There are many qualified people all over the world who conduct vision quests. Because these experiences break into more hidden places within, the transformative experience can be powerful and possibly unsettling.

Amy's Vision

ALTERED STATE DURING last night's breath session . . . Bear playing the drums, a pair of crows holding space for me . . . we meditate together in the cave. We start to dance and then rise into the air. We start to fly. I am taking the lead. We fly across the street and pick up a pair of red-winged blackbirds. We fly down the Baraboo River to Devil's Lake State Park and pick up a pair of turkey vultures and

---

*Please find more information about Stanislav Grof and Linda Star Wolf and their work in the Resources section at the end of this book.

then to the Heron rookery and pick up a pair of herons. We fly past the South bluff and pick up a pair of eagles. Down the Wisconsin River now . . . past Ferry Bluff and Spring Green. We hit the Mississippi River and pick up pelicans. We fly to the Platte and pick up two sandhill cranes. Down to the Gulf of Mexico, inland to pick up my friend Tamara, who is on vacation in Mexico. Central and South America . . . we pick up butterflies and more cranes. We all fly East across the ocean to Africa and pick up more cranes.

To India . . . a few more cranes and then head North to Tibet. We fly into the mountains. I am in the lead . . . we form a "V" formation. Deep into the mountains . . . up, up, up. High rock walls to the Buddhist temples, The Lost City, the home of the Dalai Lama before Tibet was invaded by the Chinese. I AM CROW now. I hear Buddhist monks chanting, singing the most beautiful song. I start to circle . . . I am Home. I now remember who I am. I AM CROW and I used to guard the temples of the Dalai Lama. I used to protect the monks. I cry. The monks are pleased that I have returned. I ask, "What is my purpose?" They tell me I am Shiny Black. I build nests one stick at a time. I REFLECT. I am all colors of the rainbow. I am wise and old. I am here to reflect for others. I am here to help them shine their purpose; I love shiny objects!

We fly back exactly how we came and drop off all the other birds and cranes. Back through all the ancient flyways . . . Returning all the birds home, Tamara back to her vacation in Mexico . . . Back to the Mississippi, the Platte, the Wisconsin, Devil's Lake, the Baraboo River, and into my backyard.

Crow shows me old trees and driftwood. The trees want to be photographed in black and white. Take pictures of the trees . . . the wood, the rings, the wisdom. Make notecards and sell them and share them. The rocks want special treatment too. Pick them. Collect them and bring them into my backyard. Collect more. Make my backyard a sanctuary—a Zen garden. I am told the crows will help me. They see my garden . . . a Wheel of Initiation in the center of the yard with plants and flowers from the Circle . . . crushed gravel, rock, and beautiful flowers. A fence encloses this space, and it's private. I am told, "You hold gatherings here."

People come to relax, restore, and learn . . .

Haiku

Frost covers the bark
River listens to the cold
Birdsong melts it all

Amy, 2008 Initiation Circle

THE NEXT STEP: INITIATORY TRIAL AND MEETING THE GUARDIAN OF THE THRESHOLD

In myths and fairy tales the main character goes on some challenging quest that takes him or her out of the comfort zone of reliability and predictability. In traditional and contemporary rites of passage, the initiate is given a challenge, a test to complete. The Wheel of Initiation is also a path of tests and trials—trials from the teacher (or practices), tests from the deity, tests from the self, and tests from the world. To move through these challenges is a clear "yes" to your initiation and means of real awakening, while the one who does not undertake these trials will be wasting time (as Ian mentions above, those who do not have the courage will simply think about them and talk of these inner places).

The initiation ceremony acknowledges your successful quest up until this point. It acknowledges that you have gone through the Wheel of Initiation and brought forth parts of your true nature. Given your intention and your vision, what will generate outward and inward movement in your life? What will both challenge you and prove your readiness?

What action, if you were to take it now, would not only express your initiatory intention but also generate needed movement in your life? What action would help fulfill your vision? If you were to take this one action, and perform this one activity, you would have the power to move through some habitual ways of seeing yourself or of being in the world. If you are in an initiation circle, the circle can help you choose your trial. *This is where you choose something that further creates the outward conditions for initiation, for an awakened life.* The emphasis here is on an outward action.

In the story of Sir Galahad, the knights agree to go on a quest but thinking it would be a disgrace to go forth in a group each "entered into the forest, at one point or another, there where they saw it to be thickest, all in those places they found no way or path." Where there is a way or a path, it's someone else's way. Each knight enters the forest at the most mysterious point and follows his own intuition. What each brings forth is what never before was on land or sea: the fulfillment of his unique potentialities, which are different from anybody else's.

JOSEPH CAMPBELL, *A JOSEPH CAMPBELL COMPANION*

Nothing can truly interfere with your destiny, be it an overprotective parent, age, resistance, or poverty. If creating a beautiful painting, becoming enlightened under a Bodhi tree, or finding your Holy Grail is in your destiny, much is conspiring to make it so. Not even your pain story can stop you from this destiny (your destination). In fact, as we have discovered in this pilgrimage, all your experiences are part of the initiatory journey; you are living your initiatory tale. You are creating the conditions for awakening. You are upon the horse, you see the central mountain, you have hold of the Sacred Thread.

Now go and test your spiritual commitment through a trial.

Traditionally, something of great significance must be at stake, otherwise the initiation will lack power and be unable to move the initiate into the new reality. Here in the Wheel what is at stake are tightly held beliefs and assumptions about yourself and the world—all the agreements that keep your pain stories active.

What may be at stake is a dead-end job or relationship or how others perceive you in the world. Carlos Castaneda jumped off a high cliff and dissolved his body into another reality to convince his magus, Don Juan Matus, that he was a worthy candidate. In the old forms of esoteric Christianity and occult initiations, a disturbing encounter with your pain story (and karma) and soul was called Meeting the Guardian of the Threshold.

The Guardian may reflect the habitual self, but it also really represents hidden aspects within your soul or unconscious. You must meet the Guardian face to face, as it were, with your light, with your intention to be initiated, with your vision. In my view, the Guardian protects the threshold itself because it shows how we are in need of a threshold to cross. If we were fully awake, there would be no need to cross thresholds, and therefore no Guardians. The Guardian holds a paradoxical role, saying, "Cross if you dare," but at the same time she is making sure you *can* pass through the threshold.

Our habits, fears, and reactive emotions (and past lives) can take on the form of the Guardian and *appear* to keep us from crossing the threshold into initiation. Some would call this the egoic self. You must be willing to leave some of what you identified with, and ways in which you have seen yourself up until this point, at the threshold. Leave some of the past at the feet of the Guardian so she will allow you to pass.

Your trial will help you meet the Guardian (and you thought you were done!) and move through the threshold. Many people feel they shouldn't have to deal with this final challenge before moving through the threshold. But there it is, facing you. What can you do to get past it? Remember too that the Guardian is your ally. This will help you to move past her.

Greet the Guardian as you would a precious loved one and complete your initiatory trial. Give her what she wants.

Here are some trials that were created during the Initiation Courses:

- Attend a meditation retreat. "My trial was to attend a four-day meditation retreat where noble silence was practiced. The resistance that arose within was unbelievable and an indication that this quest was truly a good battle with the false self. My false self constantly tells me I must have everything in control, and that I must take many preventive measures so that my vulnerability will not be revealed to the world. I honestly thought the quest would kill me. But it did not kill me, it killed the strong hold that the false self had on me."
- Take horseback riding lessons.
- Take piano lessons and give a recital. "My trial was to take piano

lessons and then be part of a recital. If I hadn't named this as my quest to a few others, I would have found a reason to back off. Instead, I gave my first recital, which became part of my initiation ceremony."

- Go on a solo trip. Explore a new area of the world on your own.
- Take a retreat in another state or country.
- Learn a new skill.
- Complete three paintings.
- Throw yourself a celebration. "My trial was to throw a party in my honor! For some this may seem like such an easy quest. But I found myself spinning emotionally down a road that made me struggle with my worthiness. I worried no one would show up, or that if they did, they would get bored. I struggled with all the times I felt alone, ignored, and abandoned. My old self identified strongly with 'feeling alone.' The quest was perfect for me."
- Put together a chapbook of poems; have a poetry reading.
- Pursue new jobs that resonate with your vision.
- Build a sweat lodge. "I knew this was the right one because I was instantly confronted with a mind full of rules. I told my initiation circle that the Guardian was thrashing me with the question, 'Who do you think you are?' I knew too she would let me through when I could answer her."
- Attend a Nyung Nay ritual.
- Attend a Sun Dance. "Preparing for this was a major part of the trial. I prayed to be gifted with a pipe to honor my native heritage. I prayed to be given the courage to go through with it. At the Sun Dance I got back so much that was lost to me! I offered skin and knew I could do whatever it takes to fulfill my life's destiny. I felt ready for my initiation."
- Become a volunteer for a cause you believe in.
- Finish a manuscript and send it out to publishers.
- Go on a vision quest under the stars for one to four nights/days.
- Quit your job.

Steven's Story

I FELT DISCOMFORT when my trial was chosen for me by my initiation circle. It also seemed too easy. Then came all the habitual stuff—the thoughts and emotions that have kept me from moving forward in my life. At times I felt overwhelmed and confused, but I knew I had to stick with my trial. I called on all the wisdom and skills acquired during my year of initiation. Part of me just wanted to grit my teeth and get through it, but I knew better; I went into it with eyes and heart and mind wide open. What I received in return can never be taken from me. Now, as I prepare for my initiation ceremony, I know what I am going to leave at the threshold because I am no longer who I was."

Remember your willingness to do whatever it takes to fulfill your initiatory intention. Your trial is a "whatever."

Your Initiation Threshold

> There are many circles in life. . . . Remember, do not get caught on just one circle; if you do, you will forever be going around in circles. Grasp the knowledge of that circle and then move on to the next. One day you will look up, and you will be at the center, and the mystery of life will be revealed to you.
>
> WA'NA'NEE'CHE' (Dennis Renault),
> Native American Spirituality

To fully understand and incorporate your trial, you will have to step through the threshold. It can feel both scary and exciting to do this. The tension you feel is emanating from the rules, agreements, and belief systems of the old paradigms that are attempting to hold on. Your inherent potentialities rise up in your defense in different ways: in your dreams, body signals, synchronicities, physical symptoms, and sometimes illness. The liminal (nonphysical) threshold within the consciousness is the place of one's old identity and the edge of the new paradigm.

What are you going to leave at the threshold? What are you willing and ready to let go of, to let die? What are you clearly no longer in agreement with? This is a time pregnant with power. When you begin to build your liminal threshold, you can consider all that you are ready to let go of and place it at this inner threshold. These can include agreements, beliefs, relationships, clutter, *anything* that will not serve your initiation into the new paradigm.

I have worked with people who are suicidal and others who obsess about death. Some have come to me with repeated dreams of death. They want help. And I rely on the wisdom borrowed from Carl Jung when I ask them, "What in you needs to die?" Their soul is calling out for a death. Not an end to life, but an end to whatever prevents them from living fully and from moving on. They need to leave something at their liminal threshold.

So what wants to die? Notice I don't ask what are you *willing* to let die but what *wants* to die. The Threshold Guardian is holding on and mirroring what needs to go. First ask yourself: "What wants to die?" and then check in with your willingness and commitment to do whatever it takes to fulfill your intention and live your vision. What agreements need to die? What relationship is dead? What are you giving your life force to? If your job is killing you, why not kill your job? *Leave it at the threshold.* Is your addiction to alcohol ruining your life and your relationships? Let it die. What are you going to leave at the threshold as you complete your personal initiation? I once left my television at the threshold. Another time what I left was my attachment to receiving acknowledgment for my efforts.

Jessica at the Threshold

FOR ME, THE TIME at the threshold gave me something I had needed my entire life—the ability to say no, let go, and leave behind someone or something as I moved on. It never really occurred to me that I could dump dead weight, end lifeless relationships, and release the stuff of the past. And when I say stuff, I mean boxes of stuff. Once I got started, my first threshold was stockpiled with things, both material and psychological. And when I stepped through . . . I felt newly born.

At this point, many people feel distrustful of the new paradigm that is not fully known. How can we let go of something familiar when we are not certain what lies ahead? In one of my more recent initiations, I let go of a beautiful life, letting myself open to what was next. I must admit that I did hesitate at the threshold. But then I confronted the Guardian and moved on through. We are not always just letting go of old, useless stuff; sometimes it is just time to move on.

What makes it initiatory and transformative is your courage to cross the threshold into the unknown. There are sure to be surprises along the way! The threshold takes on the symbolic image of the snake shedding its skin again and again. And in this shedding, we create a new world for ourselves and for others.

✳ Your Corporeal Threshold

The threshold is seen as a portal from this side of your life into the other side. Create a physical threshold somewhere outside (if possible). It can be made of cornmeal, stones, a line in the snow or sand, with twigs sticking up out of the snow, or whatever creates a physical identity for your threshold. Ideally, the threshold faces East, so when you move through it you are heading East, the direction of initiation, possibilities, the sunrise, and new beginnings. (But no rules.)

My recommendation is that you build your threshold a week or two before you walk through it, to let it build up some energy. This will also give you time to meet the Guardian of the Threshold and to have dreams that may help you move through the initiatory threshold during your ceremony. As you build your threshold, begin to hold in your heart-mind an intention that represents the new paradigm, what you are moving toward. For some this is an entirely new intention, for others, a natural evolution of their initiatory one.

Then either visualize or create a circle, a Wheel of Initiation (with the four directions) on both sides of the threshold. This too can be with stones, cornmeal, or other natural objects.

When you are ready to move through the threshold, approach the threshold with all that you are prepared to release. Also, hold your new intention in mind, the one you want to manifest in the world. Step into the center of the Wheel that is on this side of the threshold, the side that represents where you are now and what you will be leaving behind.

Begin by facing the South and making it clear what you are no longer in agreement with; what you are leaving behind. Say these words out loud: "I no longer agree to . . . (be afraid, hold myself back, give up, collect Beanie Babies, watch television, drink alcohol)." Then, moving clockwise, do the same thing for each direction, repeating the statements until you are facing East and the entrance to the threshold.

Leave behind all that is dead or all that represents the remainder of your pain story. You may leave actual items at the threshold as well. (I suggest they be organic and left to dissolve and perish.)

When you are in the directions, releasing the past, you are also meeting the Guardian. As you do this, the Guardian dissolves into you and lets you pass. Take as long as you want. Say a prayer or sing a chant. Call for help from your root guru. Follow your intuition and do what comes naturally.

Then step through the threshold. Know that you are entering a new paradigm, a new way of being. You are stepping into the Great Unknown of your beautiful, evolving life.

Now step into the center of the other Initiation Wheel, which is on the other side of the threshold. Facing East, state your intention out loud. You may include your core principles once you are through the threshold, calling these out to (and within) each direction as well. ("I live fearlessly and compassionately. I rejoice in the good fortune of all beings.") Move around this Wheel counterclockwise now until you are facing the South. When you are in each direction of the Wheel, state your intention and your affirmative agreements and principles out loud. Here you can recite a prayer or your vow (see page 243) as you complete your personal ritual of moving through the initiatory threshold.

You may keep your threshold in place and use it for future rituals or let it disintegrate and make a new one for future use.

❊

Out Beyond the Threshold

We want to be continually holding ourselves accountable to our spiritual and ethical lives and not have our initiatory experience be too much of an intellectual one. An intellectual understanding alone will not generate transformation or initiation. While you may agree with and understand deep spiritual principles, if they remain something you keep tucked away in your intellect, you will continue to be caught up in your habitual states.

We are reminded again and again that the journey never stops. It continues on and on like a spiral, always moving closer and closer to the center, to the still point of the Wheel. Don't wait. The polar ice caps are melting, the sun is rising, we are aging, the evening sky waits, languages and cultures are going extinct, there is beauty and death everywhere . . . the time is short and precious. Don't waste a moment! We belong to one another. Move on through and beyond your threshold now. Everything you have done up until now has prepared you for your spiritual initiation.

- Listen during the Great Conversation, the hour of predawn, at least once a week. If you do this every day, you will learn everything you need.
- Be still in calm abiding every day, and you will hear the voice of your root guru.
- Practice getting energy from the sun or be in nature at least once a week. Do this regularly, and you will have an abundance of energy and courage.
- Engage only in activities that are in alignment with your intentions, and you will have the power to create and manifest anything.
- Respond to choices and difficulty with a spiritual principle, and you will be free of suffering and know lasting happiness.

How the Snake Got Its Medicine

*Adapted by Peyta Wigmnunke Winyan from a
traditional South American story*

LONG AGO, *when creatures told time only by the rising and falling of the sun and moon, all the birds lived in the Great Green Forest. At that time all the birds were black or white, or black and white. In the First Forest there also lived a large green snake. One morning, as it slithered along, the snake noticed some red flowers. Without much thought or effort, she went and ate them all. As she glided on, the snake caught sight of her tail and turned her head to have a better look. Along her lower body were circles of red. "Strange," she thought, "but how beautiful." Later, the snake came to some orange flowers, and without much thought or effort, she ate them too. Then she turned to see that bright orange circles were beginning to appear. The snake was delighted. She was surely the most colorful creature alive. She wound her way through the forest, eating up the yellow flowers, then the bright green ones, and then the ones that were the color of the sky . . .*

By the end of the day, her skin had circles of red, orange, yellow, green, blue, indigo, and purple. "I am a most beautiful snake!" She hissed and coiled around so she could behold all her beauty. And her entire body did shimmer like a beautiful rainbow.

But the birds of the forest were angry. They gathered around the snake, whistling, singing, and chirping. They pecked at her. "Look what you've done!" they cried. "You've eaten all the flowers of the forest, and now green is its only color."

The snake looked around her, and she knew the birds were right. "What good was all this beauty if only for one snake?" she thought. She felt bad and crept away out of the forest, where she began to tremble and shake. She trembled for a long time until finally her skin began to split. As she continued to tremble, the entire skin split open and shed off of her body. She quickly slid away in her new skin and left behind her rainbow skin at the entrance to the forest. She looked upon her green skin, noticing how it shimmered with silver and gold and many shades of iridescent green, and she realized its radiant beauty for the first time.

The birds soon found the rainbow skin at the entry and without much effort tore it up with their beaks and draped pieces of it over their bodies and wings. Soon their feathers turned the colors of red, blue, orange, yellow, purple, and indigo. And the forest was beautiful again in all its greenness and color.

8
IN THE EAST

Initiation and the Return Journey

You Reading This, Be Ready

Starting Here, what do you want to remember?
How sunlight creeps along a shining floor?
What scent of old wood hovers, what softened
sound from outside fills the air?

Will you ever bring a better gift for the world
than the breathing respect that you carry
wherever you go right now? Are you waiting
for time to show you some better thoughts?

When you turn around, starting here, lift this
new glimpse that you found; carry into evening
all that you want from this day. This interval you spent
reading or hearing this, keep it for life—

What can anyone give you greater than now,
starting here, right in this room, when you turn
around?

WILLIAM STAFFORD, "YOU READING THIS, BE
READY," IN *THE WAY IT IS*

The survival of all Species depends on our grasping the significance of
what was learned during the Beginning Times. And what we learned
was this: The Ceremony is life itself: it is the way we do things; it is
the way we maintain Balance and Harmony with all our Relations; it
is the way we Honor our Ancestors and protect the Earth for the Yet
Unborn Generation.

GKISEDTANAMOOGK, FROM *ANOQCOU*

THE CALL FOR CEREMONY

In the East, you look around, and what you see is the larger world you have created through your initiatory journey. Across the threshold, you meet your true self and begin the return journey. Passing the trial that you have chosen is the induction into more of your life. In the cycle of life/death/life, the ending is also a beginning.

The wolf with the spiral on its body is the totem animal of the East. He represents your transformation and initiation—your ability to go out past the threshold and "call forth" your life. The initiation ceremony enacts and symbolizes your successful passage through the Wheel and demonstrates your abilities and commitment as a spiritual hero or heroine, as one who has undergone great challenges through your own inner pilgrimage. You have been initiated through the renewal of your mind. You are now ready to celebrate, by and in ceremony, before returning to the community with your "boon" (your renewed self, intentions, agreements, and visions). At this point it's as if you can hear the drumming of the elders calling you back out of the woods.

In *Black Elk Speaks,* Black Elk says that he did not get power from his visions until he acted them out for his people. The power comes from understanding the visions and sharing them with others through ritual, creative expression, and most importantly, right action. Anything that we initiate also revitalizes our community—that is the core historical intention of initiation.

> *For those who are interested in a spirited intimacy, listen more to the ancestors, to spirit, to the trees, to the animals. Focus on ritual. Listen to all those forces that come and speak to us that we usually ignore.*
> SOBONFU SOME, *THE SPIRIT OF INTIMACY*

When my daughter was eight, she and I went shopping for paint at the local hardware store. Of course, she wanted to browse the toy aisle. She stopped in front of the Barbie accessories. One of the packages had accessories for Barbie's adult life—a set of workout equipment, essentials for her office, and party supplies. It crossed my mind that these accessories were representative of an uninitiated adult. Not only was this "adult life" missing several valuable components of a spiritual life, its packaging was excessive and seductive.

In buying into the Barbie kits, we are seduced into the appearance of things, and, in this case, we are also passing this image of the "successful adult life" down to our children through the toys we purchase for them. Many of our current health problems arise from this agreement to be sold on what comes to us in neat, seductive packages. Even in good times, there is an average of 16 million new cases of depression in the United States every year, leading me to ask, "What is really wrong here?"

The desire to be seduced by these attractive packages that keep life on the surface is one reason why some individuals forgo completing their initiatory journey via the initiation ceremony and the recital of their vows. (For help in choosing your spiritual vow see page 243. The fully initiated life, in contrast to the uninitiated life, is unpackaged and raw and continually takes us through many thresholds into the Great Unknown, where things are not tied up in neat, simplistic boxes. We could not possibly fit all that goes into an initiated life into one little package.

An initiated life that includes ceremony and conscious ritual, on the other hand, helps break us out of the package. It lets us choose our *own* accessories and create our *own* lives. Ritual brings out the jewels of our initiatory journey in celebration and acknowledges our spiritual achievements and evolution. Ritual calls upon us to *create,* and in so doing, it honors our creative role in the dynamics of this world.

Preparing for the Initiation Ceremony

You can hold a personal initiation ceremony in your yard and gather people together to participate in it with you, or, as I show later, you can do one on your own, alone. If you have gone through the Wheel with a group, you may create a ceremony together that includes individual initiation rituals within it. Below is a template of the initiation ceremony I have done with various circles over the years. Borrow what you like. Following this are examples of personal initiation rituals (which are performed within the larger ceremony). Plan your ceremony a month ahead of time (to give everyone involved enough time to prepare as well). This also helps build up energy for this important ceremony. And once the ceremony is enacted, the return journey begins.

Receiving a Spiritual Name

A change of names typically plays a central role in initiation ceremonies. Many individuals follow the ancient Hindu, Buddhist, and Sufi traditions of taking a new name to mark their initiation by a guru. Most teachers you are working with will give you a name if you ask. You can also give yourself a spiritual name. Each of us, I believe, knows our true name, but sometimes others can help us hear it when we cannot. Many individuals have the experience of being named as they move through the Wheel.

Remember: You are the meaning-maker *and* often the name-giver. One woman wanted me to name her in a personal ceremony, and I did so. But the following night I had a dream that she already knew her name. So I called her the next morning and told her about my dream.

"I was told you already know your spiritual name."

"Yes. I had a dream a while ago where I was given a name. And the dream felt like a vision to me."

"We can trust that!" I replied emphatically.

She had asked me to give her a name hoping that I would either "get" the same name or bestow a more suitable one on her. But she too knew that the name she had been given in her dream was hers to carry.

Sometimes a name is so obvious. For instance, if you love to watch birds, Woman Who Watches Birds would be appropriate. Or a name may hold a more symbolic meaning, such as Blue Lotus One.

As Prudence Tippins, a poet, teacher, and retreat owner, said, "At our initation ceremony when Julie asked me to come up with my spiritual name, all that would come into my head was 'Calliope.' I thought I must be nuts because this word meant nothing to me. Then I discovered the meaning of the word (Calliope was the Greek Muse of heroic poetry) and how well it fit my efforts as a writer and poet. It is now the name of my retreat center as well."

Once you are given a name, you must go about the task of living up to it. A name can also be a reinforcement of your vow (see page 243), in that it is a spiritual name that reflects your spiritual commitment. Traditionally, in shamanic cultures, the elders of many indigenous tribes would send young men out into the wild alone, without food or shelter. The youths were expected to have a formative vision—an animal spirit or perhaps a tribal ancestor would present a symbolic vision to him and give him a new name, which validated that he was worthy of adulthood. For young women, a spiritual name was often bestowed during their first menses ritual. A change of names typically plays a central role in mythological initiation stories. After crossing a threshold, a name reveals and marks a successful crossing.

It's All Only Tap Water

MY FIRST SPIRITUAL INITIATION was when I chose to be baptized at the age of thirteen. I did this with a wonderful Lutheran minister as my teacher. He instructed me to read and study the New Testament and then asked me questions about it at our meetings. He knew I wanted to be baptized because this was not offered to me through my family, and I had some concern about the afterlife if I was not baptized.

After a bit of study, the minister and I got together one Saturday for my baptism. I sat in the room as he shared a few prayers and some doctrine with me. Then he got up to retrieve the holy water that I would be baptized with.

I sat in anticipation. I felt ready!

He reentered the room carrying a little bowl of water. When he saw the eager, expectant look on my face, he said to me, "It's only tap water, Julie." And then he said a few prayers over me and baptized me.

Only tap water.

Somehow, for me, this "only tap water" generated a more meaningful initiation into a new way of being than if it had been sanctified water. The threshold I passed through inside my heart was profound—I began to understand how it *is all just tap water*. I started to become my own meaning-maker. I would stumble quite a bit along the way, but here I began with a new map of the world, a map that showed me that all sacred objects start out as mere tap water.

This story also points to the value of allowing for surprises and new insights during and following your initiatory journey and ceremony. Spirit has been called forth into your ceremony and may have something unexpected to reveal to you. Savor whatever comes.

THE CEREMONY ITSELF

Designate an area where you want to hold the group initiation ceremony; this will be your ceremonial site. I recommend that it be outdoors if possible. The physical layout of your initiation ceremony can include an altar in the East, a threshold (which has a small path leading out) to walk through (West to East, if possible), and a fire pit near the center somewhere. However, there are no set rules.

One year our ceremony was in January, and due to the fact that it was forty degrees below zero, we held it indoors with a fire burning in an outdoor cauldron. We used the dining room table as the altar and set it under the windows in the East. We cleared the living room for the ceremony and went out to the fire in the cauldron when someone needed to burn something as part of their personal ceremony.

Our threshold was downstairs and went from West to East. The larger the space, the better, and an outdoor space that affords some privacy is best. We have a ceremonial site on our property that is a clearing in the woods. Years ago we cleared a large circular area of approximately a thousand square feet. The space itself doesn't have to be circular for you to create a circle within it. Some groups have rented group camping sites to do ceremonies, while others create a space in their yard. Privacy and space are important so people have the room to act out their personal ceremony.

An initiation altar typically holds images of root gurus, loved ones, symbols of power and beauty, and any and all objects that symbolize one's spiritual initiation and initiation intention. You may want to have your vows and intentions written out and placed on the altar. Typically, flowers, incense, and water are placed here too, for the spirits that are invited into the ceremony.

Your personal ritual will be an expression of your initiation intentions. Take at least a few weeks to design your personal ritual, which takes place within the bigger ceremony if you are doing a group initiation. Your personal ritual should be twenty to thirty minutes long. You will want to prepare others for their role in your ritual. You are responsible for bringing the necessary materials. Also, during the ceremony you will first talk everyone through your ritual and then go enact it. This places the responsibility on everyone, rather than just one person, for the facilitation of the rituals.

THE DAY OF THE CEREMONY

The predawn of your initiation ceremony is a wonderful time to sit in silence and listen to the Great Conversation and to meditate as the sun rises. Then go to where the group is meeting for the ceremony. I recommend you begin early in the morning, which will allow enough time for everyone's personal ritual. Once you meet up, take material for your ritual and place it somewhere accessible that is in or near the ritual site. After everyone has gathered and everything is set up, dress the altar and lay a fire that will be lit later on. If you haven't made a physical threshold ahead of time, build it the day of the ceremony. As a group, you will have decided who is responsible for doing the various setups.

Next, set the boundaries of the ceremonial site, which typically includes the threshold, the space for the rituals, the altar, and the fire pit. However, as I suggested above, work with what you have. Take the time to smudge the ritual site with sage or/and place cornmeal or buckwheat around its borders. If the fire pit is outside the site, simply have someone smudge a path to it and around it. Do the same for the altar and the threshold. When setting the boundaries, ask for protection and imagine setting the psychic container for the ceremony. Now take the time to add the medicine pouches or what you are releasing at your threshold. (See below. Borrow from the previous chapter when deciding how to use your threshold.)

When I hold group initiation ceremonies, I have open medicine pouches on one side of the threshold to be filled up by everyone participating. Initiates place small gifts, such as stones, herbs, relics, or notes, in each other's pouches. You can do this now as you set up the threshold. After everyone has placed their pouches down, others can put their gifts inside the open pouches. The initiate will wear or keep his or her respective pouch for a year, after which time the initiate is invited to open the pouch again and review the items, as well as fill the pouch up with new items if desired. New, sacred items can be placed inside the pouch any time a successive personal initiation ceremony is enacted.

If you are conducting a group initiation ceremony, each person's name can be written on a slip of paper and placed next to his or her pouch. In addition, items to be blessed may be set at the East end of the threshold. The West end of the threshold holds everything that needs to be released. The items to be released can be left at the site after the ceremony is done. The medicine pouches are collected later by each initiate as they cross the threshold. This represents their completed initiation and their return to the community. The pouch carries the medicine of the circle and the power of their initiation.

BEGINNING THE CEREMONY

Once everyone is gathered at the site, each person present is smudged with incense or sage. This cleanses and purifies them. Then everyone will take fifteen to thirty minutes (decide ahead of time) to sit in nature and pray or meditate. Take this time to consider your ritual (which you have already designed). Pray for help to fully appreciate what you have accomplished and for you to continue to fulfill your vision. Have someone drum to call you back to the ritual site, and once there, light the fire that has been set. When you come back into the ritual site, pass through the threshold from East to West, entering into the sacred space of ceremony (one at a time if in a group) as the initiation ceremony begins. (Everyone will pass back through from West to East after all the individual initiation rituals are complete.)

The template I give you here is just a guide, a possibility—because, remember, there are no real rules. Trust yourself and follow your own intuition. As the meaning-maker, design your own ceremony. Don't make this a strict religious experience but a fun and powerful spiritual experience. Use the template to keep you focused, but don't be attached to anything—let it unfold naturally.

Now is the time to call in the directions and other spirits that you want as Guardians and support for your ceremony. To honor the pilgrimage through the Wheel of Initation, you may want to begin in the South, where the journey first began.

- Call in the South, the direction of intentions and aspirations, and the Horse.
- Call in the West, the direction of the Thunder Beings, of recapitulation and transformation. The Thunderbird.
- Call in the North, the direction of one's deities and guides and that of Blue Bear.

- Call in the East, the energy of the rising sun, of successful initiations, and the Wolf that carries the sacred circle.
- Call in the Mother Earth/Creator.
- Call in the Father Sky/Creator.
- Call in the Grandmothers and Ancient Ones.
- Call in any other spirits you want—the stone people, the trees, the winged ones, and any others that you want to be at your initiation. (And remember to release them at the end.)

When you return, do not pass through the threshold, but come back to the group (gathered in front of the eastern altar).

At this point you will begin the *individual initiations*.

If you have chosen to acknowledge your spiritual name, this will be done during your own personal initiation ceremony through a recitation. You can decide how you want this done. You can call out your spiritual name and have others call it back to you. Drumming and rattling may accompany this!

PERSONAL INITIATION CEREMONIES

These are designed at the same time you are building your liminal threshold. The personal initiation ceremonies within the larger ceremony are the core aspect of the bigger ceremony. All have prepared themselves, and others, for their role in their own personal ritual.

Everyone's personal ritual is unique and holds a special intention. Design your personal ritual from your initiatory intention and from your vision. You may have something literal or symbolic from your trial as part of your ritual. Let it express and celebrate your journey through the Wheel. Keep it simple and meaningful. Through the initiatory journey, you have obtained a jewel, and you have gone to the center of the Wheel at least once. How can you reveal this boon in your ritual? What boons will you be bringing back to the community?

Individual rituals often include reading prose; creating artwork (including body painting); and enacting performances, such as weddings that represent the inner marriage, funerals and resurrections, indigenous dances and chants, skits, graduation ceremonies, and parades.

Here I share some ceremony stories for you to borrow from for your own ritual if you choose.

Alexandra's Ceremony

MY RITUAL IS ABOUT visibility. It is about true freedom: being who I am, being who we each are. My vision is really about seeing one another. So much that is now visible was hidden to me. I want to keep my life visible. In my ritual, everyone participating will gather in a circle, and I will be at the center. I will give others pens and a colorful ribbon to write on. On the ribbon, they will write the qualities that they see in me. Everyone will then say these out loud as we tie the ribbons to a red dogwood tree. Then we will remain in the circle, and, with our eyes closed, I will present myself to the others and, blindfolded, will tell each of them what I "see" in them.

Alexandra had a beautiful branch of a dogwood tree with ribbons of different colors to take home with her that day.

Jerry's Ceremony

JERRY'S CEREMONY is designed to fully integrate his experience of initiation so that he may teach others to do so as well. He will start out by sitting in a hole that he dug earlier in the ground. He will be covered in a cloth by another circle member. There will be quiet drumming and humming, and as the drumming gets louder and louder, the cloth will be removed. Then others will help Jerry out of the hole. As Jerry emerges from Mother Earth, someone else will say, "I'm so happy you are here." Jerry will then be helped into a new robe, and cedar twigs will be placed in his hair. Then his spirit name will be called out, and he will take everyone through a brief chant and teaching. As part of his ritual, he prepared an article to read on health and wholeness. As part of his trial, he wrote three articles to be published in a health magazine.

After the individual initiation rituals, gather everyone together to chant, drum, breathe, and finish dancing off the old and calling in the new. When you are dancing, release anything that still needs to be released into the fire. Throw tobacco and sage into the fire too, praying and releasing and chanting and calling out. Send out your prayers to all the directions. More often than not, people have done some releasing as part of their personal ritual, so this part of the larger ceremony is brief. Also, depending on how many personal rituals there are, the ceremony can take all day. I recommend that there be breaks between every couple of personal rituals to snack or have a small meal. Sometimes people offer food as part of their individual rituals. You decide, but what we found is that some protein and water are good to keep the physical energy up.

Now is the time to go back through the threshold. At this point, pass through the threshold as an initiate, as a spiritual steward (see pages 244 and 247), calling out your spiritual name and reciting your vow. As you pass through, pick up your medicine pouch and bring it through with you. Face East and feel the energy of the new paradigm. Look East, out over the new world.

Once everyone is through the threshold, gather in front of the altar and chant a song that you have selected beforehand to celebrate the completion of the Wheel and the ceremony. Then release your spiritual helpers and Guardians, open the circle, and celebrate further by eating a meal together. Before you close your medicine pouch, you may want to check out its contents first, either alone or with the group. You can do this at mealtime or wait until a follow-up circle where you say farewell and share what went into the pouch. When you close it up for the final time, say your spiritual name out loud and blow it into the pouch with your breath. Then keep the pouch closed for a year. It holds the medicine of your initiation pilgrimage.

Henry's Personal Ceremony (conducted by himself)

HIS INTENTION: "I fulfill my personal destiny." For my ritual, I will shed the old and put on the new, like a snake.

I will create a skin out of burlap. I will slide across Mother Earth as she helps me shed this old skin. The old skin is itchy and cloudy and dry and unnecessary and too tight. It binds me. I need to leave it behind and let it go back into the Mother. The Mother has taught me much. I am now open to Her new lessons. As I shed the skin, I will play a CD of drumming and rattling. Underneath the burlap skin is a rainbow skin (made of beautiful colors; from it I will make a rainbow tie-dye T-shirt). My new colors will be the brilliant colors of vegetables. The vegetables bring me closer to the Mother. They also represent the vision I have of my new business of selling organic vegetables. The energy that comes forth from the land will bring me wisdom.

My altar will be colorful and represent the map of my new world. On it I will have a bowl of many colorful vegetables. A snakeskin will also be on my altar, as well as candles of many colors: red to root me; green to be my heart guide in my evolving business; and purple for communication as I continue to find my voice and express what is best for me.

After I have shed my skin, I will reveal my new, truer colors of the rainbow. As I am becoming this new, beautiful snake who will connect with the Earth in a healthier way, the sun will be rising.

After the sun has fully risen, I will take the old skin and bury it in my yard, and then I will move through the threshold.

Once through the threshold, we enter the world of our new paradigm. Having been on the pilgrimage for so long, everything now looks new.

A New Map of the World

I saw my first Upsidedown World Map in the Syracuse Cultural Worker's catalog (please refer to the Resources section of this book for more information about this map). This map challenges our culture's insistence, reflected in the more standard and accepted maps of the world, that North is on top and South is on the bottom. I admit to being surprised when I discovered how maps of the world are typically *interpretational,* biased designs.

In other words, mapping conventions simply reflect the social, psychological, and navigational assumptions of the mapmakers. They are not fundamentally or universally accurate. They are made through the mapmaker's intentions, beliefs, and agreements. Maps imply a truth, but it is relative to the view of the particular mapmaker.

We all tend to hold cultlike mind-sets of what it means to be on top and what it means to be on the bottom. If we are shown a map and told, "This is a map of the world," most of us will agree that this is so, without questioning it at all. What *is* true is that *one true map* of the world doesn't exist. To agree to one universal view of a map of the world is to be in agreement with the mapmaker's view, which may not necessarily be your own. Obviously, our maps of the world influence us on many levels.*

In the same way that maps of the world are different from one another, each person has his or her own individual map, one that is unique to him or her. Since entering the Wheel, you have been redesigning the map of your world. And on a personal level, this means aligning your life with your truer nature, your inner coordinates.

Depending on where we want to go and how we want to get there, our maps can change. How we get around may change. But some things remain constant: the world is, in fact, round; there are real distances between here and there; mountains and oceans remain in place. Similarly, there needs to be some consistency in how we navigate our lives, and this comes by way of our spiritual practices, which include our principles and vows.

We can use our vows to remind and align ourselves with our spiritual and ethical commitments as well as our principles. Our intentions and

---

*For more on this, please read *Seeing through Maps* by Denis Wood, Ward Kaiser, and Bob Abramms. They have also produced an educational video for use in the classroom; please see the Resources section in this book for more information.

principles make up our map (along with the sacred texts and teachings that sustain our practice); our vows are considered our compass. Together, these tools offer skillful means to navigate our new map of the world.

Taking a Spiritual Vow

> *The bodhisattva vow is a living vow that we reaffirm every day, not just once in a lifetime.*
>
> LAMA SURYA DAS, *AWAKENING THE BUDDHIST HEART*

A vow is a simple statement or prayer recited each day to bring attention to your spiritual aspirations, intentions, and principles. Express and say your vow often enough (ideally, every morning as you arise), and your entire life will begin to come into alignment with it. My personal vow is borrowed from Shantideva's *Bodhicaryāvatāra: A Guide to the Bodhisattva Way of Life*. It contains a total of fourteen lines that are recognized as the entire Bodhisattva vow. I have borrowed and memorized eight of them:

> *Just as all the Buddhas of the Past*
> *Embraced the awakened attitude of mind*
> *And in the precepts of the bodhisattvas*
> *Step by Step abode and trained,*
>
> *Just so and for the benefit of beings*
> *I too will have this awakened attitude of mind*
> *And in the precepts of the Bodhisattvas, step by step*
> *Abide and train myself.*

Each day this vow reawakens my commitment to the spiritual and ethical path of the Bodhisattva and of an initiated adult. It connects me with others who have successfully gone before and reminds me that I too have the means necessary to transform my mind and my life, *step by step*. It helps remind me of my overall intention: to make the world more beautiful through the transformation of my own mind.

This is an important objective to aim for when you devise your vow. When so doing, you may borrow, as I have, from a particular spiritual tradition, or make up your own. With our vows we recommit to uplift our lives, step by step, every day. We continue to be willing to do whatever it takes to fulfill our intentions and be 100 percent responsible for our lives.

Your vow is intended to keep you enthusiastic about and committed to your life as a spiritual steward. In stepping through the threshold and returning to the community with your boons, you have become a spiritual steward, a steward of the ethical life. As well, your vow is a reminder to take care of yourself. "You have made me a keeper of vineyards and yet my own vineyard I have not kept" is a reminder from the Song of Solomon to tend to your own vineyard first as the best means to help others.

Your vow is what you take out into the world.

By having a vow, *we keep things real; the wisdom obtained through initiation can't and shouldn't be assumed.* Your vow holds you to the conscious life, to your new, truer map of the world.

However, a warning must be given here: many people lose their way at this particular point of initiation.

This happens when the hero(ine) of many myths, having gone through initiation, has decided not to take a vow, not to return to their home or community (both metaphorically and literally), nor to bring back the boon they received during initiation. Sometimes it is too difficult to live in the world in a more awakened state (because often much is asked of the initiate), so these individuals who hold such promise run away to a place where there will be no expectations of them (either internally or externally).

Refusing to Return

> On the brink of illumination,
> the old ways are very seductive
> and liable to pull you back.
>
> JOSEPH CAMPBELL,
> *A JOSEPH CAMPBELL COMPANION*

Your refusal to return may show up as your refusal to apply your newfound wisdom to your family and immediate community, your refusal to really *put your spiritual wisdom into practice.* This refusal to return can also manifest in the desire to be a teacher or a spiritual leader while not really bringing the practice home to close family members and friends.

There is also the *false return.* You jump right into wanting to show others how to wake up, but you bypass your own continued process. In truth, a proper return *starts with yourself and the activation of your vow,* then at home in your relationships with all your loved ones and friends, and then moves outward from there by putting your spiritual principles and vision into practice. But it should also move outward to your workplace and community, transforming the world around you.

Lisa Hartman's Return Dream

OCTOBER 13, 2007. The night following my initiation ceremony, I had this dream as I fell off to sleep:

I am in a pitch-black cave, brought here by perpetrators who are torturing a young woman. I know that if they connect me to this woman, she will die. They physically tie my body to hers. It isn't the manner in which they tie me to her that will extinguish her life, but simply my physical attachment to her. I neither protest nor resist the perpetrators, even though I am horrified by the sounds coming from the woman and the fear between us. I realize that my resignation makes me an active participant in her death, and I accept that she will die as a result of my bondage to her. I feel secure in my actions, despite the fear I hold for the woman. As I stand witnessing all, the cave lights up with a strong, full-bodied flash of radiance. I see pictograph-like shadows of the woman dangling by the waist from the cave's ceiling with me attached to another part of her. Our shadows are motionless, but I can tell from them that she is dead and I am alive.

I awaken knowing this was a nightmare, but the feeling of nightmare passes swiftly from me and I fall into a deep sleep. My initiation means that some phase or aspect of me has died, no longer to live. I agree to let it (her) go and move into the radiant light.

THE HERO'S RETURN JOURNEY

Out past the threshold you begin the return journey where you share your boons with your family and community, and then you may be drawn to take your gifts further out into the world. In so doing, you might experience resistance and opposition from some in your family and community. People may tend to hold on to the old view of you for quite some time. Because the old view of you also resonates with their familiar view of themselves and the world, it takes a continual exposure to your new way of being for others to come around. And indeed, some may choose to hold on to a pain story view of you or themselves. This continual effort on your part to remain true to your path makes you a hero among us.

This calls to mind the story of Superman. He had to be a hero in secret, while his persona to others was that of a bumbling news reporter. Even the woman he loved could not see who he really was. That is why this journey is often referred to as the Hero(ine)'s Journey—you wake up in order to bring your more awakened self back to your community to benefit others; you don't do it for acknowledgment or recognition.

The knights most honored in the Grail tales were those who brought back their skills and gifts to their communities. If we hide our acquired skills and wisdom (don't practice our principles or share our gifts), how are we of any real value to the world? The Buddha (while in *his* Wheel of Initiation) took the path of an ascetic for years, but he discovered through the process of his travels (inward and outward) that it is the middle path that is truly ethical and virtuous. Furthermore, once enlightened he didn't remain under the Bodhi tree or in retreat; he took his teachings and practice out into the world.

There once were two brothers. One day the elder brother decided to take to austerities and departed for the bleak mountain. However, he returned home after twenty-five years, greatly emaciated, looking like a skeleton.

"Where have you been, brother?" said the younger one, who had stayed in the native village. "What have you been doing all these years? Your body has been punished enough to make a man weep. What have you learned?"

"Twenty-five years of asceticism have given me the power to walk on water."

"My poor brother," lamented the younger one. "Have you really wasted so many years on such folly? Why, if I hail the ferryman he will take me to the opposite bank of the river in a few minutes."

SUDHIN N. GHOSH, "A TALE OF TWO BROTHERS,"
IN *TIBETAN FOLK TALES AND FAIRY STORIES*

Spiritual Stewardship

Spiritual stewardship means *maintaining an ongoing intention that arises from the altruistic desire to take personal responsibility for uplifting our lives and bringing benefit to others.* Every action we take then holds this underlying spiritual intention. In undergoing initiation, we have each made a very real (karmic) agreement (vow) to ourselves, and to all sentient beings. Our choices and behaviors will continue to reflect what's in our consciousness and what we choose to cultivate. What will you choose to cultivate? The initiation ceremony is the result of a successful pilgrimage and a new recognition of oneself as a spiritual steward.

Sometimes we hold our spiritual aspirations in our back pocket, not really constructing a life from them. Back-pocketing our vows and intentions can become a form of passive resistance to staying awake. This often happens when we identify with such titles as spiritual steward or Bodhisattva or yogi instead of *cultivating what they represent.* Saying we are evolving into something means that we are moving more and more into a natural state of being in the world. We are evolving past the identification with who and what we are. In so doing, we come to understand that we are not our creations, just as we are not our thoughts. We are not so much spiritual stewards as we are *stewarding.*

We are the movement. We are where life happens.

Tonglen: *Cultivating Fearlessness*

> *Tonglen is the quickest way to enlightenment.*
>
> THE FOURTEENTH DALAI LAMA,
> MADISON, WISCONSIN, JULY 2008

The greatest expression of spiritual stewardship is the practice of *Tonglen*—of exchanging self for others. I have mentioned that my path is that of Mahayana Buddhism, which is where we are given the practice of Tonglen. Even so, you can be a Christian or humanist and still use this technique to awaken your courageous heart. I find that Tonglen is my most powerful antidote when I am stuck, afraid, or angry. Here we learn to work with our own fear, which makes us fearless. With this practice we discover that an open heart is our best protection on the spritual journey. The practice of Tonglen takes courage and a willingness to open our hearts again and again. With Tonglen we are willing to feel and acknowledge the pain in the world. Anytime we feel another's suffering or are caught somehow in a painful cycle ourselves, Tonglen can be applied.

We all feel scared, confused, and angry at times. Through Tonglen we can open up to our own vulnerable feelings and touch our own humanity. Then we take any difficult feelings into our heart on the in-breath and send out an attitude of love or spaciousness on the out-breath. It is simple and transformative at the same time. Through the opening of your heart in this way you recognize deeply just how much we truly belong to one another.

✳ Tonglen Meditation

This may be done as part of your sitting practice or "on the spot" when suffering arises. First bring to mind a sense of belonging and love. Flash on a time that you felt completely loved and accepted by someone. Then become aware of the present difficulty or painful emotion and begin breathing it into your heart. On the out-breath, breathe out an uplifting state. For example, breathe in anger, breathe out patience; breathe in resentment, breathe out love; breathe in fear, breathe out courage. Have the in-breath and the out-breath be of equal length. On the in-breath take it all in and on the out-breath aspire to free the other person (or yourself) from suffering. Then end your Tonglen session (which can be as brief as a few minutes) with a wish for everyone's happiness.*

We have not even to risk the adventure alone, for the heroes of all time have gone before us. The labyrinth is thoroughly known. We have only to follow the thread of the hero path, and where we had thought to find an abomination, we shall find a god. And where we had thought to slay another, we shall slay ourselves. Where we had thought to travel outward, we will come to the center of our own existence. And where we had thought to be alone, we will be with all the world.

JOSEPH CAMPBELL, THE POWER OF MYTH

Initiation goes beyond ceremony and the Wheel and becomes an evolutionary fulfillment through our return journey to our communities. Our journey through the Wheel deepened the condition of causality—with each step we became *the cause of our own lives.* The knowledge that we are the cause of our lives, and not the effect, has taken root deep in our being. As meaning-makers, we continue to create the conditions for our true nature to emerge. Through the process of setting intentions, naming principles, trusting intuition, and getting to the root of some of our habitual habits and beliefs, we are ready for the return journey, initiating more of our true nature into the world.

As I shared earlier, in 1995 I took the Bodhisattva vow. I said yes and consciously chose to live by the thirty-seven practices of the Bodhisattva and the Lojong principles. I said yes, and this opened the door. I signed up for the continual renewal of mind and spirit through the practices I chose. I signed up to spiritually steward the world.

This means we stay on the hero's path no matter what arises. Like the

---

*For more on this powerful practice, please refer to Chögyram Trungpa's book *Training the Mind and Cultivating Loving-Kindness,* or any of the many other books or CDs on Tonglen that are readily available.

spiral on the Wolf in the East of the Wheel, our spritual path is a continual journey inward and outward, reentering the Wheel and returning out to the community revitalized again and again.

BEYOND THE THRESHOLD AND WHEEL

Quo Vadis

Sometimes I choose a cloud and let it
Cross the sky floating me away.
Or a bird unravels its song and carries me
as it flies deeper and deeper into the woods.

Is there a way to be gone and still belong?
Travel that takes you home?

Is that life?—to stand by a river and go.

WILLIAM STAFFORD, THE WAY IT IS

This Isn't It

Having gone through the Wheel once or having had a successful or transformative spiritual pilgrimage and/or ceremony, we need to be careful about taking on the mind-set that "This is it" or "I've done it!" "It" quickly becomes the past and, in reality, is merely a reflection, a pointer to what's next. It is already time to move on, to open to what is moving toward us now, in our continuing commitment to our spiritual evolution.

Initiation is the agreement to *always* be moving eastward through the circle of life and at any given moment being ready to face East—to bring forth the vision held within the rising sun and within you, the spiritual pilgrim. Hopefully you'll reenter the Wheel again and again as you strengthen your spiritual practice and live a life of your chosen intentions and principles.

God is primarily a Creator. He seeks to create new life, and His kingdom generates a continual source of new energies and possibilities.

*This is why, on an experiential level, no human being ever reaches
the end of his inner journey; for, as the kingdom begins to become
a reality within him, there is generated from within a host of new
possibilities which his consciousness can fulfill. So the life of the
kingdom is dynamic and continually evolving. This is the inner meaning
of the story of the great catch of fish in Luke 5:4–7.*

JOHN A. SANFORD, *THE KINGDOM WITHIN*

One morning I took my walk later than usual because I had seen
my daughter off to her first day of middle school. With her Superman
T-shirt and long, loose hair, she got on the bus. When the bus disappeared, I felt some sadness, but I soon realized how all that I had experienced before this very moment had led up to it—this moment of release
and letting go, this moment of movement, this moment of initiation for
us both.

As I entered the prairie spiral, a red-tailed hawk flew East while
six sandhill cranes called out from the South, initiating their purposes
through migration. Walking the spiral, my attention was drawn to the big
bluestem grass, rising in small clusters above most of the other fall prairie
plants, preparing to go to seed. The brown-red seeds dropped down from
the blades like droplets of sun-drenched dew. A fine thread held the seed
to the stem until it was time to be released.

In the same way, the perfect and natural time will come for the
release of each seed that *you* carry. And the sun and the soil as well as
the wind know what to do and will help create the perfect conditions
through their agreements, just as you have created the perfect conditions through your agreements. Finally, wind and time will assist the
mother plant to let go.

Not knowing exactly where they will land, the seeds take flight.

The initiation is complete—the seeds are fully ready to become
another big bluestem. Some of the seeds will find fertile soil, while others will be crushed by beak, or spread by bird. Some seeds will land on
unfriendly ground and not take root. This is also part of the agreement
the mother plant has with the natural world—her agreement is to send

out an abundance of seeds. Enough will take root. And a natural balance with the land will continue.

See your life now ready again for seed. Imagine sending out many seeds to find places to root, germinate, and grow. There is a promise of blossoms to come. There is a guarantee that your seeds will add to the beauty and integrity of the prairie (your family, community, and the world). *But you must actively send out all you've got.* Every day! Today!

The poet William Stafford got up every day before dawn to write in his journal. His aspiration generated many, many seeds of poetry, prose, and essays. I am one of the fertile soils in which his seeds of words and wisdom took root. So I become his soil and now, in the sharing of his poetry, his wind. There is a great agreement going on in the world, a natural conspiracy to have us all send forth our inner wealth to benefit everyone.

Winter's Next Spring

Winter's next spring will wake on fields
furrowed for seven seasons,
in extremes,
topsy-turvy.
Nature calls our better natures
to crack the crust to light,
in concert,
right-side up.
Whatever would be green must bide
its darkest times timelessly,
incandescent,
shoulder to shoulder.

DAVID ROZELLE

DEDICATION

We have been in this Wheel together, you and I. I may not have been there in physical form to witness your initiation journey, but my spirit was, just as you were with me as I transcribed my experiences on initiation into this book.

I would like to reiterate that our efforts should be dedicated to helping all beings wake up to their true natures. Dedicating our good efforts reminds us that we belong to each other. Our initiatory work is transpersonal; it goes beyond each of us. In the following passage, I borrow from Shantideva, in his dedicational verses in the *Bodhicaryāvatāra*. Please borrow from this as a prayer of dedication to use as you complete this round through the Wheel.

> *By all the merit I have accumulated*
> *By completion of this Wheel,*
> *May every being walk the path of initiation and*
> *   awakening.*
>
> *May all beings everywhere who are hooked by fear and*
> *   drama*
> *Who suffer in mind and body*
> *Have by virtue of my efforts*
> *Relief from victimization*
> *And have joy in boundless measure.*
>
> *May all beings realize their True Nature due to my efforts.*

And here is my prayer of dedication for *you*, dear reader:

> *May all your intentions be fulfilled and may your efforts*
> *be supported, may harmony prevail in your life, may you*
> *feel a strong connection to self and spirit, and may your*
> *purpose here be fully realized in the world. May you find*
> *peace and quiet to replenish yourself and with ease move*

through any habitual ways that may arise. May you always be able to access your inner wisdom and seek refuge and guidance in your chosen principles and root guru.

May your agreements to live a more sane, awakened life be sustained.

May all your dreams come true, and may you always have the resources and means to adhere to your spiritual practice. May you always know where you are in the Wheel (South, West, North, or East) and may you move through the Wheel again and again with little resistance and much joy.

And finally, may you always feel loved and blessed, knowing that we all belong to each other.

To My Initiation Circles

Belonging

Two cranes rise out of the creek, heading southeast
calling out their farewell
and their salutations.
I want them to land in our pond,
but they keep going.
Like an end of a circle
the sound of coming and going
are one and the same.
Always leaving to arrive
Always arriving to leave.
This is what Belonging sounds like—
the calling out of the cranes
as they pass.
This is what Belonging feels like
the longing to follow
while one stays.

The cranes land somewhere out of sight and sound.

And all this must bring me happiness
the passing of their call
the distance of where their beauty rests.

A moment of grace with you.

TEACHERS AND GROUPS

The Tao of Not Following

Not in Utopia, subterranean fields,
Or some secreted island, Heaven knows where!
But in the very world, which is the world
Of all of us, the place where, in the end,
We find our happiness, or not at all!

WILLIAM WORDSWORTH, FROM *THE PRELUDE*

Whatever affects one directly, affects all indirectly. I can never be what I ought to be until you are what you ought to be. This is the interrelated structure of reality.

MARTIN LUTHER KING JR.

You cannot own the power and the magic of this world. It is always available, but it does not belong to anyone.

CHÖGYAM TRUNGPA, *SHAMBHALA: THE SACRED PATH OF THE WARRIOR*

IN SEARCH OF THE PREMIUM TEACHER OR GROUP

Throughout the Wheel and this book, I recommend you find your own spiritual practices, resources, and related traditions. This investigation will likely lead you to spiritual teachers and groups. This chapter encourages you to undergo your search with caution and acute awareness.

When we set out on a pilgrimage to a sacred site, or plan to meet up with a spiritual teacher, or gather in a group to do spiritual work, the truly transformative experience will be in what we meet up with within ourselves. The spiritual pilgrimage or initiation may be deepened and supported by a skillful teacher or dynamic circle of peers. Martin Luther King spoke about how the "interrelated structure of reality" means that we are in this together—that we belong to each other. Due to this interrelated structure, seeking out a group or community to support your initiation makes sense.

The group or spiritual community is a wonderful place to practice all that you learn from texts, teachers, and other spiritual encounters. It can be an ideal place to progress through the Wheel. However, groups have the power to both transform and inhibit. They can be an avenue of encouragement or of control. The emphasis of any group, teacher, or process should be to get you in touch with your inner resources and your best qualities. The outer means needs to be a path to all the innate riches we carry within. The group or teacher must be a trusted ally for this transformation to take place.

But participation in a group is not essential, because all the practices within the Wheel can be done in an initiation circle or on your own. For those of you who want to join or create an initiation circle, I recommend that you first read Parker Palmer's book, *A Hidden Wholeness: The Journey Toward an Undivided Life,* as well as this chapter. For those who come into my year-long Initiation Course, reading Palmer's book is a prerequisite.

> *But this I can claim: every time we get in touch with the true source we carry within, there is net moral gain for all concerned. Even if we fail to follow its guidance fully, we are nudged a bit further in that direction. And the next time we are conflicted between inner truth and outer reality, it becomes harder to forget or deny that we have an inner teacher who wants to lay a claim on our lives.*
>
> PARKER PALMER, *A HIDDEN WHOLENESS*

Question Authority

Recently I attended a public-school gathering where the Pledge of Allegiance set the stage for the day. I overheard a mother direct her child of eight years, "Keep your eyes on the flag. Keep your eyes on the flag!" Of course, many of the adults around this child seemed to follow this rule and appeared to have their eyes on the flag as well. Apparently it was the right thing to do, without question.

Teaching a child (as well as employees, a congregation, or students) to follow rules and traditions without question generates a passive attitude to life. It teaches us to *follow* rather than listen. One doesn't have to question the way things are because one puts their trust, automatically, in the established dogma. And it often appears as if everyone else is following the same rules. Rules help to some degree if we are to function as a community. The danger is when we cut off our ability to hear our intuitive wisdom. Our intuition may be saying, "This isn't right!" while we follow the prevailing rules and dogma.

This is particularly troublesome, if not downright dangerous, in psychological and spiritual settings. The teacher or the doctrine may suggest that there is something wrong with you (not the situation) when you feel ashamed, afraid, or threatened. You may put expectations on yourself to assume the prevailing belief system. This pressure may be particularly strong in a group setting where most of the people present agree with and conform to a particular mind-set.

Being able to question authority and its attendant doctrine and rules is necessary for personal spiritual initiation. Spiritual initiation and pilgrimages purposefully remove initiates from their accustomed surroundings so that they will question how things are. This helps bring forth a transformation in their consciousness. The teacher or group you choose must be able to help you shift your perspective "from the flag" and onto other phenomena. The group or teacher should not insist that your eyes be upon their "flag." Instead, the group or process should lead you to inner doors, doors you will move through in your own way.

Some are afraid of the responsibility that goes along with such independence. They want the backup of set rituals, rules, or dogma, rather than taking the continued journey inward to discover and bring forth their own inherent qualities. Indeed, a healthy group (like the Truth Circles described in Parker Palmer's book, *A Hidden Wholeness*) can be quite helpful to one's transformative process. But too many of us have been trained since childhood to follow, copy, fit in, and do whatever we can to be part of a group. Many people just want to feel part of something and to know they are appreciated. When you are part of a group, there is also a tendency to lose the motivation to continue a given practice of meditation or contemplation on your own.

A woman once shared the story of how her son had died in a tragic accident at the age of three. It was a hard story for me to hear, having a young child myself. She told me how her minister told her if she had prayed hard enough and in the right way, her son would have been saved. She not only had to deal with the loss of her son but with the shame and blame put on her by this church elder and the congregation. Although she was deeply upset by what the minister had told her, she felt compelled to return to the church and feared for her immortal life if she did not.

When we set ourselves up to follow in this way, we never have to deal with the discomfort of the unknown or answer the difficult questions for ourselves. But alas, we also cut ourselves off from the beauty and mystery of personal spiritual experience. The real impetus of the word *initiation*, which is related to *initiative*, is that we take our own direction instead of going in the direction of the crowd. When this happens, some religious fundamentalists will say that we are heathens. Some of our friends or family may say we are being imprudent, and those who are somehow attached to us not taking a new direction may call us ridiculous.

Believe Nothing

Believe nothing just because a so-called wise person said it. Believe nothing just because a belief is generally held. Believe nothing just because it is said in ancient books. Believe nothing just because it is said to be of divine origin. Believe nothing just because someone else believes it. Believe only what you yourself test and judge to be true.

BUDDHA

The Buddha reminds us to discern for ourselves because he wants us to wake up to our truest selves, to awaken to our innate gifts, not to be Buddhists and not to follow him. Most of the major spiritual traditions and practices of the world hold one fundamental principle: that the purpose of this life is to wake up to our true nature—our Christ light, our essential selves, our Buddha nature, love, or our shakti, for instance. In his book *The Kingdom Within,* John Sanford points out how Jesus set the example of everyone's ability to awaken: "The whole self is in each of us as a potentiality, and seeks to be realized in the life process."

Euripedes said, "The wisest men follow their own direction and listen to no prophet guiding them." Ancient and contemporary truths hold *pointers* to the truth for all of us but should not be followed at the expense of the loss of a connection to one's own inner guidance and journey. The Buddha also said, "My teachings are like my finger pointing to the moon. Don't mistake my finger for the moon." The idea is to *experience* the moon for yourself, to take your own pilgrimage, to be familiar with personal initiation; in short—to be your own meaning-maker.

As we seek guidance, we can ask ourselves, "Am I in the mind of awareness, or am I merely following?" We can ask this question throughout the day, every day. Are we just following a schedule, plugging ourselves in, so to speak, and moving through the day without rocking the boat, without taking a conscious look around? Are we aware of our intentions and principles, or just reacting to what comes up for us in each moment? We can ask ourselves, *"Where in my life might I be following rather than creating and manifesting something of my own?"*

Partners in a marriage can fall into this rather easily, into a groove of following a certain way of being with each other, rather than opening up to the rawness and unpredictability of the moment. We too often see ourselves as "married," rather than *creating a marriage* with someone. If you follow the spiritual or religious ideas presented by someone else, you may have some powerful spiritual experiences, even peak experiences, but you will not be waking up. Peak spiritual experiences can be very seductive and can be valuable when one maintains a wakefulness, a mindfulness, and a consciousness with them, integrating them into daily life. Without this integration, these experiences are about as consequential as reading a very good novel.

One size does not fit all when it comes to a spiritual initiation. Find what fits you, what moves you consciously through your pilgrimage and your life. Don't eat the poisoned apple just because someone else offers it as a gift and you are hungry and lost in the woods. Discern for yourself— ask yourself, is this the right person or group to learn from and practice with? Perhaps it is best to go hungry for a while, to take your time. Spiritual truths, fortunately, come in a diversity of flavors. All truths need to be listened to with a curious heart and mind.

> The important thing is not to stop questioning. Curiosity has its own reason for existing. One cannot help but be in awe when he contemplates the mysteries of eternity, of life, of the marvelous structure of reality. It is enough if one tries merely to comprehend a little of this mystery every day. Never lose a holy curiosity.
>
> ALBERT EINSTEIN, SOURCE UNKNOWN

What to Keep Your Eyes On

Whereas many spiritual practices are thousands of years old, modern psychological principles are considered to have originated with Sigmund Freud. Of course, such practices as Lojong, mind transformation (Buddhism), the Four Agreements (Toltec), and *zikr* (Sufism) can easily be considered both spiritual and psychological.

The best teacher or group to support your personal spiritual initiation might offer both spiritual (ethical) and psychological practices and therefore be transpersonal. A safe and transpersonal practice will offer you an organic template of guidance free of dogma, rules, or rigid assumptions. It will be rich in tradition and linked to historical practices (such as yoga, Tibetan Buddhism, or depth psychology). But it will not forfeit present intentions and personal awareness for tradition.

Masterful teachers will often simplify techniques to make them accessible to their many students. I find this true of Geshe Tenzin Dorje and other teachers at the Wisconsin Deer Park Buddhist Center. They willingly present material in both advanced as well as simple formats for the diverse level of students who attend their classes. Realizing that Buddhism is not for everyone, they also encourage people to seek out the spiritual practice that suits them best.

Trust Your Experience

Choosing a teacher or group should be done through a rigorous investigation on your part. Geshe Tenzin Dorje reminds us that a teacher is choosen by the student, not the other way around. When choosing a group or teacher, let your *experience* be your guidepost, not the doctrine or practice. When a group process or teacher supersedes a person's intuition, a divergence between what one truly experiences and what the group or teacher insists one should experience may erupt. The moment you feel this divergence, question the process. Turn the questioning mind outward. I find myself at times uncomfortable and unnerved because I am either adventuring into new mental or spiritual territory, or old habitual ways are being challenged.

I now know enough to trust the process and move through these emotional states of mind on my own. When I feel ashamed, belittled, or stupid in my investigation and search, I question the origin of these feelings. *Am I still just bumping up against some internal baggage, or is there something in my environment that generates these negative emotional and cognitive states?* Am I being asked to place my eyes on the flag while my inner guide is nudging me elsewhere?

Be ready to ask yourself these same questions should disturbing feelings arise while investigating a teacher or group.

Use A Transpersonal Benchmark in Your Selection

A transpersonal process is more concerned with recognizing the needs and intentions of the seeker rather than enforcing some formula. Techniques such as meditation or mind-training practices may be provided, but the teacher always takes into account the abilities, willingness, and uniqueness of the students. The more transpersonal the practice, the more empowering it is likely to be for the seeker. A transpersonal practice is easily integrated into one's life and does not require a long-term financial commitment or a big down payment. A transpersonal practice does not recruit followers. Instead, it emphasizes personal responsibility and freedom. You are not encouraged to recruit others to this "way." Personal progress is attributed to the student's commitment and efforts, not to the healer, teacher, formula, ritual, or doctrine.

Such a practice unifies rather than divides. It connects the client/student to his or her local community and own intuitive wisdom. In fact, community service is an integral part of a truly transpersonal effort. In a transpersonal practice, the language is humane and not loaded. Loaded language is used as a source of directive control. Such vocabulary is meant to define various personal experiences and thoughts that the teacher or group wants the student to see and respond to. For example, you may be told you are either in or out of "integrity." Or your "commitment" or "understanding" may be challenged when you question authority. A charismatic recruiter may imply that there is something wrong with you if you don't sign up (and put up a finacial down payment) for their workshop.

Loaded language implies the teacher knows something that you do not have access to (even through your practice). Use of such loaded language may cut you off from your own intuitive judgment. The teacher or group is telling you when you have your eyes on the flag and when you are veering off in directions they are not happy with. Skillful therapists, group leaders, or spiritual teachers, on the other hand, may frame a response in a question, directing you to ask and trust yourself. They always give you room to discern for yourself.

Transpersonal teachings are fundamentally ethical, teaching one to be more socially, environmentally, and spiritually responsible. This kind of work also relies on science and natural law. Much can be revealed through contact with nature and through the laws of science (such as cause and effect, relativity, the interconnectedness of all living things). Transpersonal teachings view the student as part of a whole (not just part of a given group).

In transpersonal work, no one is out to convert anyone to a given way. As Joel Kramer and Diana Alstad write in *The Guru Papers,* "The power of conversion experiences lies in the psychological shift from confusion to certainty." Conversion often takes place without the one recruited really understanding the actuality of the experience. The conversion experience messes with our minds and emotions. So any time you are feeling confusion is a time to remain alert. When the group or the teacher insists that the confusion is *proof* that you must embrace *their* view—that they hold the way to certainty—then seeker beware! They may be setting up a conversion experience.

I once attended a retreat where the teacher showed a PowerPoint presentation that went on for two hours. It articulated all the atrocities we have done to each other, to the planet, and to ourselves. Many of the people in the group were already followers of this teacher; a few, like myself, were not. By the end of the presentation, most of us felt confused, ashamed, and *ready* for someone to show us how to save the world.

This was a strong and effective setup, in that everyone felt beholden to the teacher for guidance. One student came up to me so full of shame that she was ready to do whatever the teacher told her to do to help herself and the planet. No one challenged the teacher, so it *appeared* as if everyone was on the same page.

The reality is that the facts presented in the PowerPoint presentation were true, but the *spin* put on the presentation was one of fear, shame, and blame. The teacher's spin included how pissed off the spirits must be at us. (He, of course, claimed to have a special relationship with the spirit world.) When I later challenged his spin, he took the opportunity to publicly humiliate me. Fortunately, I knew where the exit doors were and left. Many remained, however, and those who did attributed their shift from confusion to clarity to the group process and to this teacher; they became ready converts.

In transpersonal work, we give most of the credit to our own willingness and courage when the transformation takes place. Before entering a group or working with a teacher, have a sense of your own intentions and ideals. When you are grounded in your intentions and values, it is not so easy for others to manipulate you. When you are vulnerable, or are searching for truth outside yourself, or lack your own value system, you are more likely to be manipulated and even converted. This does not mean you should never join a circle when you are vulnerable; simply be more aware of who or what you are joining.

The Sacred Circle of Initiation

If you decide to be part of an initiation circle, I recommend that everyone agree that the circle only go on for a year as you progress through the Wheel together. If there is a teacher or facilitator, she or he should not create another need to gather once the year is complete. The sole intention of the group and the leader should be to facilitate the personal initiation of everyone involved. Furthermore, I recommend that the circle be focused on the process the Wheel offers and not be distracted by other topics.

Ultimately, everyone in the group has lives, commitments, and intentions that are outside the group. This group is a temporary structure that supports personal spiritual initiation and holds space for transpersonal work. As you may have already discovered while reading this book, group members typically hold different spiritual practices while participating in the initiation circle together. (People in the same initiation circle may not even be from the same community.)

This diversity helps with the dynamic and purposes of the initiation process. It is not about belonging to this particular group; instead, the energy goes into everyone's personal initiation. Groups or teachers whose primary intention is to maintain the group on an ongoing basis will end up directing too much energy to attendance and doctrine. We have witnessed too many times the harm that can come when a group's intention is somehow to form a following.

The integrity of a given group is defined by the intent and motivations of the group and its facilitator. Always be conscious of the intention of the group, as well as the process and teachings offered. Also, be aware that the intentions of the group may change over time; remain alert to this.

A small circle of limited duration that is intentional about its process will have a deeper, more life-giving impact than a large, ongoing community that is shaped by the norms of conventional culture.

PARKER PALMER, *A HIDDEN WHOLENESS*

Whereas you have a shared focus of personal spiritual initiation and certain agreements while in the circle together, there can be great diversity of spiritual traditions and aspirations among members, as mentioned earlier. For example, when in the North of the Wheel, everyone is supported in finding a personal root guru. This may be central to some and less valuable to others. It is not expected that everyone in the group will have the same root guru—this is an individual choice.

The initiation circle should simply create a container for personal inquiry and an organic template for raising one's consciousness. The first part of creating or being part of an initiation circle is to create a place that is safe for the soul to emerge. Respect for the shared agreements and known intentions make the circle safe for this emergence. Circle members need to feel a strong commitment to these agreements and to be skillful mirrors for one another. This safety will be up to you to discern and maintain. Don't leave this solely in the hands of even the most skillful teacher or facilitator.

The initiation circle can be considered a *borderland,* a place where the next new paradigm is dawning for you. After you have gone through the Wheel once and been initiated, you can reenter the Wheel on your own, initiating more intentions and aspects of your true self. Ultimately, all types of initiation are about movement—from one place of consciousness and experience to another, more evolved one. This is why I get concerned when people "join" groups and then become trained to become facilitators of the same group, promoting certain set beliefs and practices that give the illusion of movement and growth but actually may keep the individual's eyes "on the flag," as it were. It keeps their view on someone else's agenda.

My first teacher in the Vipassana tradition, Shinzen Young, reminded us regularly to "seek other teachers and teachings" to strengthen and deepen our practice. He believed that to receive instruction from only one teacher would inhibit one's progress.. This is not about bouncing around from practice to practice. As I suggested in the North, we must choose and keep to our principles and spiritual path if we want to evolve spiritually. But an exposure to diverse teachings helps expand our view and enables us to see that there are indeed many paths to truth.

> But we know very little about creating spaces that invite the soul to make itself known. Apart from the natural world, such spaces are hard to find—and we seem to place little value on preserving the soul spaces in nature.
>
> PARKER PALMER, A HIDDEN WHOLENESS

IN THE CIRCLE

If you have been hurt in your family of origin, and this remains active as an unconscious wound (pain story), you will come into an initiation circle (or most any group, for that matter) and attempt to recreate the trauma (the dynamic surrounding the wound). You do this with the unconscious motivation to heal the wound. We unconsciously repeat the conditions of the wound so we can change the outcome.

The underlying reason for this is that we all want to experience the love, appreciation, or acceptance that was lacking, not because we want to keep on suffering. We also will repeat the habitual patterns that allowed us to survive the family dysfunction (bullying, sarcasm, defensiveness, addictions, feeling righteous, feeling wrong, for example). These provided us a means to survive a difficulty (our pain stories) and therefore benefited us, so they are hard to give up.

We then either assume that if we find ourselves in a similar painful situation, we can control the situation (reinventing the pain of the past) and finally get the love, appreciation, or acceptance we did not get from our families; or we rely on our habitual patterns of survival. We all have done this in our relationships, and it always results in more suffering, not less. (The adult child of an alcoholic is a magnet for an alcoholic partner in the hope—albeit unconscious—that this time they can sober up their loved one and receive love in return.) Therefore, when we enter the initiation circle, we must consciously challenge these agreements so that we don't get hooked into the story lines of our pain stories. The pain stories will arise while in the Wheel, of course. But we simply agree not to act them out within the circle. We take 100 percent responsibility for our experience (a strong motivation for this agreement).

Neither can we put any of our own issues on anybody else in the initiation circle. (This is a gateway to freedom from within and without—we will not transfer our stuff to someone else.) Only we ourselves can initiate what needs movement and healing in our lives. So, we let the Wheel of Initiation bring forth what needs transformation, and we let the circle be the sacred *borderland* for this process while agreeing to consciously and intentionally heal and transform our own lives.

Remember, both conscious and unconscious agreements are energetic contracts. Over the year that you spend in an initiation circle, you will be strengthening life-enhancing agreements and freeing yourself from those that are not truly serving you. You will get to the root of one or several agreements and uproot them. You will retrieve energy you have lost to negative agreements. This journey will transform relationships and agreements as long as you keep the integrity strong by staying focused on your own internal process and use this book to move through the Wheel (borrowing from the group practices articulated in Parker Palmer's book *A Hidden Wholeness* as need be).

A typical group session may include starting with everyone checking in about his or her progress through the Wheel. Then there would be a reading and a practice from this book. The session would then end with closing statements. A group session is typically three hours long. Mirroring is practiced with one another, except in closing statements where everyone shares a brief statement without a response. On a night where someone is sharing his or her life story, the entire evening is given to listening to and mirroring the storyteller. The facilitator of the circle is the one guiding the participants through this group process.

THE ART OF MIRRORING

Reexamine all you have been told at school or church or in any book, dismiss whatever insults your own soul, and your very flesh shall be a great poem.

WALT WHITMAN, PREFACE TO *LEAVES OF GRASS*, 1855

In a healthy, dynamic family, a child is born, and the parents understand, "I am here to help this child become who they are intended to become. I am here to help them fulfill their destiny and needs." And the parents naturally mirror the child. Reflected in this mirror are the child's true nature and all the potential that goes with this. In an unhealthy, non-dynamic family, a child is born, and the parents believe (consciously or not), "This child is here to fulfill my needs, to make me happy. This child is here to assist me in fulfilling my destiny." And the child is not mirrored the truth of who they are and what they can become.

I recently watched the movie *Guess Who's Coming to Dinner*, which starred Sidney Poitier. A favorite scene of mine is when Poitier, playing the fiancé, confronts his father with his intention to marry a white girl. The father, who is opposed to this plan, reminds the son just how much he and his mother have sacrificed for him. The son reminds the father that the son owed him nothing for doing what a father is supposed to do.

Like this family, most families fall somewhere between the ideal and the extreme. It is likely that some mirroring went on in your own family. However, most people come into my groups and sessions with a serious lack of mirroring and find profound healing occurs when they are mirrored, as well as when they learn how to mirror others.

Mirroring is a key dynamic in Parker Palmer's *Circles of Truth,* and it is a central skill in my initiation circles. This skill is essential to practice when going through the Wheel in a group setting. When we share our life stories with each other, the rest of the circle mirrors back to the story-teller what they have witnessed—the true nature of this person and their all their potentialities, as well as how they handled their challenges. In a group, the sharing of life stories begins around the second month, because it takes an entire evening to do a story. My groups typically comprise between ten and fourteen people, so this takes up three to four months of the year's gatherings.

Telling one's life story is quite transformative, because often the person has never shared their life story and has never been mirrored. We learn and practice deep listening to each other without projecting our internal struggles and assumptions on the other.

Cindy's Experience of Mirroring

MIRRORING WAS FOREIGN to me. I was raised in a family that discussed problems in an effort to find solutions, but this was not always done in the most pleasant way. When my story was mirrored in the initiation circle, I felt affirmed. I suddenly felt seen and accepted, even valuable. I was not viewed as damaged goods to be repaired. Learning to mirror was also a challenge. Taking time to listen and not interpret opened my eyes. Just being with someone in their story and their memories was an honor. This new way of listening allowed me to see that person's beauty and strength. If I'd been stuck calculating solutions to their problems, I would have missed the big picture. I would not have been able to accept and affirm them for exactly who they are.

Mirroring and being mirrored have helped me in my daily life. I am in less of a hurry to give advice (although I do notice how others are always wanting to advise me!). I view others as being more capable and wonderful than I used to. I also feel stronger and more valuable. I trust myself. I feel a solid core of love from my circle and myself. Somehow this acceptance of the cycles within my friends and myself gives me hope for humankind and the planet. Mirroring has been a huge blessing for me.

When mirroring, you become the other's *Terton*, which in Tibetan means a Treasure Revealer. Those who can see and hear beyond illusions and projections can then reveal other's treasures to them. (Historically, secret texts, called *terma* in Tibetan, were hidden until such time that their treasures could be revealed to those ready for such knowledge.) As a Terton, you can point the way to the other's inner hidden treasures. Those qualities were buried but not lost and have been waiting to be discovered. When you are mirroring, you are able to do this, and as you practice it you become a mirror outside your circle too; you begin to apply this practice in the course of your waking day. As a mirror, you know yourself as a Terton, and this is healing as well.

When we hear other people's stories, numerous levels of healing occur within each of us. Stories touch us where we are vulnerable and help us notice what may need our loving attention in our own lives. Listening deeply to others' personal stories shows us how agreements generate experiences and patterns, and how changing agreements can transform the direction of our lives.

> *We are all shaped by conventional culture. So we all come into a clearness committee (Truth Circle) carrying a gravitational force that tries to pull our relationships back to fixing, saving, advising, and setting each other straight.*
>
> PARKER PALMER, *A HIDDEN WHOLENESS*

To be a mirror, we agree to put our full attention on the one who is sharing. We actively listen. We can notice what comes up within ourselves, but we set that aside for the time being. When the person is done sharing, two or three individuals who have been selected ahead of time will mirror the storyteller's story back to him or her. In so doing, they shouldn't make suggestions, give feedback, or counsel the person in any way. (The facilitator of the initiation circle has the right to stop anyone who is doing just that.) Instead, the mirror paraphrases what he or she has heard from the person sharing the story.

In mirroring a story, we listen for the themes of beauty and truth that weave this person's life together. We reflect back to the other his or her qualities and strengths. When you listen to the story, you are a witness— so you can ask yourself, "What am I witnessing here?"

Lynee Lets Go

AFTER TELLING MY STORY and being mirrored, I felt like I was being heard and known at a deep level for the first time. It was like being forgiven (in a letting-go sense) and releasing the past, just to have others hear my story in that way. It made me realize how we hold onto things because we think nobody else understands. When I was mirrored and felt understood, I no longer needed to hang on to the past.

When they are mirroring a story, mirrors can take some notes if they like, because the story can go on for up to two-and-a-half hours. Mirrors spend their time in *understanding* others rather than trying to be understood. When we get into defending ourselves, projecting our views, or proving ourselves, or are attached to our perspective, we no longer clear the way for understanding and lack the clarity to mirror.

Within the initiation circles, we borrow from the process invented by the early Quakers called the "clearness committee" (more on this can also be found in Parker Palmer's book, *A Hidden Wholeness*). Its name comes from its ability to help provide needed clarity. In my training on the clearing process, I observed the power and medicine of being a witness for others. I noticed how those who have to share their opinions are often the ones protecting the false self.

As each of us evolves and opens up to our own truths, it is important that we do not make anyone else the reason for our success, happiness, or growth. No matter how dynamic the teacher or profound the spiritual experience, what happens is due to our own awareness and opening. A skillful group will create the dynamics that makes it possible to go through the Wheel or to practice one's spiritual principles without getting entangled with dogma, rules, or personal drama, thereby offering a place where personal spiritual initiation can occur.

A'cha'rya, Murshid, Guru, Teacher

The teacher's role is to show the student the possibility of presence. The pointing-out instructions are the transmission: together the teacher and student create the conditions in which the student sees what the teacher is pointing to.

KEN MCLEOD, WAKE UP TO YOUR LIFE

At a teaching I attended at Deer Park in Wisconsin, Geshe Lhundub Sopa spoke on the importance of finding a skillful teacher. He emphasized "seeing the difference between a teacher that shows the inner path versus one that shows the outer path." Mark the difference between these two types of teachings, he suggested. Ask yourself, is the inner path of discipline, meditation, and contemplation emphasized, or are the externals such as ritual, appearances, and traditions emphasized? Choose a teacher that focuses on the inner path.

In the words of A'cha'rya Jina'neshvar (James Powell), a teacher:

I think a good teacher practices what they preach. In yoga I am considered an *acharya*. This is a name for teacher, but on a more subtle level it means, "One who leads by example." This does not imply perfection or mastery, but instead a sincere attempt to practice (not perfect) the spiritual lifestyle. I take this as a tough challenge to myself. My shortcomings keep me humble and therefore help me be understanding of and empathetic to the struggles of those I have a teacher's responsibility toward. Being a teacher should be an inspiration to keep working on oneself.

I would want a teacher to respect where their students are in their development and not push their own agenda at the student's expense. In other words, healers and teachers should have a higher proportion of love and compassion and keep their own will on a leash. Too many teachers are not aware of their own shadows and therefore lean too much on their students to validate their teaching. Not that there is anything wrong with being validated or liking validation; it is the attachment to it and hence the subtle message that you'd better embrace my way or you're not okay. A good teacher knows they are in service of a higher power and hopefully this comes through in their demeanor.

A good teacher has a softness about them. They have a love and respect for others. They also convey an innocence. This brings the Dalai Lama to mind—He is a Guru that is a model for teachers to aspire to. A good teacher speaks to your soul. Someone may be a good teacher but they don't "speak" to you. So not all good teachers are right for everybody. This should be respected. One doesn't have to necessarily figure out if a teacher is good or not but rather are they good for you? Do they speak to what you need for spiritual growth? A good teacher will not force their message on those who do not have ears to hear.

Finally, a teacher should understand the power dynamic that they potentially have with their students and not exploit this transferential relationship.

When you are choosing a teacher, it is also beneficial if you have knowledge of some of the techniques that you will be practicing; often these are passed down through a lineage of teachers. A'cha'rya Jina'neshvar uses cooking as an example—"It's good to know the recipe before you cook." Whereas someone who trusts their intuition can create their own meals with what they have, most of us need at least some basic instruction. You don't become a skillful biologist simply by proclaiming, "I am a biologist."

You must study with those who are knowledgeable and seasoned. A tradition or practice, as well as a skillful teacher, carry years, likely even lifetimes, of knowledge within them, and they are willing to share the benefit of this with you. By means of a skillful teacher, this information is accessible to everyone. In Geshe Lhundub Sopa's book *Steps on the Path to Enlightenment,* he offers an entire chapter on the student-teacher relationship, "Relying on the Spiritual Teacher." In this tradition, the teacher-student relationship is the cornerstone of a successful practice, emphasizing the qualities of a worthy teacher and a prepared student.

I don't favor conversion.

THE FOURTEENTH DALAI LAMA,
MADISON, WISCONSIN, JULY 2008

A GOOD TEACHER

- Helps you contemplate and consider your world of choices.
- Points a clear way based on proven wisdom but does not insist that you follow it.
- Asks you skillful questions rather than relying solely on feedback.
- Generates movement and transformation. You experience shifts in consciousness and real transformation when you follow through on what the teacher points to. You don't feel "stuck" for years.
- Answers your questions in a way that you understand and can use.
- Witnesses and honors your power and skills. A teacher is a masterful mirror.
- Never expects you to be part of a following or to recruit others. Does not encourage converts.
- Does not "pick" you as his or her student; you have chosen the teacher through a rigorous investigation.
- Directs you to other teachers and resources.
- Is up front and open about his or her own beliefs and practices.
- Sets an example by practicing and demonstrating what he or she teaches.
- Expresses true humility. The teacher knows and shows how he or she is just like you (even though the teacher should be more versed in a given tradition).
- Has a sense of humor and incorporates this into the teachings.
- Is willing to admit to mistakes, or lack of knowledge.
- Money is not a big factor in the exchange. You do not have to put up a lot (or any) money to receive spritual teachings.

The best teachers have been preparing for their roles as guides and examples for a very long time.

SURRENDERING TO THE TEACHER

In various traditions, including my Buddhist practice, we are often asked to surrender to the teacher or teachings. We do this because we find a spiritual teacher that we can rely on. I surrendered to all my teachers. For me, "surrendering" allows me to be the student practitioner; to be open enough to receive the teachings and alert enough to discern what is being taught. With surrendering, you can absorb it all, listen, learn, and then decide for yourself what works for you and what doesn't. We can surrender fully to the teachings while always remaining centered in ourselves.

Each lesson, although it may be difficult, should empower you somehow and strengthen your relationship to your spiritual practice. The teacher isn't in a position always to make you feel good, but should point to the inner teacher. When a lot is blocking the way to this inner source, some lessons will likely feel painful and difficult.

The skillful teacher will continue to give you the means to aspire and practice. Without this willingness to surrender to the teacher and the teachings, a personal spiritual initiation is unlikely. After all, an internal revolution and transformation of consciousness takes a serious commitment and some guidance from someone who has experienced it for him-or herself. This can come in the form of a transpersonal counselor, a spiritual teacher such as His Holiness the Dalai Lama, a meditation teacher, or a yogi, for example. Find someone who is versed and practiced in your chosen spiritual path. As Geshe Lhundub Sopa explains in *Steps on the Path to Enlightenment,* "Spiritual teachers who try to teach others self-discipline must first experience for themselves how to tame their own body, speech, and mind. Then they can teach based on their own experience and accomplishment. They will lead by example."

Even though we may receive great benefit from a teacher, if the teacher clearly crosses an ethical boundary, you must find an exit strategy. As a heads-up, however, there may be many shades of gray here. It may be the case that a teacher causes you a great deal of pain, but the teacher may not be irrefutably unethical. I view someone claiming powers that they do not actually have, or scamming people in various ways, as unethical, but such a teacher may not be viewed this way by others. We must stay alert enough to discern this for ourselves. Again, go through a lengthy investigation of a given teacher before claiming them as yours.

> *Each student must be encouraged to take responsible measures to confront teachers with unethical aspects of their conduct. If the teacher shows no sign of reform, students should not hesitate to publicize any unethical behavior of which there is irrefutable evidence. This should be done irrespective of other beneficial aspects of his or her work and of one's spiritual commitment to that teacher.*
>
> THE FOURTEENTH DALAI LAMA

Beware Spiritual Seduction

Spiritual seduction occurs when we are attached to receiving spiritual insight, connections, appreciation, recognition, or validation from someone we deem more spiritually gifted than ourselves. In spiritual seduction, someone seduces you with "spiritual compliments." The statement "You are an expression of the divine" is not a lie; it is the *intention* of the flattering remark that is the problem. *Seduction is a compliment with a twist.* Wherever we feel separated from our own inner truth, seduction can be employed to make us feel better about ourselves, albeit only temporarily.

When I was in my early thirties, I had been meditating for nearly twenty years, had recently found the Mahayana path of Buddhism, and had a strong community of friends. I felt strong in my practice, yet I carried a secret assumption that some people were spiritually more potent than others and therefore more connected to spiritual truth. And thus, like many other people, I had a hidden tendency to give myself over to someone I felt was "better" than me. But this tendency was repressed (and therefore in my shadow), because I saw myself as a gifted meditation teacher and therapist and one unlikely to give myself away to anyone. I was single at the time, and this too had its share of shadow and vulnerabilities as well. Put these elements together and introduce me to an ex-Buddhist monk—and viola! a setup for seduction was in place.

It did not take long for me to give myself away to seduction. Like a moth blindly going to the flame, we can find ourselves in agreement to seduction because we get hooked by "feeling and being" special somehow, forgetting we are on our own, extra-ordinary. The ex-monk would make comments about my special spiritual skills. Not believing in myself enough, I was easily seduced. If I had been stronger in my sense of my spiritual self, his compliments would have simply been a mirror. (I would take it as an acknowledgment of the obvious.) Furthermore, we often *want* others to have special abilities so that we can depend on them instead of our own efforts. This is the agreement to look outside ourselves for what we think we need, because spiritual seduction is fundamentally an *agreement*. You can't seduce someone who is strong in themselves. Spiritual seduction also plays out the culturally endorsed agreement to be in a state of needing something. Wherever we lack self-esteem is an entry point for seduction.

Fortunately, my primary teacher at the time worked with me. I freed myself from the grip of spiritual seduction and went on to research and study the dynamics of mind control, narcissism,* and the shadow found in different aspects of the spiritual student-teacher relationship.

> It may seem clever to know and accept others
> Yet accepting oneself is the way to Wisdom.
> It may feel powerful to overcome others
> Yet disciplining ourselves is true strength.
> It may be noble to honor others
> Yet respecting oneself is deep self-esteem.
>
> CHUNGLIAN AL HUANG AND JERRY LYNCH,
> *MENTORING*

---

*For more on narcissism, read James F. Masterson, M.D., *The Search for the Real Self.*

SIGNS OF SPIRITUAL SEDUCTION

Spiritual seduction occurs when you are vulnerable in entering a spiritually significant relationship and do not remain alert. You should always maintain a presence, a questioning view. Ask yourself, "Does this feel true to me? Does this feel right?" Even when I "surrender" to a teacher or teachings, I remain alert and present to my experiences. Of course, a skillful teacher grounded in his or her practice would never knowingly enter into a seductive relationship.

Common signs of spiritual seduction include:

- You somehow are made to feel special to this person. You are given a special role in the group, or the teacher implies a special bond between you. The teacher may speak of spiritual dynamics in a way that states there is a karmic bond between you ("It is destined").
- Promises are implied or made by the teacher with regard to your role in his or her life.
- You come to believe that this relationship is somehow your destiny. This prevents you from challenging it.
- The teacher controls your behavior and often your appearance, influencing what you do and wear. Again, this can be implied or stated.
- You let this other person make decisions (often big ones) for you. It may seem as if you are making the choice, but you cannot diverge much or at all from what the other wants.
- At some point your energy feels drained.
- You need to go back to that particular person for a fix. You find you have to be with this person. As a result, you may give up other relationships or goals. (The teacher does not discourage this dependency.)
- Isolation and control are part of the relationship's dynamic. The teacher may further isolate you from friends and community and doesn't recommend you seek others for insight or guidance unless the teacher approves of them.

- The teacher often depends on a following (even if it is a small one). The teacher needs to be viewed as important to others.
- You doubt yourself. (This is a big one, a pointer that something is not right.) You hesitate and doubt your ability to make the right choices.
- It seems to you that your relationship with this person gives you special privileges or access to the spiritual world or to spiritual truths.

Often people are drawn to the more seductive, charismatic, but self-serving teacher. To remain with such a teacher, you have to dissolve yourself into the teacher's "light" (not the light of god, or your own inner light). The light may be a false light, dependent on some outside source—you—for energy. When in the teacher's presence, you must pretend not to have your own light. In a seductive dynamic your light cannot outshine that of the teacher.

A challenge with spiritual seduction is that we have to become conscious of it, but the seduction itself makes this difficult. Beacause we feel special, we don't want to question the relationship. Also, when a teacher has given us access to the spiritual dimensions we crave, it's hard to notice that this is problematic. In general, if you feel dependent on a teacher, this is a warning to step back and gain more perspective on this relationship.

ENDING SEDUCTION AND GAINING FREEDOM

I have taught the way without making any distinction between inner and outer teaching. For in respect of the truth there must be no such thing as the "closed fist" of the teacher, who hides some essential knowledge from the pupil. Secrecy is the mark of false doctrine.

THE DIGHA-NIKĀYA,
FROM THE SUTTA PITAKA DISCOURSES

If you believe you have been seduced by a teacher or group, let them think what they want to while you put your energy into getting away from them. Be like the lizard that drops its tail and then leaves it behind in order to get away from a predator. They may think they "got you" as they chew on your tail, but you have escaped to freedom. Sacrifice what you don't need—approval, praise from the teacher, or recognition (the tail), and leave. The lizard's tail grows back, as will your sense of self.

Because our need for outside validation is so strong, spiritual predators are ever present. (Both the predator and the victim are dependent on outside validation.) Interestingly, the same dynamics and steps to freedom found in spiritual seduction are also found when someone is in the grips of any kind of controlling relationship. Because you cannot influence or change the mind of the other, focus your attention on getting out of the relationship. Don't let anyone hold you captive. Only be part of a group that has an open door, and that encourages you to be part of other groups and teachings.

When attending a group or receiving teachings from someone, pay attention to your dreams. Dreams can warn you if you are in danger; they can point out discrepancies. Our dreams are not concerned about the teacher's feelings but are wholly invested in *our* integrity and well-being. If you are in a problematic relationship or group, dreams are likely to point this out to you. If you need help in interpreting them, get a skillful dream partner or coach. If a teacher or group is in question, seek outside help.*

Ultimately we honor the outer teacher by *not* following them; instead we honor the teacher through our ethical and spiritual practices. In an appropriate spiritual student-teacher relationship (when done ethically), we respect the teacher by nourishing ourselves spiritually. When we agree to become a student of a spiritual teacher, we agree to live a principled life, knowing this benefits our teachers as well.

Below is a checklist to use if you are considering joining up with a

---

*A dream consultant I often use is Laurel Reinhardt, Ph.D. She is a dream coach who resides in North Carolina. More information about her can be found in the resources section of this book.

teacher or a group. It may also be used to assess a teacher or group you are presently working with. Because our hearts tend to be open and vulnerable when searching for a teacher, using these questions can be helpful in evaluating a given teacher, healer, therapist, or group. I recommend you do this even if you are certain the group or teacher is acceptable.

1. Are you mistaking knowledge or spiritual gifts as proof of a skillful teacher? One may be gifted but not be safe, ethical, or qualified to teach.

2. Does the group feel separate and shut off from the surrounding community? Beneficial practices will be easily integrated into one's daily life and community.

3. Does the teacher admit to mistakes right there on the spot? A questionable teacher may tell stories of "past" mistakes but not come clean when challenged on the spot. Instead the teacher may point to the student as being at fault in some way. Or the teacher may rely on doctrine or credentials to back himself or herself up. After all, the teacher has proven somehow that he or she has a special connection to god or to the spirit world.

4. Is there too much emphasis on ritual and other outer practices and little on internal processes such as meditation and personal analysis and inquiry?

5. Do the group members or students progress after a while? If no one progresses, something is wrong.

6. Are the teacher's words and actions in alignment? For instance, the teacher may say something like, "No shame or blame," while the teacher does, in fact, shame and blame. The teacher's actions must match his or her words. To discern this, you must pay attention to what the teacher says and how it feels in your body when he or she says it.

7. Is the teacher dependent on a following? Does the teacher seem always to be surrounded by followers (even a small group?). The teacher may well rely on your continuing to feel inadequate to meet the need to have a following.

8. Do you feel small around the teacher? I have never felt small in the presence of the Dalai Lama or Geshe Lhundub Sopa, even though I recognize that their knowledge and skill level far surpasses mine.

9. Does the teacher push rules and doctrine? As Geshe Lhundub Sopa pointed out, the skillful teacher emphasizes the *internal* path of meditation, contemplation, and analysis. Although his teachings are steeped in tradition and ancient doctrines, the student must rely on the inner path of investigation and practice.

10. Are boundaries and agreements blurred? Too many circles become incestuous (emotionally and psychologically), and boundaries and agreements get blurred. To hold a safe, dynamic, and spiritually oriented circle is inherently precarious—sometimes for the teacher, but more often for the students. A teacher must have clear boundaries and agreements with self, the students, and spirit. A teacher must get his or her emotional, spiritual, and social needs met outside the circle the teacher is working with. *Good boundaries allow the teacher and student to focus on the practice rather than getting caught up in relationship dynamics.* I have witnessed many groups where the teacher or facilitator is a friend of everyone in the circle, and inevitably jealousies develop, people feel betrayed, and dramas ensue.

11. Does the teacher have a closed fist? Does the teacher maintain an authoritarian certainty that he or she has some secret knowledge or insight that the followers tend to lack (unless you have a special alliance with the teacher)? Masterful teachers are motivated to share all they have come to learn and understand with an intention to benefit their students.

12. Does the teacher or group use fear to manipulate? Wherever fear is used as a means to bring you into the practice—run, don't walk—away. Fear is a method of control. Someone once forwarded me a group e-mail sent out from an angry teacher. There was some dissent in his group of followers, and a few students were challenging his methods and claims (and rightly so). His four pages of threats included "Those who pray alone, pray with the devil," warning wandering students that they cannot deal with the spiritual world on their own.

13. Are you allowed the means to process the experience in the group or outside the group setting? Inside the group, are you told what to feel and experience? Outside the group, do you feel you are betraying the group or the teacher if you speak up about your concerns?

14. Are authoritarian rules of conduct enforced? Irvin D. Yalom, an expert on group dynamics, states, "Authoritarianism will not breed personal autonomy but, on the contrary, always stifles freedom. We will go to any length to avoid responsibility and to embrace authority even, if necessary, if it requires us to pretend to accept responsibility." Yalom points out that the authoritarian group pushes its members to take personal responsibility for their lives while at the same time maintaining an authoritarian stance. When I attend Deer Park Buddhist Center in Wisconsin, I prostrate because I choose to, not because it is required. (Many attend the teachings without prostrating first.)

When any of these factors are present in a teacher-student relationship or group, the relationship is questionable. If more than one is true, you may be in jeopardy of being spiritually seduced or may be in a controlling situation or caught in the grip of a narcissist teacher.

If this is the case, you cannot hope to have a personal or real shift in consciousness. Basically, you cannot have life-altering experiences that lead to freedom, transcendence, and lasting happiness if you are following another's path or are in the grips of a cultlike group or charismatic teacher. When we continue to travel the path of consciousness, to reenter the Wheel of Initiation (while engaging in our own chosen spiritual principles and practices), we will continue to experience the various stages of initiation for ourselves. There will be times of great, even profound, awareness, and times of experiencing how little we know. We are, however, led to similar universal truths, which can be condensed into the realization that we are each sacred and holy. We each carry an inner light.

What kind of group we join to help us on our spiritual journey or the qualities of a given teacher are strong influences on our path. But even with the best of teachers and the most beneficial of practices, we are still ultimately on our own. At some point we must do the return journey and practice and live what we know in our day-to-day lives.

> *The return is seeing*
> *the radiance everywhere.*
>
> JOSEPH CAMPBELL

Hidden in View

Grace

> *The woods is shining this morning.*
> *Red, gold and green, the leaves*
> *lie on the ground, or fall,*
> *or hang full of light in the air still.*
> *Perfect in its rise and fall, it takes*
> *the place it has been coming to forever.*
> *It has not hastened here, or lagged.*
> *See how surely it has sought itself,*
> *its roots passing lordly through the earth.*
> *See how without confusion it is*
> *all that it is, and how flawless*
> *its grace is. Running or walking, the way*
> *is the same. Be still. Be still.*
> *"He moves your bones, and the way is clear."*
>
> WENDELL BERRY,
> *THE SELECTED POEMS OF WENDELL BERRY*

This day, on our walk down the driveway to catch my daughter's school bus, a bald eagle graced us. This impressive bird sat perched on a tree only a few yards from the house. We took time to admire it. The eagle remained in the tree after the bus took my daughter out of sight. I stood in silence watching as the eagle looked out over the field. Then I went inside for my morning meditation. Later I came out to find the eagle leaving its perch and flying across the field to the distant eastern hill of trees.

This wet March day created a view of white snow still lingering in spots among the grays and blacks of the oaks and pines. As the eagle flew East and landed in a tree across the valley, it disappeared, blending in with the trees and the patches of snow and grayness. Seeing the beauty of this bird so unusually close was a gift, but watching it blend into the eastern hill and trees offered a greater lesson. I knew that, hidden *yet in full view, the eagle sat looking out over the valley, too.* I wondered how many mornings that eagle had been perched there, across the valley, looking out, present but unseen?

The eagle expressed for me what some call the omnipresence of the Creator or the Buddha; others name the luminous void or the invisible but unifying principle, the Tao. Though it may be hidden or disguised, *it is always there.*

Everywhere present, hidden in view.

RESOURCES

ALTERNATIVE PRODUCTS

For alternative children's toys, progressive gifts, and books for the initiated adult, go to www.SyracuseCulturalWorkers.com.

BREATHWORK RESOURCES

Transpersonal Breathwork should be done with a trained breathwork facilitator such as Stanislav Grof; his website is www.holotropic.com. Please refer to it for training in Holotrophic Breathwork as well as links to other Holotropic facilitators around the country.

Noted breathwork facilitator and shamanic healer Linda Star Wolf's website is www.shamanicbreathwork.org. Her book *Shamanic Breathwork: Journeying Beyond the Limits of the Self* is a wonderful resource for anyone interested in pursuing breathwork; it is available through her website.

DREAMS

For a professional consultation about your initiatory dreams contact Laurel Reinhardt, Ph.D., at www.innerlandscaping.com.

GROUP DYNAMICS AND LEADERSHIP

For more on healthy group dynamics and leadership skills go to Parker Palmer's official website: www.couragerenewal.org/parker. It includes information about his Circle of Trust Retreats, as well as interviews, books, and a dynamic blog.

For useful information on cults and unsafe groups and leaders check out Rick Ross's website: www.rickross.com/warningsigns.html.

For an example of leadership in the media go to Bill Moyer's online journal, which includes archives on Joseph Campbell: www.pbs.org/moyers/journal/blog.

MAHAYANA AND BUDDHIST RESOURCES

The website of the Deer Park Buddhist Center in Oregon, Wisconsin, is www.deerparkcenter.org. This website includes photos of the Stupa, a schedule of teachings, and Geshe Sopa's biography.

For news, a calendar, and updates directly from His Holiness the Fourteenth Dalai Lama go to his official website: www.dalailama.com.

For information on the Mahayana Tradition and its practices, go to the Foundation for the Preservation of the Mahayana Tradition: www.fpmt.org. This is the official website of Lama Zopa Rinpoche and includes information about practices, free online classes, and referrals to many other related websites.

MAPS

For new ways to see the world, visit the website: www.ODTmaps.com. They offer a free online newsletter and educational material concerning alternative maps of the world.

NATIVE AMERICAN SPIRITUALITY

The website of Eagle Man (Ed McGaa) is http://edmcgaa.com. Ed's focus is on nature spirituality. At his website you will find a lot of useful information as well as a biography of Ed and a photo gallery. His book *Mother Earth Spirituality* is recommended for anyone interested in building a sweat lodge. You may purchase any of his several other books through his website as well.

TAROT

For information on the OSHO Zen Tarot deck, please refer to the following website: www.osho.com.

TRANSPERSONAL PSYCHOLOGY

For more information about all aspects of transpersonal psychology, please visit the website of the Association for Transpersonal Psychology at: www.atpweb.org.

THE WHEEL OF INITIATION

For more on the Wheel of Initiation, spiritual journaling, and Bindu breathwork, go to the author's website: www.julietallardjohnson.com. She offers a blog, useful links, and a calendar of events. The author is available for two- and four-day workshops on "Entering the Wheel."

For more information on shadow work and the use of poetry in one's spiritual pilgrimage, contact Prudence Tippins at www.calliopecenter .com. Prudence also offers workshops and a yearlong course on the Wheel of Initiation.

BIBLIOGRAPHY

Altman, Donald. *Art of the Inner Meal: The Power of Mindful Practices to Heal Our Food Cravings.* Moon Lake Media. Portland, Oreg.: 2002.

——. *Meal by Meal: 365 Daily Meditations for Finding Balance through Mindful Eating.* Novato, Calif.: New World Library, 2004.

Arterburn, Stephen, and Jack Felton. *Toxic Faith: Experiencing Healing from Painful Spiritual Abuse.* Colorado Springs, Colo.: Waterbrook, 2001.

Baker, Ian. *The Heart of the World: A Journey to Tibet's Lost Paradise. A Memoir.* New York: Penguin, 2004.

Berry, Wendell. *Collected Poems: 1957–1982.* New York: North Point/Farrar, Straus and Giroux, 1985.

——. *The Selected Poems of Wendell Berry.* New York: Counterpoint, 1998.

Black Elk. *Black Elk Speaks: Being the Life Story of a Holy Man of the Oglala Sioux.* As told to John G. Neihardt (Flaming Rainbow). Lincoln, Nebr.: Univ. of Nebraska Press, 1979.

——. *The Sacred Pipe: Black Elk's Account of the Seven Rites of the Oglala Sioux.* As told to Joseph Epes Brown. Norman, Okla.: Univ. of Oklahoma Press, 1989.

Bolen, Jean Shinoda. *The Tao of Psychology.* San Francisco: Harper & Row, 1989.

Browne, Brian Walker. *The I Ching or Book of Changes: A Guide to Life's Turning Points.* New York: St. Martin's Press, 1992.

Campbell, Joseph. *A Joseph Campbell Companion: Reflections on the Art of Living.* Edited by Diane K. Osbon. New York: HarperPerennial, 1991.

———. *The Power of Myth.* With Bill Moyers. New York: Doubleday, 1988.

Chödrön, Pema. *No Time to Lose: A Timely Guide to the Way of the Bodhisattva.* Boston: Shambhala, 2005.

Dalai Lama. *The Dzogchen: The Heart Essence of the Great Perfection.* Edited by Patrick Gaffney, translated by Geshe Thupten Jinpa and Richard Barron. Ithaca, N.Y.: Snow Lion, 2004.

———. *Ethics for the New Millennium.* New York: Riverhead/Penguin, 1999.

———. *How to See Yourself As You Really Are.* Translated and edited by Jeffrey Hopkins. New York: Atraia/Simon & Schuster, 2006.

———. *Shantideva's Guide to a Bodhisattva's Way of Life and Kamalasila's Middle Stages of Meditation,* July 20 through July 23, 2008. Available to order on DVD by contacting www.deerparkcenter.org.

———. *Stages of Meditation.* Translated by Venerable Geshe Lobsang, Jordhen Losang Choephel Ganchenpa, and Jeremy Russell. New York: Snow Lion, 2001.

Das, Lama Surya. *Awakening the Buddhist Heart.* New York: Broadway, 2001.

———. *Natural Radiance: Awakening to Your Great Perfection.* Boulder, Colo.: Sounds True, 2007.

Dodd, Ray. *Belief Works: The Art of Living Your Dreams.* Charlottesville, Va.: Hampton Roads, 2006.

———. *The Power of Belief: Essential Tools for an Extraordinary Life.* Charlottesville, Va.: Hampton Roads, 2003.

Douglas-Klotz, Neil. *Prayers of the Cosmos: Meditations on the Aramaic Words of Jesus.* San Francisco: HarperCollins, 1990.

Eliade, Mircea. *Rites and Symbols of Initiation: The Mysteries of Birth and Rebirth.* New York: Harper Torchbooks, 1958.

———. *Shamanism: Archaic Techniques of Ecstasy.* Princeton, N.J.: Princeton Univ. Press, 2004.

Ghose, Sudhin N. *Tibetan Folk Tales and Fairy Stories.* New Dehli: Rupa, 1993.

Gkisedtanamoogk, and Frances Hancock. *Anoqcou: Ceremony Is Life Itself.* Portland, Me.: Astarte Shell, 1993.

Gold, Peter. *Navajo and Tibetan Sacred Wisdom: The Circle of the Spirit.* Rochester, Vt.: Inner Traditions, 1994.

Grof, Stanislov. *The Adventure of Self-Discovery: Dimensions of Consciousness and New Perspectives in Psychotherapy.* Albany: Univ. of New York Press, 1988.

Hassan, Steven. *Combatting Cult Mind Control.* Rochester, Vt.: Park Street Press. 1990.

Hawkins, David R. *Power vs. Force: The Hidden Determinants of Human Behavior.* Carlsbad, Calif.: Hay House, 2003.

Huang, Chunglian Al, and Jerry Lynch. *Mentoring: The Tao of Giving and Receiving Wisdom.* New York: HarperCollins, 1995.

Huang, Alfred. *The Complete I Ching: The Definitive Translation.* Rochester, Vt.: Inner Traditions, 1998.

Kain, John. *A Rare and Precious Thing: The Possibilities and Pitfalls of Working with a Spiritual Teacher.* New York: Random House, 2006.

Kongtrul, Jamgon. *The Teacher-Student Relationship.* Translated by Ron Garry. Ithaca, N.Y.: Snow Lion, 1999.

Kramer, Joel, and Diana Alstad. *The Guru Papers: Masks of Authoritarian Power.* Berkeley, Calif.: Frog, 1993.

Kyabgon, Traleg. *The Practice of Lojong: Cultivating Compassion through Trainging the Mind.* Boston & London: Shambhala, 2007.

Leopold, Aldo. *The Sand County Almanac.* New York: Ballantine, 1966.

Levine, Stephen. *A Gradual Awakening.* New York: Anchor/Doubleday, 1979.

Mails, E., and Thomas Fools. *Crow: Wisdom and Power.* San Francisco: Council Oak, 1991.

Masterson, James F. *The Search for the Real Self: Unmasking the Personality Disorders of Our Age.* New York: Free Press/Simon & Schuster, 1988.

McGaa, Ed (Eagle Man). *Mother Earth Spirituality: Native American Paths to Healing Ourselves and Our World.* New York: HarperCollins, 1990.

———. *Nature's Way: Nature's Wisdom for Living in Balance with the Earth.* San Francisco: HarperSanFransisco, 2004.

McLeod, Ken. *Wake Up to Your Life: Discovering the Buddhist Path of Attention.* San Francisco: HarperSanFrancisco, 2002.

Mehl-Madrona, Lewis. *Coyote Healing: Miracles in Native Medicine.* Rochester, Vt.: Bear & Company, 2003.

———. *Narrative Medicine: The Use of History and Story in the Healing Process.* Rochester, Vt.: Bear & Company, 2007.

Miller, Alice. *The Drama of the Gifted Child: The Search for the True Self.* New York: Basic, 1997.

Miller, William A. *Make Friends with Your Shadow: How to Accept and Use Positively the Negative Side of Your Personality.* Minneapolis: Augsburg, 1981.

Mipham, M. O. *Tibetan Divination System.* Translated by Jay Goldberg and Lobsang Dakpa. Ithaca, N.Y.: Snow Lion, 1990.

Mohatt, Gerald (Joe Eagle Elk). *The Price of a Gift: A Lakota's Healer's Story.* Lincoln, Nebr.: Univ. of Nebraska Press, 2000.

Pabongka Rinpoche. *Liberation in the Palm of Your Hand: A Concise Discourse on the Path to Enlightenment.* Edited by Trijang Rinpoche, translated by Michael Richards. Boston: Wisdom, 1991.

Padmasambhava. *Advice from the Lotus Born.* Edited by Marcia Binder Schmidt, translated by Erik Pema Kunsang. Berkeley: North Atlantic Books, 2004.

——. *Natural Liberation: Padmasambhava's Teachings on the Six Bardos.* Commentary by Gyatrul Rinpoche, translated by Alan B. Wallace. Boston: Wisdom, 1998.

Pagels, Elaine. *The Gnostic Gospels.* New York: Vintage, 1979.

Palmer, Parker. *The Active Life: A Spirituality of Work, Creativity, and Caring.* San Francisco: Jossey-Bass, 1990.

——. *A Hidden Wholeness: The Journey toward an Undivided Life.* San Francisco: Jossey-Bass, 2004.

Pressfield, Steven. *The War of Art: Winning the Inner Creative Battle.* New York: Rugged Land, 2002.

Renault, Dennis (Wa'na'nee'che') and Timothy Freke. *Principles of Native American Spirituality.* Thorsons Principles Series. San Francisco: HarperCollins, 1996.

Ruiz, Don Miguel. *Beyond Fear: A Toltec Guide to Freedom and Joy.* As told to Mary Carroll Nelson. San Francisco: Council Oak, 1997.

——. *The Four Agreements: A Practical to Guide Personal Freedom.* San Rafael, Calif.: Amber-Allen, 1997.

Sanchez, Victor. *The Toltec Path of Recapitulation: Healing Your Past to Free Your Soul.* Rochester, Vt.: Bear & Company, 2001.

Sanford, James A. *The Kingdom Within: The Inner Meanings of Jesus' Sayings.* New York: Paulist Press, 1970.

Shantideva, *A Guide to the Bodhisattva's Way of Life (Bodhicaryāvatāra).* Translated by Vesna A. Wallace and B. Alan Wallace. New York: Snow Lion, 1997.

Sogyal Rinpoche. *The Tibetan Book of Living and Dying.* San Francisco: HarperSanFrancisco, 1992.

Sopa, Geshe Lhundub. *Steps on the Path to Enlightenment: A Commentary on Tsongkhapa's Lamrim Chenmo.* With David Pratt. Vol. 1, *The Foundation Practices.* Boston: Wisdom, 2004.

———. *Steps on the Path to Enlightenment: A Commentary on Tsongkhapa's Lamrim Chenmo.* With Beth Newman. Vol. 3, *The Way of the Bodhisattva.* Boston: Wisdom, 2008.

Stafford, William. *The Way It Is: New and Selected Poems.* Minneapolis: Graywolf, 1998.

Trungpa, Chögyam. *Shambhala: The Sacred Path of the Warrior.* Boston: Shambhala, 1984.

———. *Training the Mind and Cultivating Loving-Kindness.* Boston: Shambhala, 2003.

Yalom D., Irvin. *The Theory and Practice of Group Psychotherapy.* 5th ed. New York: Basic, 1995.

Zopa, Lama Rinpoche. *Transforming Problems into Happiness.* Boston: Wisdom, 1993.